OFF THE KING'S ROAD

OFF THE KING'S ROAD

LOST AND FOUND IN LONDON

PHYLLIS RAPHAEL

Other Press • New York

Copyright © 2006 Phyllis Raphael
Production Editor: Mira S. Park
Text design by Kaoru Tamura

This book was set in Filosofia Regular 11.5 point by Alpha Graphics
of Pittsfield, NH.

10 9 8 7 6 5 4 3 2 1

Library of Congress Cataloging-in-Publication Data

Raphael, Phyllis.
  Off the King's Road : lost and found in London / Phyllis Raphael.
    p. cm.
  ISBN-13: 978-1-59051-259-3 (acid-free paper)
  ISBN-10: 1-59051-259-6 (acid-free paper)   1. Raphael, Phyllis—Homes
and haunts—England—London.   2. Raphael, Phyllis—Divorce.   3. Authors,
American—20th century—Biography.   4. Americans—England—London—
Biography.   I. Title.
  PS3568.A6Z46 2006
  813'.54—dc22
  [B]

                                                     2006008843

For the one and only R.L.

I met a lot of people in Europe. I even encountered myself.

—JAMES BALDWIN

AUTHOR'S NOTE

While everything in this book is true, not everything is exactly factual. I've changed or omitted many of the names and altered occupations and physical characteristics in an effort to protect the privacy of those whom I suspect might prefer it that way. In many cases I've assumed the cloak of fiction to invent probable dialogue and imagined likely gestures and details of atmosphere and nuance rather than subject the reader to the mystery of a half-remembered episode. But the major part of my story is essentially true—not fictitious—and as faithful to my experience as I was able to keep it. I was aided in this endeavor by letters, my own writings and the writings of others, and by my vivid recollections of a period that was not "everyday life." Most of all I tried to convey as accurately as possible the spirit of the time, the place, and the person I was—and became.

LOS ANGELES

August 1968

LAST TANGO IN WESTWOOD

MARLON BRANDO IN A BROWN velvet jacket with a black broadtail collar has his arm draped casually over Rita Hayworth's shoulders, but his knuckles—light as a firefly's wings—are tracing the upper flank of my left arm. No one else seated in the semicircular leather banquette floating mid-floor in Matteo's Italian restaurant in Westwood can see those knuckles—not Rita Hayworth, who appears to have difficulty seeing anything; not Bob, my young turk of a husband, who is seated at the opposite end of the banquette from Brando in a poor viewing position; not even the dapper Hollywood agent on my right, who was having dinner alone with Rita Hayworth until Bob and I, unwilling to wait thirty or forty minutes for a table, joined them. Of all of us, that agent might be the most amused at knowing the whereabouts of Marlon Brando's knuckles. "Phyllis," he said, when Brando materialized above us and lowered himself into our booth, "you're flicking your cigarette into your salad."

Although no one at our table knows that Marlon Brando is sending me a signal with his knuckles, his touch is heating up my skin like a sun reflector in the California desert. Heat is traveling up my arm, through my body, and into my head. I am being careful not to move, even when I breathe. Neither Brando nor I make any visible sign of what is transpiring between us. Since I became aware of his touch I haven't altered my expression, and Brando, even when looking directly at me, appears oblivious. His face, at once both tender and cruel, is not what it was over twenty years ago when I watched alongside my mother as he hulked across the stage as Stanley Kowalski in *A Streetcar Named Desire*, or even seven years later when he played the tragic small-time punk Terry Malloy in *On the Waterfront*. But now, in 1968, his body thicker but not yet shrouded in fat, he is still mesmerizing to me, never more so than at this moment as he bends the force of his charm on Rita Hayworth while beckoning me to him with his knuckles. He's looking directly at her with a gaze of such pitying commiseration, such concern, that it's difficult for me to watch them without feeling as if I'm seeing something I shouldn't. She in no way resembles the Rita Hayworth of memory, the beloved of the bad-boy genius Orson Welles and of the playboy Prince Ali Khan; no trace of the glamorous actress who looked out from the covers of the fan magazines I read in high school under the hair dryer in my Brooklyn beauty parlor. Her face is puffy, her hair is pulled back in a severe bun, and she's dressed in a strict, buttoned-up Glenplaid suit and laced-up oxfords. She doesn't look so much like a movie star as like a woman who if she even had a film career would have spent it playing the matron in British orphanages. But Brando is treating her as if she's still the luscious Gilda, her silken leg extended from the slit in a long, strapless black gown.

He'd crooned her name, looming above our table while the diners in the surrounding booths shifted to watch them. He told her how thrilled he was to see her again, how happy he'd been when he'd spotted her from across the room. His voice was whiny with a hint of brass. He took her hand, which she unfurled from a glass of scotch, and held it safely between the two of his like a small white bird. They went back some years together, he explained to us. They were old, old friends. She'd been there for him, saved him from himself, and they'd had some great times together. She shook her head and smiled like a woman who has just gotten a prize but isn't sure for what. Behind the surface recognition her eyes looked vacant, and I wondered if she knew who he was. He slipped into our booth and began talking softly to her—betraying nothing, his eyes fastened to hers—while his knuckles began their conquering march upon my skin and while Bob, the agent, and I conducted a parallel conversation, superficial and labored, about real-estate prices in the San Fernando Valley, how Angie Dickinson reshaped her body, Japanese gardeners we had known.

The restaurant was crowded that evening when Bob and I drove in from Pacific Palisades for dinner. We took one look at the packed bar and the crowd waiting for tables lined behind a velvet rope and did a quick turnaround. We thought we'd go to a natural-foods place we liked in Topanga Canyon, or maybe to one of the fish joints on the Coast Highway. But when I returned from the ladies' room, Bob pulled me to him and said, half laughing, "Brando's here. You'd never forgive me if we left." That's when we spotted the talent agent. We both knew him. We had met him at a party thrown by a New York actor friend of mine who had come to L.A. to shoot a TV series about a mild-mannered gas-station attendant who swallows a pill and becomes "Mr. Terrific." We waved and he beckoned us over.

"Is your name really Rita Hayworth?" I asked as I slid into the booth alongside her, thinking her an impostor who had borrowed the name.

"No," she said in a rhythmic Spanish lilt, "it's Margarita Carmen Cansino."

Which in fact, although not the answer I expected, it was.

Our booth was in the center of the floor and had a high back. Unless I climbed on my knees and peered over the top I had no way of seeing Brando. I went to the ladies' room again, this time from inside the restaurant out to the bar, passing in front of his table, looking but not looking as if I was looking, seeing but not acting as if I had seen. Another man sat across from him. There were espresso cups, glasses, crumpled napkins. I was wearing a clingy blue minidress, and I made it a point to walk as if I knew something, as if I had inside information, as if I were a person who never turned back, always moved straight ahead. The walk had paid off. Now here he was. What was I going to do about it?

There are those individuals, I'd learned by then from literature and from life, who pluck such a moment and others who let it sail by. I had always been in the sailing-by school myself, and this time my inclinations were in that direction. I had sent Brando a message, but the invitation was meaningless. I wanted attention but had no plan to follow through. I was not yet a person who took responsibility for her actions, did not believe that the laws of cause and effect had anything to do with me. When it came to flirtation there was no honor in me. I had married Bob while I was in college and he was in law school, and we had three children under the age of seven. Bob and I had our differences and I was not incapable of infidelity, but mine would be of the more clandestine variety and it wouldn't be with Marlon Brando. He wasn't real. I knew that and so did Bob. That's why we stayed; to see the unreal made real. Seeing Marlon Brando at Matteo's was like spotting JFK buying ties on Fifty-seventh Street or Marilyn Monroe in temple with Arthur Miller on Yom Kippur. You want to see them, but you don't want anything more. One snowy night in New York after a meal and a bottle of wine Bob and I had passed the Carlyle Hotel when JFK was in town. "Is he here?" I'd asked the doorman, a little loopy.

"Are you good?" he asked. Over my head he'd winked at Bob. "You can go upstairs if you're good." My face had heated up. I felt it burn in the cold air. Although I'd joked about the invitation all the way up Madison Avenue to our parking space, being solicited to pay a call on the president had made me uneasy. No, I didn't want to go upstairs or home with celebrities—or bring them home with me, physically or emotionally, not even the short distance down Santa Monica Boulevard to the mansion on the Palisade where in one intersection of fantasy with reality—as befits a young turk and his wife—we were living.

His due-a-due with Hayworth concluded, Brando gathered up the rest of us and launched a paean to her: what a sensitive actress she was, how much she'd taught him, the Stanislavski side of her, the degree to which her insights had shaped his performances. Hayworth leaned back, nesting under his shoulder,

suddenly younger, even glowing. He'd moved her into the spotlight and she was enjoying it. Waiters and patrons craned their
necks. She crossed a leg and arched a foot from the booth. From
time to time she demurred, "No. Not really!" But Brando hushed
her. This was his game. We murmured appreciatively but none of
us spoke. I'd watched men commandeer dinner tables before and
understood that this was a courtship dance. I knew what he was
doing and where he was headed as he extolled Hayworth, her
beauty, her talent, her intuition. They'd spent time together, he
inferred. A distant past floated over the table, impossible to nab,
a location where their paths had crossed. No one—no one—was
more fun than Rita. They'd shared plenty of laughs, but there was
more. He wanted us to know. In a business like theirs, a hotbed
of lunatics with massive egos, a magnet for crazy people, lustful
and betraying, she was a rare lady. A pure soul! An amazing
woman! He kissed his fingers in tribute. His eyes pressed mine.
I nodded to let him know I understood. And I did, including the
subtext. The louder he praised her, the better he got. Rita
Hayworth was the star of this story, but Brando was the hero. Like
all stories men tell about women, this one was really about the
man who was telling it.

A braver woman than I—and I knew some existed—would do
something other than simply sit there. Bob had told me about the
young New York actress who had packed her bags and flown out
to L.A. after one night with an actor. The guy, a short, sweet-faced
character actor, was working on the film Bob was producing, and
he told Bob how she'd just rung his doorbell and moved in. I'd
seen them together at a screening. His face gauzy with love, he'd
introduced her, a thin, shiny, midwestern blonde, stylishly with-

out lipstick, and said—looking foolish (though I may not have thought so then)—that she'd changed his life.

Women did such things, I knew, and I began to wonder if I shouldn't do the same. I saw myself breaking into Brando's tribute to Hayworth and pulling him out of the booth. I imagined he was just waiting for me to do it, to drag him with me across the floor of Matteo's, dodging waiters with trays of clams casino and fried eggplant, past booths of men in body shirts and Gucci loafers and women with hair sprayed into bouffant towers. Just thinking about it my heart began to beat rapidly. I could see all of it: the unsettling whiteness of Rita Hayworth's powdered skin as I yanked Brando from her, the agent's knowing smirk, the crimson tinge of rage that would erupt and color Bob's pale, freckled face. I could see myself with Brando outside in Matteo's parking lot, him leaning against a yellow Karman Ghia, doubled over with laughter, shaking his head, my cheek against the rich velvet jacket. I could hear him saying, "Oh Phyllis, you got it, honey. You did just right!"

Brando's voice, soft and metallic, began to wind down. Even the century's greatest actor could take this riff only so far. The thought entered my mind that he was preparing to leave us. I hadn't considered this possibility and it pained me. I had believed somehow that he'd come into our lives and would stay for a while. The pressure on my arm subtly decreased. He'd finished. Now what?

"I'm an actress," I said. "I did the lead in a play at the Mark Taper." The words coming out of my mouth surprised me. Until that moment I'd had no plan to speak. Brando's eyebrows rose just enough to let me know that there was nothing he would like less than to hear about my starring role in a downtown L.A. showcase. This was not a man built for listening.

"I played Kitty Genovese," I told him. Like my walk across the floor of Matteo's, I was about to go someplace I had no map for, no way of knowing where I would end up. "I was killed in Queens," I said. "I lay in an alley while all the witnesses who watched my murder from their windows explained why they didn't lift a finger to save me. They all had real parts," I said. I could feel my autobiography surging up to meet his impassive face. "I was the star, but all I had to do was lie dead on the stage," I said. "They marched around my body during the whole second act—all of them telling why they hadn't come down to stop the killer. The afternoon of the final dress rehearsal there was a small earthquake. The stage trembled; I could feel it moving beneath my cheek. The audience began rustling programs and moving around. A few headed up the aisles for the exits. But these actors all had monologues. There were casting agents there. Careers could be made.

"I was dead—forty minutes of death—I couldn't get up unless the stage manager brought down the curtain and this was theater-in-the-round. There was no curtain. Finally, at the end of the act, I stand up. Then Winston Mosely, the killer, stalks me. The stage goes dark. The audience sees only my silhouette." I showed Brando how I walked and Mosely stalked—hunched over the table in Matteo's, looking into my salad. "Backstage—when it was over—not one of those actors admitted there had been a tremor. 'Earthquake? What earthquake?' An agent who saw the show liked the way I lay dead on the stage and liked my silhouette, the way I was stalked. He called me afterward, and I went to see him. The meeting was the shortest in history. He said I looked much younger on stage than off, so he didn't think I'd be right for film!"

At that Brando's expressionless face slipped into laughter. He threw his head back and really laughed. I felt his touch change, his knuckles bolder and more insistent, moving in rhythm with his laughter, beating a rat-a-tat on my skin. I kept going. I told him how I played Eurydice, the tragic Queen of Thebes, in *Antigone* at Judson Church in a Japanese Kabuki outfit, all of us white-faced, in masks. I was too young for the part, but under the makeup no one could tell. I told him how Warren Finnerty played Creon, drunk and high, late for every performance, how we struggled every night to get Finnerty made-up, into his Kabuki costume and onto the stage. We never knew what he would say; he made the lines up as he went. The director wore Granny glasses and spoke in a whisper. The worse Finnerty got, the lower the director's voice sank. The Kabuki concept was his idea, his artistic baby. He'd been planning this production for years, all the time he was at college. Miraculously, the show was a triumph. A friend in the audience said, "You've made theatrical history, adding improvisation to Kabuki and Greek drama." Geraldine Page and Rip Torn came twice. By closing night the director's voice was audible. He went on to direct another Kabuki *Antigone* with a new (and presumably sober) cast. I told Brando how I danced in a black slip to "That Old Black Magic" played on voodoo drums; how I rose out of the audience and leapt to the stage at Café La Mama; how I auditioned for Valerie Solanas in a sleazy rehearsal hall in the East Village. (She would go on to shoot Andy Warhol.) I told him how another actor and I adapted a scene from a Philip Roth novel and got Philip Roth to come watch us perform it. When it was over Roth said "Thank you," and left. I told him how I improvised four nights a week for a year for no pay in a club on West Ninth Street, "a toilet on lower death street."

When I'd gone through nearly everything, the odyssey of my entire career—from my early acting classes with Uta Hagen right up through the Maxwell House Coffee commercial I auditioned for but didn't get because my hands shook so badly I nearly dropped the cup—I stopped. The table was silent. No one had spoken for all the time I'd been talking, and I had no idea how long that had been—it could have been twenty minutes or two. I had been skimming along like an ice skater, pirouetting, doing figure eights. I loved being an actress, bad as I was, and I suppose I wanted to let Brando know that I knew something about what he knew, that I'd put in my time in basements and churches and dark bars where actors imitated and idolized him. Brando was sitting back in the booth, an indulgent, paternal, amused look on his face—Sky Masterson in *Guys and Dolls*, betting he can make it with Sarah, the Salvation Army captain, played by Jean Simmons in a prim uniform. His arm still encircled Hayworth. I had the thought that he was probably laughing at me, that whatever set me off on my monologue had been ill advised.

Several months earlier Bob had brought Lee Marvin back to our house. He'd stretched out on the grass. While I poured him a drink he warned me sternly never to talk about acting. "Talk is for amateurs!" he said. "An actor without a job should keep his trap shut!" I remembered that Uta Hagen once told our class that upon meeting those she idolized—like the Lunts—she was stunned to silence. She thought Brando was a genius. If she ever met him she doubted she'd be able to speak. I should have listened.

I consulted the rest of the table. Rita Hayworth oozed contentment. She hadn't been listening to me. She gazed around the banquette like a bright bird and smiled as I imagined the Hayworth of old might have while sailing on Ali Khan's yacht sipping scotch. Bob had heard all these stories before and in any event took a dim view of my acting career; he now wore an expression I knew well—the smile of a man thanking his hostess for a dinner party that he didn't want to go to and was now in a rush to leave. Only the agent actually looked happy. Of all three bystanders to this scene, he seemed to have enjoyed it the most.

A waiter appeared with plates on his arm, steam rising from veal and peppers. I couldn't remember ordering, but something red was put in front of me, something swimming in tomatoes. Brando mumbled fuzzily that he had to go, he'd kept the friend at his table waiting too long. I felt his knuckles lift off my arm, the skin naked and weeping. He whispered something in Hayworth's ear and she laughed. "See you, Mar," the agent said. Bob flapped a couple of fingers.

From above the table Brando looked down. "Phyllis," he said in his soft, buttery whine. "I live on Mulholland. Up at the top, honey. You can't miss it. Why don't you come over later? I'm always up late." He added a line of numbers to his address. I felt them dance up and down in my brain. My mouth went very dry and the rims of my ears burned with heat. But I smiled as if nothing had happened. And he walked off without seeming to notice.

By the time we left the restaurant Brando was gone, his booth cleared of his espresso cup and wine glass, his crumpled napkin and his bread crumbs. A blonde model or dancer with skin as white as Wonder bread sat in his place across from a man with a receding hairline who looked vaguely Chinese. We drove back to Pacific Palisades, Bob teasing. "Don't you want to go?" he asked. "You're leaving the poor guy alone and rejected."

"Oh please," I said. "He has about four thousand numbers to call and all his old movies to watch."

"Don't be so sure," Bob said. "I think he expects you."

Bob was behind the wheel of the little two-seater sports car he had bought for me that was supposed to make California driving, which I hated, more fun. We drove with the top down out Santa Monica Boulevard to our house. After Bob and I divorced I would discover a car just like that one in a movie starring Audrey Hepburn and Albert Finney. It was a movie about an architect and the girl he fell in love with and married and the trips they took across France when they were young and carefree before he was successful and she was unfaithful. There was a breeze from the Pacific hitting the open car and blowing over me, and I found myself secretly covering the spot on my arm where Brando had touched me, as if I could save what was left of him from blowing away.

L O N D O N

December 1968

ST. LEONARD'S TERRACE

THE HOUSE I WAS LIVING in when my marriage ended belonged to Lord Henry and Lady D'Avigdor Goldsmid, he of the House of Lords. My husband Bob had rented it for us and our three children while he was producing a film in London and I saw it for the first time the morning after I'd flown there from L.A. We'd spent the night in a suite at a hotel in Park Lane under down quilts in a bedroom darkened by heavy draperies and I'd gone to the house in a midnight blue Bentley driven by a small handsome driver, formally dressed. Inside, the car was soundless with windows tinted against the misty white London light. It was only 10:30 when I met Lady Goldsmid but she offered me a scotch and soda and potato chips (crisps) from a small glass bowl in the library. She'd had her butler bring up some ice ("I know Americans like it") but I'd never drunk hard liquor at that time of day except at a bris, so I just shook my head no. She poured some for herself anyway and downed it before she took me on a tour of the house.

The D'Avigdor Goldsmid house was an imposing five-story brick townhouse in Chelsea, SW3, just off the King's Road at Royal Avenue, across from an expansive green parade ground and the Royal Hospital where every May the annual London Flower Show is held. It was furnished with antiques—well worn sofas and chairs and wallpaper that curled up from the baseboards from the "rising damp"—a sort of combination of mildew and green mold that I would learn all the very best English houses have sprouting from their basements in wet weather. Bob made a big fuss over the house. He was very impressed by it. He had discovered it through an English film executive who had taken him to dinner at an exclusive club in Pall Mall, but—like many of the symbols of wealth people in the movie business fall in love with—I didn't get it. It looked as if it could use some fresh paint and new carpets.

There were paintings in the house too. Lady Goldsmid had the kind of paintings museum curators collected. Bob lowered his voice when he talked about them, as if he were whispering about something illicit. If I hadn't known about them beforehand I would have thought they were knockoffs or just something she'd picked up in the odd gallery while she was bopping around London. But since I was on the alert I could spot them: the fragmenting, crazy cow by Jean Dubuffet and the large dark blue mournful canvas by Mark Rothko. There was something unreal about living in a house with paintings that belonged in a museum. In L.A.

we had friends who bought a Monet in Paris and hung it in the living room under a picture light. At their decorator's suggestion they hired a contractor to panel the living room in walnut just for the painting. But Lady Goldsmid's art wasn't like that. Except for the Rothko which she'd placed at the end of a long icy blue formal sitting room where I had the feeling people rarely sat, her Ladyship's paintings were all over the place, in her bedroom, even in her carpeted bathroom where they hung on the grasscloth wallpaper. I suppose it was a sign of her good breeding that she said nothing about them as I trailed through the house behind her. I would have liked to ask her how she chose them, but since she didn't mention her art collection neither did I.

The precise spot where the marriage ended—where Bob, opening and closing his palms at his side and shifting from one foot to the other, said, "I have something to tell you"—was in her Ladyship's walk-in closet. The closet was part of the bedroom suite that took up the entire third floor, bedroom, bath, and closet. Her Ladyship was emptying the closet for her departure on the day I visited. An elegant trunk swimming with cashmere stood half full in the center. It was a large closet with racks and shelves and I hadn't brought enough clothing with me to come anywhere near filling it. On the night Bob made his announcement a few things hung on the pole in front of me, dresses and shirts with the shape of my body. It was three weeks after I'd arrived, the week between Christmas and New Year's. We had come back from a party and I was getting undressed. I had just pulled off a pair of brown boots with red and green stripes on top and they were lying on the pale blue wall-to-wall carpeting like crumpled dead animals with collars while he told me about the eighteen-year-old actress he was having an affair with.

I'd had plenty of days when I'd longed for another life and as a wife I'd been less than perfect. I'd tried to do better, but Bob had a way of confounding me; my best intentions could evaporate when he simply asked a question in a particular tone of voice. "What do you mean by that?" could send me off on a rant. Most of the time, though, our unhappiness took the form of a low buzz, a sound you know is there but don't really hear. Periodically there were tears, explosions, vows to do better. Once he'd moved out for two months and taken a sublet on Central Park South. But in spite of all that, I didn't want our marriage to end. I assumed, like all unreasonable people, that one day our unhappiness would disappear and we'd be happy again. As I stood in the closet, a creeping terror rose inside me, a panic akin to what I'd felt only once before being wheeled in for surgery.

I knew I should keep quiet, that good sense dictated that I not argue with him, that I was half naked in another woman's closet in a country not my own and I wasn't holding a winning hand. I should stay silent and hope it would all go away. But I couldn't keep my mouth shut. Tears, like hot ash, were on my cheeks. I didn't really want the answers to the questions I was asking:

"Who is she?"

"I can't tell you that."

"Why not?"

"She's not the point."

"She's not?"

Finally he said, "She's very young, an orphan, an actress, this isn't her fault." He said she loved him so much she wanted to be our au pair, just so she could live under our roof and see him every day. They could meet late at night under the stairs. How could he live without passion? he asked me.

We'd started off in the closet, but at some point we moved out, to the bathroom and then to the bedroom. The night wore on.

"You're my best friend," he said. "No one knows me like you do. I feel like shit. Do you think I want to do this?"

"Then don't."

"Don't you think there's more to life than what we have?"

"No. I think this is it. In fact, we have more of it than most."

A vast longing whirled in the center of my panic, a conviction that I didn't want to lose the life we had. I loved Bob, or thought I did. I'd pulled a red caftan over my head in the closet and it sailed behind me as I moved through the rooms. Fear twisted inside me like a tornado. "Do you want a divorce?" I asked finally, digging my grave.

"Divorce is even stupider than marriage," he said. "I'm seeing a psychiatrist here who's opened my eyes. It's a new world. There are all kinds of arrangements. All kinds of possibilities. Monogamy isn't the only way to live."

The answer flew out, words I never meant to say. "No arrangements," I screamed. "Tomorrow morning get the fuck out."

"I knew I couldn't talk to you," he said.

After she'd shown me her bedroom I followed her Ladyship up one flight to his Lordship's bedchamber. The room was chaste and bare with a mahogany highboy, a stern four-poster double bed and a threadbare Oriental rug. It looked like a room that nobody any longer lived in, the kind of room you might see while touring a historic house. I assumed at first that his Lordship slept downstairs in her Ladyship's bedroom, that this was a room for the occasional guest or the nights when His Lordship had a cold or her Ladyship a headache. But that conclusion was contradicted by the David

Hockney drawing of an elephant on the closet door. I'd seen David Hockney's paintings in shows in New York and Los Angeles and I knew he was British and famous in London. Why would this artist of the moment, who I imagined partying with the Beatles and the model Jean Shrimpton and Antonioni, the maker of "Blow Up," hang here, out of sight, unloved and unlooked at? Surely, I thought, his Lordship did sleep here, in exile (as I'd heard about highborn European marriages), a man who left no imprint on anything.

While she was pouring the scotch her Ladyship apologized for taking her servants with her, her butler and cook and maid. She was "dreadfully sorry." She had replaced her personal staff for me with servants she had located through friends. I was "not to worry" (a very English phrase which could be translated as "don't bother your pretty little head" . . . but to me always served as a cue to start worrying immediately), she had checked their letters of reference and thought they would "do nicely." "Shall I have a look round for a nanny?" she asked. I told her not to go to any trouble, and she paused and looked at me closely as if waiting for me to change my mind. Finally she said she hoped I would "manage."

As she showed me through the house, opening closets and drawers with stores of china and silver and linen, she continued to fret about the servants and admonished me to keep a strict eye on the ones she'd found. "Be firm with them from the start," she advised. "See to it they do what they're meant to and things should swim along."

She left the telephone number of a laundress and a "char" under the desk blotter and clasped my hand when we parted. She was a beautiful woman, in silk and tweed and good leather pumps, with a fine-lined unhappy face. I had never had a butler, a cook, or a full-time maid although we'd had an au pair from USC to baby-sit back in Los Angeles and a Mexican woman who came in to clean three afternoons a week. What I was supposed to do with all those people, I had no clue. But I felt for her Ladyship as she took my hand in her fine-boned jeweled one. I wanted to soothe her Ladyship, to relieve her of the distress painted on her face and to save myself and her from her learning how ignorant I was. Most of all I wanted to flee, so I pressed her hand quickly in mine. "Don't worry. Everything will be just fine," I promised before escaping down the worn burgundy stairway runner and out of the house.

Since I had no notion of what to do with the servants I took the path of noblesse oblige. Staff administration wasn't a skill I had cultivated even before Bob left and with him gone it was out of the question. Joe, the Spanish butler, was a round-faced young man in his twenties, with white skin and unruly curly black hair and a wet pink mouth and he blushed every time he came near me. He wore a white jacket and appeared in the library every morning with a tray of coffee and the *London Times* and asked me haltingly, "Madam, what you want the cook to make for dinner?" And then his face and neck turned a bright scarlet and we stared at each other in utter disbelief that we were in this awful position. I had no notion what she should cook. The English names for cuts of meat and varieties of fish, even some vegetables, were like a third language and the entire operation of coming up with an appropriate menu felt completely beyond me. The less I knew what to say, the more he blushed and the longer I sat and he stood, backing up, both of us mystified as to what would happen next. I finally developed the technique of asking him to have her make a suggestion and then, to save himself a trip downstairs, he would name a few dishes that I would OK with relief that I covered up with praise ("Oh, that's a good idea!"). If there were questions (Flounder or sole? Artichokes or French beans or "courgettes"?) I would pretend to mull them over and then pull an answer based on nothing I could think of out of the air, trying to sound authoritative and enthusiastic as I did so.

Emilia, the Portuguese maid, was a plump, dark-haired young woman, sweet faced and warm with large breasts and terrible body odor. She wore Dr. Scholl's exercise sandals, which made a soft, flopping sound as she went through the house. You always knew when she was coming. In the beginning she remained in the background, cleaning the house daily, leaving the rooms smelling faintly of Fairy liquid and body odor and afterwards playing with the kids down in the kitchen whenever she could. But after Bob left, as my tear-stained face became more and more obvious, she began to cry all the time too, and clasped me to her when we passed in the hallway, murmuring "my poor, beautiful Madammy." Sometimes I would hear the flapping of the Dr. Scholl's sandals behind me and turn to find her sniffling and I would embrace and comfort her. "It will be alright," I'd tell her and she'd burst into fresh tears. "Oh Madammy," she'd say. "How can it be alright? How can it ever be alright again?" "Don't worry," I'd insist. "It will be. I promise." I'd search for a tissue, wipe her eyes, and send her back to pushing the Hoover. When she wasn't weeping over my plight, she told me about her sorrow for me, how she had been hanging up my robe and burst into tears or had gone to a film and couldn't get through it for crying. She'd had to leave and go have a Wimpy. But her responses were light as air, a mere soufflé when compared to the leader of the little troupe, Carmele, the Basque cook.

Carmele, a passionate revolutionary and refugee from Franco's Spain, was a tall, angular woman with a small coffee-colored baby girl christened Arantja, after her best friend and fellow revolutionary, also Arantja. Carmele had body odor as strong as Emilia's, but she was not one for tears; "He will be back," she predicted, standing up tall, raising a fist. "I promise you he will be back. And when he returns you must be cruel and make him beg," she ordered, wagging a finger. Carmele managed her emotions with confrontation and action. She gathered a coterie of supporters down in that basement kitchen around the island: her baby Arantja, her friend Arantja with brightly dyed red hair, her "husband," baby Arantja's father, a short, grizzled black man always smiling, Joe and Emilia, and my kids. She turned out apple tarts and pork roasts and fish smothered in butter. She'd learned about loyalty back in Fascist Spain and never hesitated to act in concert with her code.

"I called the little bitch," she announced one day, standing up tall, her mouth curling with vitriol for Bob's girlfriend. "I told her she was a slut, not worthy to wipe your shoes, and if she comes near his children I will murder her in her sleep." She made this announcement as I entered the kitchen on my way to a cup of afternoon tea. (Joe had started off bringing me mid-afternoon tea on a tray, but I could never get used to being waited on in my own house and discouraged him.) Joe gathered up the children into a game with trucks (lorries) on the floor. Emilia stood up and began to weep. Big Arantja took little baby Arantja in her arms and stood beside her, and Arantja's father stood alongside the two of them. Carmele stood at the end of the line waving a fist, breathing heavily, her eyes bright. "You shouldn't have done that," I said, trying to summon ten centuries of British breeding into my tone of voice. "You must never do anything like that again!"

But Carmele opposed me; "No, Madam," she said. "I will never obey!"

When I began inviting guests to stay in the house—there was so much room upstairs, after all, why not—they told me that the bathing facilities up on the fifth floor were less than adequate—one very small tub—and that explained all the body odor. My guests slept upstairs where there were plenty of extra bedrooms but used her Ladyship's bath (now mine) on the third floor or his Lordship's on the fourth (now the kids). I suggested to Joe, Carmele, and Emilia that they do the same but they ignored the suggestion as they did many of my American eccentricities and went on as they were and continued to smell. I had failed yet again to follow Lady Goldsmid's advice and take a firm hand.

RUNNING

IT WAS PAST MIDNIGHT WHEN the scene we'd begun in the closet ended. I lay at the opposite side of the bed, curled as close to the edge as I could get. Towards morning I let myself out and ran to the King's Road. I wasn't much of a runner nor was I dressed for a race but running felt like the thing to do.

The running was a relief. I'd cried most of the night and I had a headache. I was wearing the first clothing I'd grabbed, a pair of jeans and boots and a sheepskin coat I'd bought in Portobello Road that was heavy as lead. It wouldn't stay closed and flapped around my calves. Wearing it was like carrying another person on my back. But I needed to move; there was a small motor of anxiety whirring inside my chest and when I stopped running it sent powerful currents up the back of my neck into my arms and legs. The motor got hyperactive every time I slowed down, so even though I was breathless, I didn't stop.

At a certain point I heard Bob's footsteps behind me. I'd thought he was asleep.

He caught up to me and reached out and grabbed my coat and we stopped, panting and breathless in the middle of the silence of the King's Road. He was wearing an aviator style jacket he'd been wearing on the movie set and it was unzipped over a shirt he'd buttoned on the wrong buttons and his face was pink from exertion.

"Don't do this," he said. "Come back. We can talk . . ."

"Why did you want me to come here?" I screamed.

"I didn't know this would happen," he said. "I couldn't help it."

"You couldn't help it?"

Tears were rushing down my cheeks and I searched in the pocket of my coat for a tissue but there was nothing there except some loose grains of tobacco. I ran my sleeve across my wet face and nose. Bob's expression was blank, emptied of everything but fear, like a kid who's gotten lost in a department store.

"You couldn't help it?" I said again.

"No," he said. "I didn't want to . . . I never wanted to do this."

His being out of control seemed the worst thing I'd heard so far, as if his falling in love with someone else was a force of nature, something that had been destined to happen, a truck that had been fated all my life to hit me, even if I'd known it was coming and tried to avoid it.

"You shouldn't have made me come here," I screamed again.

I'd taken the children out of school, packed, unpacked, arranged for the house watcher, stopped the newspaper, forwarded the mail, gotten someone to take the cat, start up the cars. I'd flown fourteen hours from Los Angeles on my own, trying to keep all three kids amused. Four months' worth of my eight-year-old daughter's homework was in my trunk, workbooks with exercises. It was endless what I'd done to come here.

"I don't know a soul," I said. "You fucking bastard. I don't know a soul."

My fist darted out to punch him. The motion surprised me. We'd been married twelve years and we'd had plenty of fights, some of them vicious, but I'd never struck him or anyone else.

He caught my wrist and we wrestled till the air drained out of me and he let go.

"Don't come after me," I shrieked, beginning to run again.

I listened but there were no footsteps. My steps were the only sound in the empty street. The slap of my boots against the pavement made me feel better. I just kept on going.

After a while I began to feel disoriented. Instead of taking a right turn at the Chelsea Drugstore and heading towards Sloane Square, Knightsbridge, and the parts of London that had become familiar to me in the few weeks I'd been there, I'd gone in the opposite direction, past the Chelsea Potter Pub, the Antique Market, and the Public Baths at Sydney Street and into an unknown area, a place I'd never been and wasn't likely to go. The cityscape of Chelsea was gone; no whitewashed terraces, very few small shops, pubs, or cafes. I was running past open spaces; vacant lots, looming behind them some dark buildings that were probably a housing project. I had seen only a few cars and one or two people

since I started out, lonely figures walking rapidly in a barren land-
scape, heads down and inaccessible. I couldn't see much ahead
of me. The streets were poorly lit. When I finally gave up, I was
out of breath, sweating and panting, a stitch in my side, the damn
coat half off on my arms. I was under a pub sign. "World's End,"
it said. Ahead of me the sky was almost imperceptibly beginning
to lighten. A wavery line of pinkness glowed on the horizon and I
had the thought that if I kept running towards it I might just fall
off the earth.

KIDS

WE TREATED BOB'S LEAVING LIKE something that
was barely happening, something we didn't actually notice, a
non-event.

We lined our kids up on the sofa in her Ladyship's library.
There were three of them, Jenifer, the oldest, was eight, with
white skin and freckles and long hair the color of chestnuts. Billy
was blonde, five and a half. He too had the freckles and eyes like
blue marbles. Julie was just four that month. Her green eyes
seemed to take up her face.

I said, "Daddy has something to tell you."

"Mommy and I aren't happy together. We think we shouldn't live together for now," he said. His voice was high, like the call of a distant bird.

"Why aren't you happy?" Jenifer asked him.

"We just aren't," he said. "Sometimes people stop getting along. It's nobody's fault."

"Are you mad at her?" Billy asked.

"Not mad. Just not happy," he said.

"You should say you're sorry" . . . from Julie.

"I am sorry," he said. "Very sorry, sweetheart."

"I'm not happy too," Billy said.

"Why not? What are you unhappy about?"

"I didn't mean it," Billy said. "I was joking." He looked away. He smirked at Jenifer.

"Promise you'll talk to me if you're unhappy. Billy? Billy? Will you promise?"

"OK. OK," he said, barely.

"When will you come back?" Jenifer asked.

"I don't know."

"Are you never coming back?" Billy asked.

"I don't know. But I'm going to see you all the time. As much as I can. You can call me on the telephone whenever you want."

"You're always on the telephone," Billy said.

Julie took a miniature tin horse out of her pocket. She had found it on the street and carried it everywhere. She'd also been wearing swimming trunks under her clothes, a fashion choice I'd questioned but hadn't argued with. She'd worn them on the plane from L.A. She got ideas. They came and went. When one was in play it was impossible to reverse it. The toy horse looked like it had escaped from the Queen's regiment with a regal gold and white bridle, feathers, and a saddle. She marched it along the leg of her corduroy pants and lifted it over her kneecap.

"Look, he's jumping," she said.

"Who cares?" from Billy.

"Stop it, Billy!"

"It's stupid."

"It's not stupid!" She rapped his leg with her open palm.

"Stop it," he said, pushing her hand away.

"Not now, both of you!" I told them.

"How will we see you?" Jenifer asked.

"I'll come get you, sweetheart. And I'll send a car. We'll go to the zoo. And the wax museum. And to lunch. And I'll call you on the phone every day."

"It's not a stupid horse," Julie said. Her eyes filled up and she slipped off the sofa and into my lap.

"Is too," Billy said.

I reached over and held his leg. "Enough!"

"Can we go to your house?" Jenifer asked.

"Not right away, But sometime . . ."

"Why not now?" Her face is innocent, washed in freckles, her eyes big and dark.

"It's better to wait awhile," I said.

"Why?"

"It just is."

Julie sunk deeper into my lap. She paraded the horse across her pants leg, taunting Billy. I felt as if torrents of water were thundering inside my chest, a huge, indiscriminate flood. Rivers ran into my arms and legs. My new psychiatrist told me, "It's better for children to live with one parent than two angry ones. Better a divorce than a childhood with two miserable people."

"We weren't miserable," I argued. "No more than anyone else."

"Children know what's going on," he insisted.

It sounded like good advice. I repeated it like a mantra. I said it whenever anyone asked . . . or even if they didn't. Thinking our separation was better for them made me feel better, even though I wasn't sure it was true.

"So who wants to go to lunch with me?" Bob asked. His voice was jaunty. The meeting was over. We'd told them. Now things could return to normal.

"I do," Billy said. He was off the sofa, alongside his father.

Jenifer and Julie said they wanted to stay with me and I walked down the King's Road with them to the Picasso Café, the closest thing to a luncheonette in the neighborhood. It was always filled with French and Scandinavian and German backpackers and Americans reading the International Herald Tribune and drinking coffee with pastries. You could get salads and omelets. There was sunshine on the King's Road, rare winter sunshine, thin and fine. The street looked the same as always. Tourists. Window shoppers. Locals. No drama, no epiphany. They didn't even talk about what had happened. Julie skipped along in an embroidered sheepskin jacket I had just bought for her, the little horse still clutched in her hand. She'd noticed riders, English saddle, in Hyde Park and she wanted to go. "I think you should wait till you're older," I said. "Those horses are very big . . . not like the ponies at the stable in Malibu."

"No. No." she insisted. "I can do it." Jenifer held my hand. "Will we see Daddy later?" she asked.

"Maybe not right away, but soon," I said. I put my arm over her shoulder and pulled her to me. After lunch we stood at the counter in the Chelsea Drugstore for a long time lingering over tie-dyed T-shirts, their fronts like spiderwebs of dancing rainbow colors. We spent a long time picking out which ones they wanted, holding them up against their chests while the strobe lights flashed and over the speakers Mick Jagger blasted, "You can't always get what you want."

Bob removed his clothing and belongings gradually from the house, like a slow tide sweeping shells out to sea. A pair of shoes here. A suede jacket there. He called in the mornings and asked first. "Fine," I said and hung up. The driver, a small handsome man named Billy in a dark blue overcoat and dark tie, came to the door and Joe, his face pink over his white jacket, ran up the stairs and out to the street and handed the items into the waiting Bentley. Bob called to speak to the kids all the time and sent the car to pick them up for lunches and teas. They came back from the movie set with haircuts from the stylist and photos of themselves taken by the still-shot photographer. One of the actors read their horoscopes. On a day-to-day basis you'd hardly know Bob was gone. It gave the separation a murky, indefinite quality, like milky fog.

Every morning when I woke I told myself it was the day I'd call the airlines, pack up the kids, go back to L.A. I'd never wanted to live in Los Angeles, but now it was my home. If I could get us back to Pacific Palisades it would be a beginning. From there I could eventually return to New York. Somehow the day would pass without my ever lifting the phone. I wasn't sure where the hours had gone. I moved as if through a fog, taking the kids to Madame Tussaud's, the

35

Tower of London, the Regents Park Zoo, the Battersea Fun Fair, to tea at the Dorchester Hotel. I stood while they listened to records at the Chelsea Drugstore (*Pack up your Sorrows*, Judy Collins sang, bells ringing, guitar jangling) and swam with them at the public baths. I was present in body, even making responses while floating above what was happening. When the currents of anxiety got too strong, I walked. I walked down to the embankment and along the river to the bridges, up and down the King's Road, up trendy Sloane Street to Knightsbridge, into Park Lane, sometimes as far as Oxford Street, to Bond Street and into Mayfair. Often I'd walk so far I had to take a taxi back to St. Leonard's Terrace. The days were passing but I had no notion where they went or what I would do next. It was like being on a train interminably stopped at a station without being able to get off.

"Where's Daddy?" they asked. "Is Daddy coming back?"

"Not right now," I answered.

"When?" they asked.

"I don't know," I said. "Maybe never!"

"Do you love Daddy?" Jenifer asked.

"Well . . ." I said. "Yes . . . but . . ."

"He loves you," she said. "He said so. If he loves you, why don't you let him come back?"

"It's not my choice," I said. "It's complicated," I said.

"Are you and Daddy never going back together?" Julie asked.

"I don't think so," I said.

"Too bad," she said. She was in the bathtub squeezing a big sponge full of water onto her chest. The drops rolled down her tiny body. "You're a good pair!"

"Where did you learn that expression?" I asked.

"I don't know," she said. "I just did."

"Why didn't God make me a boy?" she mourned, another time.

"Why would you want to be a boy?" I asked.

"I just do," she answered. "Like Billy," she said.

I didn't argue. She idolized her brother. She'd seen it all. My tears. Her father's life. At four she'd figured out what made most sense.

"You'll change your mind," I finally said.

At night I slept stiff, unmoving, stretched out under a corner of her Ladyship's white satin comforter, sometimes without taking my clothes off. I took baths and changed clothes at strange hours of the day and night. Time seemed to bleed into itself so the hours had no relation to an appropriate schedule. There were French lamps, a shepherd and shepherdess, with white silk shades on French nightstands alongside her Ladyship's bed under a Roy Lichtenstein painting, a comic strip of a blonde woman and a handsome dark-haired man. "Oh Brad. How could you?" I slept on one side of the bed, the side closest to the door, and I often left the lamp on that side on all night. One night I awoke and found Bob sitting on the edge of the bed. My body was leaden, as if held down by weights. I tried to reach out but it was too much of a struggle to lift an arm or open my mouth to speak. He sat without saying anything for what seemed a long time before vanishing. "An hallucination," my psychiatrist said.

"It was real," I said. "He was there."

"Yes," he said. "That's the way an hallucination is."

"Dear girl, you can't have him coming and going as he pleases," said Ian Smith, the barrister who months later I engaged to represent me. "He'll have to respect your schedule. You can't run a household with the dear boy dropping by whenever the mood takes him! One evening a week and every other weekend is customary!"

"He'll never do that," I told him.

"He bloody well better. We'll see to it that he does! You're not married to the bloke anymore, now are you?" he asked.

Julie begged so much that eventually I gave her a riding lesson in Hyde Park. There was a stable in a mews nearby and the instructor put her on a small horse and took her onto the bridle path. By the second lesson she was cantering. I bought her a black velvet helmet and she started riding once a week. She rode through the Knightsbridge arch into the park and waved back at me, her face alive with happiness.

THE RIMPOCHE

"WHERE IS YOUR PAIN?" the Rimpoche asked. I didn't have an answer. Every spot I could think of seemed wrong. Neck? Stomach? Head? I could justifiably claim that every part of my body had hurt me in the months since my marriage ended. But somehow I didn't think that was what he was getting at.

"What do you mean?" I asked.

"Where is it?" he repeated. "Your foot? Your hand? That geranium on the window sill?"

He wasn't being sarcastic. His voice was cool and without judgment. He looked honest with a smooth face. He was older than I was but didn't look old. He had fled the persecution of his native

Tibet and settled here in this cold, drafty Scottish farmhouse with an entourage of monks. You could stay here and walk the brown grass patched with snow, help with the chores, and meditate morning and evening when the gong sounded. For two pounds a week you also got vegetarian meals and an interview with the Rimpoche. I was having mine.

This was the nicest room in the house. He had draped the furniture with embroidered Tibetan fabrics and he sat cross-legged on floor cushions on top of colorful rugs. He was painting a Buddha with a brush that looked as if it had one hair in it. He dipped the brush into little pots of ink and held the sleeve of his robe each time he dipped. The brush covered an infinitesimal space on the painting. The Buddha sat in a dark sky sprinkled with white stars.

"The pain is in my head," I said. This seemed like a good answer. It was in my head, I was sure.

"Aha," he said. I thought he seemed pleased. "Now we're getting somewhere." He smiled at me and dipped the brush again, holding onto the sleeve of his robe. He pointed the one hair onto the painting. He looked at it steadily.

"Where in your head?" he asked. "Which part?"

"The top," I said.

Again he smiled, dipped, painted.

"The very top?"

"Yes."

"Show me."

I pointed to a spot between my eyes. In fact, my headaches seemed to settle there, maybe because I cried so much.

"That's not the top," he said.

"It's not?"

"You need to be precise."

"I'll try."

"Inside or outside?"

"Inside."

"That's very hard to locate," he said. He looked discouraged. "How far inside?"

"An inch or two?"

"One . . . or two? Unless I know exactly where the pain is, how can I help you?" he asked.

We'd reached an impasse. I knew he couldn't do a thing. I'd just have to go on as I was, riddled with electrical spasms of anxiety and miserable dreams. He was still dipping and painting, covering pinpricks of the dark sky on a painting that he could work on into eternity. I supposed there was a lesson I should take from this, but what it was I had no idea.

"Go for a walk by the river," he said as I gathered myself up. "When you can tell me the exact location of your pain, come back and I'll see what I can do."

The river bank was cold and the earth was hard and brown there. There were some islands of snow dappling the hills like spots on a giraffe. The revolutionary anti-psychiatry psychiatrist I'd begun to see in London told me he had ripped off all his clothes here and gotten wet just so he could savor the pain and feel alive. Ted, a playwright I'd met at a children's birthday party in London, said the morning and evening meditation had calmed him down. His eyes had bugged out when he said it and then he'd said, "Really. No. Really it's true."

My roommate at the monastery was a girl, eighteen or so. Her "Mum" had sent her here to get her off drugs. "It's pissing working," she said. Except that she could do with a platter of bangers and mash and a pint, she thought she'd stay a month, maybe two. After I'd walked along the river I decided I'd go back to London. I'd been in Scotland three days and that was enough. I hadn't located my pain, but it had no trouble finding me. At breakfast the morning I left one of the monks, just a boy, turned me around and put his hands on my back. He said the Rimpoche had instructed him. I felt a sharp crack and a streak of pain and then relief. My body felt wrung out.

The relief persisted all the way back to London on the train. I couldn't tell if it was because of what the monk had done, because I was leaving Scotland, or because I was going back to the city. On the way to the monastery the train had gone through a long dark tunnel and when it emerged the brown hills had all been white with thick, clean snow. I'd taken it as a sign that I was going someplace magical, that something mysterious would happen, that I'd find Shangri La.

Back in London I was so happy to see St. Leonard's Terrace with its colored enamel doors and flower boxes, the glitzy shops and traffic of the King's Road, all the trappings of civilization, I nearly soared with joy. The euphoria didn't last long, but that kind of happiness, I knew by then, never does. Some time later my psychiatrist told me that soon after I was there, the Rimpoche had left the monastery, moved to London, bought a Bentley. One night he'd had too much to drink and wracked up the car and nearly killed himself on the A-1. He'd been in the hospital for months afterwards and had only recently begun to walk again.

VIVIAN

"I DON'T LIKE HIS HANDS," Vivian said about Bob. She saw him only once but she'd made up her mind. "Too small," she said. "Men with small hands have small penises."

She was wrong but I said nothing. My role with Vivian I'd decided was one of the observer. Hers to talk. Mine to listen. She was a single woman. I wanted to find out as much as I could.

She was the friend of a friend. The wife of one of the actors on the film knew her from L.A. and asked if she could stay with me. "That house is so big. Could you spare a room for a single woman?" she asked. "She hates hotels and doesn't have a lot of money. She's only a single woman," she said. "She won't be much trouble."

"Sure," I said. "Why not?"

Vivian had long dark hair and was thin and sallow with deep eyes and a sharp nose. She arrived one afternoon in a taxi dressed in black with a long violet Isadora scarf flying behind her. Joe helped her upstairs with her bags, his neck turning red. "That scarf is so pretty," I said. "I always wear violet. It's my color," she said.

She brought her own tea and set it out in the kitchen, blackberry with honey. She said she'd rather live in a house without food than a house without flowers and the next day she filled the house with bouquets from the King's Road. She put violet soaps and herbs in the bathrooms and after she bathed you could smell them wafting through the house.

She was in her forties and needed a hysterectomy. "It runs in my family," she told me. "My mother needed one and her mother before her. This is my last fling. I have to go back to L.A. and face the surgery."

She swallowed iron tablets. She kept them in the kitchen next to the blackberry tea. "When I get my period I lose quarts of blood," she said. "Sometimes I get so weak I have to go to bed."

Vivian's great-uncle was a famous Viennese psychoanalyst, a disciple of Freud's, and she had roots in the old world, in Viennese coffeehouses and analytic circles. Her mother had known Anna Freud. She made her living as a stylist on movie sets, but she thought of herself as an artist. At night, after she came back from dinners with friends, she would roll a hash joint to share with me in the library, her long fingers with the antique rings she favored moving quickly, melting the hash from a chocolate-colored bar and dropping it into the tobacco from a St. Moritz cigarette. The St. Moritz cigarettes came in an aquamarine and gold box which Vivian pulled from a velvet bag.

When we were stoned Vivian would opine about art. Of Lady D'Avigdor Goldsmid's collection she didn't think much. The Dubuffet and the Lichtensteins were "non-art" she said, risen to fame only because of the privileged position of male painters. The Hockney elephant was "humorous" but "insignificant"—the Rothko she would admit "had something."

One night she showed me slides of her work—abstract paintings, large canvases covered with bright flashes of paint. "This isn't the best way to see them . . . too small," she said. She held the transparencies up to the light and I looked through them, surprised that Vivian could be so brave. "It's impossible to be a woman painter," she said. "The life is too cruel."

She began bringing me books and talked about them, saying she couldn't believe I hadn't read Colette and Simone de Beauvoir and Doris Lessing. She told me how Willy had locked Colette in her room and forced her to write, how Isaak Dinesen had gone to Africa, how Jean Rhy's women always came to bad ends. She told me how Simone de Beauvoir had written about Sartre's other woman in *She Came to Stay*, and had an affair with Nelson Algren.

I'd read my share of women writers in college but never thought about how they were formed. Listening to Vivian I began to understand that these women were real. I'd never thought of writers in this way before—as people—with lives. I'd understood them in theory, but the raw truth of their flesh and blood hadn't really touched me till now. The betrayals and triumphs they'd written about were true. The dramas they wrote about had all really happened . . . to each of them. An old Gershwin song, "How Long Has This Been Going On?," began to play in my head with its lyric, "I know how Columbus felt, finding another world."

I piled the books Vivian gave me under Lady Goldsmid's shepherdess lamp on the nightstand beside my bed and read every night. I pored over *The Golden Notebook* by Doris Lessing, reading and rereading the long section about the nights Anna made love to her lodger, the writer Saul Green. Vivian swore she'd met them both and it was all true, every word. As the tug of war between them went on and on I was stunned by Anna's patience. Saul Green was so cruel. Was there something I didn't understand? Was this what it was like to be a "free woman"? I wanted to smack him. If I were a writer I'd tell another story, I thought.

The day before Vivian left to go back to Los Angeles for her hysterectomy, we went to the Portobello Market and she pointed to a pair of amber earrings on the black velvet case of a stall. They were the color of the draft beer on tap in the pubs. "Buy them," she commanded.

"Ta Beauty, very Dolly," said the antiquier as he slapped my hand with the change.

"You can trust me," Vivian said. "I have an eye."

When Vivian left I began buying St. Moritz cigarettes. You couldn't find them in just any tobacconists. Sometimes I had to go as far as Park Lane, to the Hilton. I wore the dangling amber earrings for weeks. They made me feel like a woman in a D. H. Lawrence novel, someone wanting to learn about sex. I finished reading *The Golden Notebook* and started *She Came to Stay*, which wasn't as good. Carmele told me she was throwing out the blackberry tea bags. "They make a mess," she said, showing me the faint blue stain on the cups. "I am happy to see that woman leave," she snorted. "She talked too much."

"Who was that woman who was here?" Bob asked the next time he picked up the kids.

"Just a friend of a friend. A single woman," I said.

CHINA

THE CRASH SOUNDED DANGEROUS. A loud, clattering
smash. I'd just stepped in the front door. And then I heard it again.

Downstairs, in the kitchen, Jenifer stood with Carmele alongside her in a sea of broken china. Jenifer looked uncomfortable,
as if she didn't know how to get out of the mess.

"Only some plates, Madam," Carmele said. "They'll never miss
them!"

She waved at stacks of gray earthenware in an open cabinet.

"I told her to throw hard!" she said. "Now she feels better." She
tiptoed across the shattered china, held out a hand to Jenifer and
pulled her out. "Don't you feel better?" she asked.

Jenifer looked at me. "We only broke one good plate," she said.

"Madam. Her heart is breaking," Carmele said. "She has to break something back!"

Carmele grabbed a broom and began sweeping the scattered china. It made a low clinking sound, like someone dancing a soft shoe.

Among the shards of gray earthenware were specks of royal blue and gold Limoges, a French shepherd and shepherdess. Lady Goldsmid had shown me the set on the day of my visit.

"Are you mad?" Jenifer asked. She was my oldest child, careful, responsible. She rarely let loose. In the playground Bob and I had to tell her to take back her toys when another kid snatched them and to hit back when hit. We never succeeded. She had a sweetness about her and a vulnerability.

"No," I said. "I'm not mad."

I put my arms around her and we rocked back and forth. I tried to think of something comforting to say. Anything I could think of sounded stupid.

"You won't feel this way forever," I said, although I doubted my words even as I spoke. I thought we would all feel this way forever, that the anguish would never let up.

Carmele swept up the remaining bits of china and dropped them into the dustbin. She pointed to the cupboard. "There's plenty left. If you still feel bad you can do it again!"

"Go ahead," I said. "Throw as much as you want!"

She stepped out of my embrace and picked up a plate. Her arm rolled all the way back.

Weeks later Bob told me that he'd heard that Lord Henry and Lady Goldsmid had lost their child, a daughter, twenty one, drowned in a sailing accident. I thought of the day I met her Ladyship, of her swallowing the scotch neat from the glass. Could his Lord-ship comfort her, he of the Spartan room, so sterile and bare? I wished I had drunk with her. I saw us together belting back scotch. Maybe we would have had things to say to each other. I thought she'd understand the broken plates, even the Limoges.

A LIGHT BEHIND THE GLASS

ALLIE HAD TWO BOYFRIENDS. And they were both fighting over her. I couldn't blame them because she was very pretty
and stylish. She had long, straight red hair that moved all of a piece
like satin ribbon and white skin with freckles, and she was tall and
very thin with beautiful long legs with white kneecaps. You got to
see a lot of her kneecaps because she wore mini skirts and boots
that came up to the knee. She wore a lot of clunky silver jewelry
too. The first time I saw her she was crying and every time she
blotted her eyes with a wet Kleenex, the chains on her wrists
jingled and clanked.

I said she could stay with me. She was a friend of Vivian's and she had no place to go. She'd come to London to surprise her boyfriend, a writer—they'd lived together in New York—and when she rang his doorbell he was with someone else. A woman in a Japanese kimono opened the door. He came after Allie an hour later. He gave me a look and plowed past me to find her. He was wearing a sheepskin jacket and had curly black hair and glasses. She wept more when she saw him. She had a nervous giggle that attached itself to the ends of her sentences like an appendage and it happened when she saw him. She said "Oh" and then the giggle. She called him Michael but introduced him as Mike. I left them in her Ladyship's library and I knew that as soon as I was gone she'd be in his arms.

Three days later the other boyfriend appeared. He'd flown from New York. He was handsome, more polished than the first boy-friend but with a receding hairline, and he was very quiet. He spoke so softly you had to strain to hear him. His low voice made him seem gentle, but gave him a kind of power. I had the feeling he could be mean, but you wouldn't know it because he was so laid back. It would take you a while to figure out that he was hurting you. His name was Ben and I was surprised he was Jewish. Jew-ish men I'd known, like Bob, even when they were successful were usually more awkward, less deliberate. He had been calling her from New York ever since she got to London. He was an advertis-ing account executive and they had met while she was working on a photo shoot for one of his products, a shampoo. That was her job; she collected props for photographers.

Allie had a sweetness, a kind of innocence about her. I never had the feeling she would attack anyone or say anything awful. I couldn't imagine her throwing things or screaming. She wasn't particularly ambitious and the time I saw her happiest was when she told me about when she and the first boyfriend, Michael, lived downtown in one of the last remaining cold water flats in New York with a bathtub in the kitchen and how they rode on his motorcycle uptown every night to meet his friends at Elaine's. "That was our routine," she murmured. Another story she told was about how both boyfriends wanted to settle things so they had met for a drink at the King Cole Bar at the St. Regis Hotel and she'd come along. "It was so weird," she said, giggling. "I didn't know where to go, where I should sit."

"Settle things?" I'd asked. "Which one did you want?"

She giggled again. "I didn't know," she said. "I couldn't make up my mind."

The dual courtship went on for weeks, both of them coming and going and calling, boyfriend number two—Ben—flying from New York to London and back on the weekends. Ben was getting a divorce. He was a vegetarian and brought his own meals on the plane. Allie baked eggplant and tomatoes and went to the Food Halls at Harrods to select cheeses for him to take out to Heathrow. I watched Allie just as I'd watched Vivian, wanting to see how she managed an unmarried life. In the past whenever I'd faced being alone, I'd begun to have dreams where I ran through dark alleys fleeing killers. How would I manage? What would I do if I were free? Being on my own wasn't the same for me as it was for Allie or Vivian because I had children, but I thought there were tactics I could learn from them. I watched Allie's giggle, her hair and clothes, her innocence. She drank white wine so I began drinking it too. She dangled both men very sweetly. Neither one of them threatened to leave. Ben pressed her to make a decision. He said blandly, "You need to grow up."

She promised him she would choose but then she'd say to me, "Why do I have to? Who am I hurting? Why can't I go on this way?"

Allie could make anything look good. She could take a cardboard box and fill it with apples or bottletops and make it look like a display in the furniture department at Bloomingdale's. When she dropped flowers in a vase they fell just the right way. A cheap string of beads around her neck looked like high fashion. I knew I couldn't imitate her—the same beads on me would look trashy— but I couldn't help watching just to see how she did it. She said it was part of her job, just tricks she'd learned as a stylist. She came from Staten Island. Her father worked for the post office. "Just waiting for his pension," she said, followed by a giggle. She was older than she looked, thirty-eight, she hinted. It didn't seem possible. She looked like a child.

Late one afternoon I came home and found Mike and Allie in the library with a friend of Mike's, a blonde blue-eyed actor with the look of an unmade bed. I'd seen him on the stage in New York. He was one of those actors everyone knew about, but he'd never gotten a big break. A movie he'd auditioned for but didn't get, *Easy Rider*, was opening that weekend in London. The cameo role he'd lost would make Dennis Hopper, the actor who'd landed it, a star. The actor was joking about his bad luck. He was very funny and wry. Soon he took out some grass and we smoked it. He and I began to share Hollywood stories and we started to laugh. He told me how he'd hitched all the way from Texas to L.A. thinking Hollywood would be the way it was in the fan magazines. I told him how I'd played Kitty Genovese and had to lay dead on the stage of the Mark Taper during an earthquake and how the agent I'd gone to had said he couldn't sign me because I looked much younger on stage than off. The actor was fast and smart, with a slow Southern drawl. The grass made everything funnier. Allie and Mike were watching us as we quipped back and forth.

"That son of a bitch is after you," Mike said. "Watch out for him."

"I'm after him too," I said. "It's mutual! Mutual after-ness."

This seemed funny too. The actor kept laughing and so did I.

I felt Mike watching me from behind his glasses, his curly head bobbing forward, his hands on his knees. He wrote columns for *The Village Voice* about musicians and jazz and fringe life in London. Over the weeks he'd been coming for Allie we'd passed each other on the stairs and sat in this room across from the crazy cow painting. One day he'd reached over and taken a piece of soot off my cheek with his finger. Sometimes our jokes had double meanings—but I'd thought they were only jokes. "You're going to be free, the beautiful ex-wife of a movie producer in swinging London. What will you do?" he asked me one day.

"Probably hide," I kidded him.

"I hope not," he'd answered. And then he paused. "That would be a waste of your potential," he said, grinning. His face could be hard to read, like a window with the shade drawn. There's a light on behind the glass but you can't figure out where it's coming from. Now I knew exactly. He had moved to the edge of the couch, his head carving into the space between mine and the actor's. Allie was fading into the cushions, nothing from her but an occasional giggle. If I stole her boyfriend it would hurt her, but she'd never complain.

"Give me your number," the actor said when he got up to leave. He ran his index finger over the back of my hand. "I'll call you later," he promised. I wrote the number on a piece of typing paper I had on the desk, and he folded it carefully and put it into his shirt pocket under his sweater. We all watched him do it. "Next to my heart," he said, grinning. He was rumpled and scruffy-looking, just what I liked. We'd laughed all afternoon. We'd laughed about headwaiters and agents, Yorkshire terriers and hairdressers on Rodeo Drive, fights over parking spots at the studios. Mike was watching us, his hunger stretching towards me, thick as taffy. The four of us stood by the door in a closed circle saying goodbye. I felt an elation, a huge happiness, a giddiness, as if I was floating on top of the room. I could imagine the smell of Mike's breath and the weight of his body, feel the actor's tan hand with golden hairs on my flesh.

UNRELIABLE

"I HAVE PSORIASIS. IT CROPS up at the damndest time," said the first man I went out with after Bob left me. Ted was a writer with a play about his suicidal sister just opened in the West End and soon to close. "Don't count on me for anything," he added. "I'm unreliable. Unstable. I make no money. Get this through your head and we'll be fine." He cleared his throat a lot. He made dinner for me in his flat in Putney. He showed me files with all his work. Tall ones, they stood like sentinels in a converted closet flanking a desk and goose neck lamp. He said he'd just cleaned them out and that was a sign he'd soon be starting another play, which would make him even less available than he was now.

"That's fine," I said. "I have no problem with that. I'm busy too. I can't keep my kids here much longer. I'll probably be leaving for L.A. any day. Besides which I'm mourning a loss. You know what that means. Don't count on me either. I'm not all that dependable myself."

"I've had this psoriasis all my life," he said. "My face looks like shit when I get it which I do in times of stress. Red scales all over my body too. If I break a date with you at the last minute, don't complain. That's what it will be. I'm protecting you. One look and you won't want to see me again. Trust me."

"That's OK too," I said. "As long as you know it's a two-way street. And frankly, you're a little old for me!"

"My sister committed suicide," he said.

"How awful!"

"And my wife . . . my ex-wife, that is . . . was married to a mobster before she met me. She could put a hit on me at any time."

"That's tough."

He made me laugh. And he was a writer. I suppose that's why I chose him. There seemed, in fact, no other reason why it should be him instead of one of the other men who came across my path. This was swinging London. The tail end of the sixties. Sex was everywhere. And hash. And LSD. On every corner. Steps from my house the Chelsea Drugstore throbbed an open invitation and just up the street was the Club Arethusa with its bar packed and jumping till late into the night.

He came from Montreal, the Jewish Ghetto there that bred anxiety and ambition from its coven of unhappy immigrant souls from eastern Europe. At twenty-two he had a story in the *New*

Yorker that won a prize. Since then he'd been racing to catch up with that achievement. He had just stopped smoking—except for marijuana—and always seemed out of sorts.

I met him at a children's birthday tea in a house near Cheyne Walk. A client of Bob's, the singer Noel Harrison and his wife Sarah invited me to bring the kids. Ted walked us home and came inside just at the time Bob appeared to pick the children up and take them out to dinner. I introduced them and they shook hands, each seeming to be backing away from the other as their palms met. It looked to me as if they were both steering their hips into opposite corners. This was in the room where I'd first met Lady Goldsmid, the library with the fragmenting cow by Jean Dubuffet above the fireplace. Next door in the sitting room the mournful deep-blue Rothko wept its sad tears.

"Tell him I'm not interested in you," Ted said when Bob had left. "I have no money," he said. "Tell him that as well."

From his flat in Putney I could see the Thames, lights glittering by night on the black waters. Out back, behind his house, grass rolled down to the river. It's nice, I thought, this thing the English have about their gardens.

When his fingers landed at the back of my neck, moving slowly down the channel between my skull and spine, I leaned over and kissed him. Don't wait for someone perfect, I thought. Put this behind you. Do it now.

"The reason I stopped smoking," he reminded me in bed after the sex, "is because I'm afflicted with emphysema. It could get out of control at any time. I should have stopped sooner. It's only because I'm neurotic and self-destructive that it took me so long."

"Alright, alright," I said. "It wasn't that good. Don't worry. Relax," I said, stroking his face. He was up above me, bug-eyed, his chin on his palm, his shoulder milky in the yellow light. "I'm not staying," I said. "I have three kids. I'm going home."

Now I've done it, I thought, leaning back on the pillow, a hunger from the grass we'd smoked beginning to rise. A beginning, so to speak. There's more out there, I thought. I got married young and the sex I'd had in marriage was ignorant and ill-informed. Before the marriage my few brief encounters were incomplete, quick and on the sly, guilty and inhibited. Going back to Los Angeles suddenly seemed impossible, not a good idea at all. New York, my home, was equally wrong. Returning without a husband? What could that bring me? The decision was suddenly in front of me—lit up and flashing like the lights on a marquee. I'm going to stay in London, I thought. I've got things to do. Things to try.

CAROLINE

THE DAY WE MET I told Caroline I needed a tape recorder and she convinced me to charge one on Bob's credit card. We'd had some white wine and scotch salmon at lunch in the King's Road and it seemed like a good plan, but after the wine wore off I didn't think she'd actually make me go through with it. I'd said yes the way you do when something seems funny and you're enjoying the joke, but she meant it and when the lunch was over she grabbed my arm and paraded me from the King's Road to the electronics department at Harrod's. "He deserves it," she'd cackled. "Don't be so nice. He can afford it. He won't go to the poorhouse."

I had the credit card in my wallet but I'd never used it. I paid for things with British pounds which, now that we were separated, came once a week in an envelope delivered by a car and driver. I knew that this arrangement couldn't go on forever and that I better do something about my financial future, but whenever I thought about money my body began ringing like an unattended switchboard and I had to go outside and take a walk or a run, anything that got me moving. I'd walked a lot of London this way and had begun to learn the city, the shops and green squares, parks and gardens, the houses with their little blue plaques announcing that Oscar Wilde or Richard Sheridan or Virginia Woolf had once lived there.

London was a jigsaw puzzle of tiny streets. A turn off a main thoroughfare could lead to a square or to a secret warren of mews and closes, terraces or crescents. Mike told me taxi drivers had to memorize every street within a six-mile radius of Charing Cross; it seemed impossible. "Doing the knowledge," they called it. All those twists and turns lured me. The houses with their sparkling exteriors and covered dustbins (trash was collected regularly and there was less of it) and flower boxes and white Georgian pillars and Victorian brick fronts and turreted windows with stained glass insets pulled me to them. Walking, I wanted to live on every gorgeous London street. The city had begun to enter me; it was the ultimate distraction, the most seductive tranquilizer. London was an endless maze of places I could lose myself.

Money or the lack of it did not get in Caroline's way. She pulled the British Barclaycard right out of my wallet as if it were a playing card and she had "gin." She drummed it on the counter while I was examining the tape recorders a bald clerk with a shiny head and a fringe-like drapery decoration around his crown and a red tie and pocket handkerchief had taken out and strung across the countertop. While none of these boxes with their glittery buttons and little doors for batteries made any sense to me, she pointed to the most expensive one, the one with the most elaborate array of fixings, and said, "Take that one." I was looking at the smaller, less commanding models but she ordered, "Go first class," and laughed and pushed my shoulder.

I thought of Bob and what the repercussions of this evil act might be, most likely him asking me to return the recorder because he could get one for me from the film office. I didn't want to do anything that might bring on a conversation about my departure from St. Leonard's Terrace now that he and I were no longer together. Nor did I want to risk a discussion of a more stringent financial arrangement than a magical weekly envelope of British pounds. I didn't think he'd evict me and cut off my money, but I knew I couldn't stay there forever on the movie company's dime.

The recorder had a leather case with a little strap so it could hang from my shoulder. Caroline was an American photographer from New York and I'd already taken notice of the sexy way her cameras slung from her shoulder and hit the hip of her velvet jeans. The tape recorder would do the same for me and the professional look of it excited me. Caroline and I had met because she'd done some still shots for the movie Bob was producing and she'd called the house to drop off the contact sheets. "He doesn't live here anymore," I'd growled. She laughed and asked, "How come?"

"Too boring," she said, when I told her Bob had gone off with an 18-year-old actress.

The notion that anyone could regard my situation as less than tragic was something I'd never considered. "You're better off without him," she pronounced crisply, as if this was the only sane position to take. One thing led to another and we'd ended up at lunch at a popular spot—Alvaro's in the King's Road.

The tape recorder came to thirty-three British pounds, about seventy-five dollars. I bought some cassettes too and feeling as if I'd just unbuttoned a too tight skirt, I waved the pen and signed the credit slip and took the Harrod's bag from the smiling clerk. Even his slightly oily fringe looked happier, somehow more light-hearted after I'd spent Bob's money. Caroline took my copy of the slip and tucked it into the pocket of the St. Laurent safari jacket she'd just bought in Paris (a shop would soon open in Bond Street and we'd have to go there, she said), "so you can't return it," she said definitively. She had a way of making statements so you didn't want to argue with her. Not everything she said was fully rational but somehow you had the feeling that if you pointed her illogic out to her she'd mow you down. Her gift for acting spontaneously, always in her own favor, fascinated me. I wished I had it. I envied her boldness, her comfort in the world, her fearlessness. She was an heiress. She had money. She earned money. She strode the earth like a colossus in high-heeled boots, curly hair flying, cameras swinging from her hip.

Caroline could stay anywhere—the Connaught, Claridge's, but after that day in Harrod's she began staying at St. Leonard's Terrace when she was in London . . . which she often was. When she was there the phone would ring without cease, a stream of dates and invitations. Ted Koppel and Lord Snowdon were among her callers. She was invited to gallery openings, cocktail parties, dinners and lunches. And when she left, boxes and ribbons and clothing remained behind, cluttering her room, along with empty film containers, the telephone calls for her still coming until they tapered off like vapor from a departing plane.

That night I took the tape recorder out of its box and read the directions. I'd never had the patience to read and follow directions and I'd never been good with anything mechanical, but I wanted to make the recorder an extension of my body, the way Caroline used her cameras. I learned where to put the batteries and how to adjust the volume and how near or far a voice should be to get picked up by the machine and how to turn the machine on and off unobtrusively. I recorded the kids, Jenifer playing the guitar and all of them singing a Donavan song, "I Love My Shirt," with Joe, Carmele, and Emilia humming in the background. By the time the evening ended I could move the recorder around without looking like an amateur. Bob looked irritated. "What did you do that for?" he asked. "I could have gotten you one from the office." He shook his head as if astonished that I hadn't thought of this possibility knowing the way things worked as well as I did, but he didn't take it any further, at least not this time.

STAYING

WHEN I TOLD BOB I wanted to stay in London he said, "I don't blame you. It's a great town." We were walking down Sloane Street, leaving the stables. He'd come to see Julie ride. I felt as if every time we brushed shoulders it set me back. Old yearnings rose painfully inside me, like heat. Walking alongside him was like being a girl again, feeling I'd die if the phone didn't ring. I longed for him to put his arms around me and say that it had all been a mistake. I wanted us to be married again, to belong to each other, to live in a family with a place in the world. The past came back like an assault. The memories brought on a longing so powerful that it could strike me down. I wondered what would happen if I reached out and touched him and I dug my nails into my palms to stop myself. Walking alongside him brought being apart much too close. But I didn't know how to stop seeing him.

He was wearing a new jacket and an Indian scarf swimming with blues and pinks tied around his neck and smelled of new cologne. Since we parted, every time I saw him he was wearing new clothes. He'd told me in the closet that with his new girlfriend he could express his feminine as well as his masculine side. I guessed this was it.

"Everyplace you turn there's something charming," he said.

"Yeah," I said.

"It's great to spend time in Europe," he said. "I'd like to stay myself. Who knows? Maybe I can do another film here . . . or just take some time and not work at all."

I burned remembering all the times I'd begged him to take a holiday and spend it with me. But I didn't say a thing. A single word could take the conversation someplace I didn't want to go. I'd discussed this with my psychiatrist. Avoid dialogue that leads nowhere. It can only make you miserable.

"I'd like to stay in the house," I said.

"How long?"

"I don't know."

"A month? Two?"

I shrugged. "I'm not sure," I said.

He called me a day later and said he'd cleared it with her Ladyship. I could stay on month to month for a while.

"You have any idea how long?" he asked again.

"I'm not sure," I said.

"You want to live here?"

"I'd like to try it. See how it feels." I held my breath.

"You can't stay in the house indefinitely," he said. "It costs a fortune."

"I know."

"I'm not rushing you, mind you, but when you make up your mind, let me know your plans."

"Sure," I said.

There was a silence. Something dropping from beneath me. Like a little death.

The more I said I was staying, the more real it became. Walking through London I felt weight falling from me, as if I'd scattered everything I didn't want to think about and left it behind, as if I'd lost something I'd always thought I'd needed but now discovered I could live very well without.

In Jermyn Street I bought bath brushes and big sponges and bath oils and put them near the tub. I bought a thick robe made from turkish toweling and hung it over the heated towel rack. I'd always taken quick showers, but the English made a fuss over bathing and I began to do the same. On walks I stared into the windows of every open sitting room, imagining what the life would be inside if it were mine. I began to shop the way Londoners did. Carrying a string bag I made daily trips to the greengrocer and the fishmonger ("Very improvident, Madam," he chided me when I bought Dover sole for everyone, Joe, Carmele, and Emilia included). And in the King's Road supermarket I bought food in small amounts, cheese and vegetables neatly packaged and manageable. The English, I'd noticed, were happy with small pleasures; little chocolates and biscuits and sweets were sources of delight. The attitude was a remnant of the war, I thought, when treats were scarce. In America there was so much excess and so much waste. But I liked life better, having less. Shopping in the King's Road I felt a comfort unlike what I experienced when pushing a loaded cart past the dizzying yards of lettuce in the supermarket in Santa Monica where I could easily waste a half an hour pondering which to choose.

"Movie producers are like royalty," Bob always said, "The kings of Hollywood." Returning one afternoon to St. Leonard's Terrace from a walk through London's dazzling streets I passed the Chelsea Drugstore and turned into Royal Avenue; I'm living off the King's Road now, I thought—in more ways than one.

LA CORUNA

THEY WANTED TO GO TO Spain on a holiday, Joe, Carmele
and Emilia. And they wanted to take my kids. Joe was born and
raised on a farm in the north where his family still lived. He made
it sound like an Eden. "I'll have my own dog," Billy said. "They're
giving it to me while I'm there." His face shone like a medieval
portrait of angelic joy. My daughters, Jenifer and Julie, looked
hopeful. "Please, please let us go," they begged.

We were down in the kitchen around the island. I'd said no
already three times. I'd offered alternatives. We could all go to the
country for a weekend. How about the Cotswolds or Brighton?

"No," Billy said. "Spain!"

"Madam," Joe said. "Looka here." He flashed a wedding photo of a dozen smiling Spaniards. The bride looked sixteen and possibly pregnant, encased in stiff lace. The men were in ill-fitting suits and white shirts, the women in shiny dresses that pulled across their full thighs. "Here—my mother, my father, my sister, my sister's husband, my other sister, here my cousin." His breath whooshed past my ear, "and my sister's husband's cousin, the mother-in-law of my sister. . . ."

He took a creased map from inside his white cotton jacket and put his finger on a pale green spot. "La Coruna!" he said. Everyone gathered around, as if showing me the town on the map would make it all right. It was up towards the coast and looked to be a thousand miles from anyplace I'd ever heard of—Madrid, Barcelona, or Seville.

"They will be safe!" Carmele promised. "I will say these are the grandchildren of General Franco. No one will dare touch them!"

"No," I said. "You really can't go. Think of something else, something closer to home, something I can do with you."

They were all looking at me as if they couldn't believe I was actually going to take this away from them. My face began to feel hot. A rash of sweat broke out on my neck. They had ganged up on me and I deserved it. It was my neglect that had brought this fantasy to life. I'd left the kids with Joe, Carmele, and Emilia too much and too often. I'd used them as babysitters. They made life easy for me and I'd taken advantage.

"It's a long way away," I explained. My voice was thin and wispy. "I can't let you go that far without me or your dad."

The girls were pliable. Tears formed on the bottom of Julie's lids like little lakes but she didn't say anything. Jenifer could be bribed. I could offer her a new guitar. But Billy would make this impossible. He always did. I could see him gearing up. "Please, please, please," he begged. "I want to go . . ." He stretched the word "go" into a long, agonized moan. His eyes were the most perfect shade of marble blue and now they began to darken. "You've never been away from me for that long," I said. "You don't understand how that will feel."

"Don't worry. I won't miss you," he howled.

One night just after Bob left he'd run a fever so high he'd been delirious. I'd had to put him in a tub of cold water. "Who are you?" he'd asked me. The heat radiated off his body in waves and tiny bumps rose on his skin. The driver had come and taken us in a car to the hospital. He was a sweet, small, handsome man with bright blue eyes also named Billy and with a thick Cockney accent. He'd driven me to her Ladyship's house that first day I was in London and he carried my six-year-old child downstairs wrapped in a blanket as if he weighed nothing. The car streamed soundlessly through the empty late-night streets to an old Victorian brick building in a foreign neighborhood. He couldn't move his neck and the doctor said he'd need to tap his spine to check for meningitis. Bob had come and held him while I stood outside listening to him cry in a dimly lit corridor, my forehead pressed against a green wall.

By the following morning his fever had dropped and he asked for bagels and lox. Billy the driver had miraculously found the English approximation of a bagel in an East End shop and brought cream cheese and scotch salmon from Harrod's.

"I want to go! I hate you," he screamed. I waited it out, readying myself for the moment when he'd say, "I hate you. It's your fault Daddy left." But in fact, although he continued to scream, he left that line out.

"Come, Billy," whispered Joe, reaching out for him, trying to pull him to him. Joe was his slave and played endless games with him with his matchbox cars. He cut his food for him and helped him on with his clothes, tasks he'd long ago learned to do for himself. But now he punched Joe's hand and pushed him away. His temper was in full flower, his face scarlet, and it was time for me to act. I had to drag him upstairs away from civilized society. I had to be a firm, reasonable parental figure. When Bob was there we had done this together, neither of us well. But now I had to do it alone.

I wanted to turn my back, walk out of the kitchen and leave them all behind me. I wanted to tell them to go to Spain and not come back for a year. That way I could have all five floors of her Ladyship's house to smoke grass and screw around among the paintings and have sex whenever I pleased. I could think of at least half a dozen men I'd imagined going to bed with and the number was growing every day. I found myself looking at men on the streets, in restaurants and pubs and theaters, their legs rounding the bases at the Sunday morning softball game in Hyde Park, their square hands wrapped around glasses of wine at an art opening in the Mall. I watched men holding raincoats over their shoulders with one finger and the way a clean-shaven cheek curved up to a flat ear. I could feel their skin on my face and the exhalation of breath on my neck. A come-hither scent must have been drifting from me because I found myself in flirtatious conversations at parties and dinners and evenings with friends, exchanging sexy looks and double entendres.

"Don't look for a relationship," advised the singer Georgia Brown, who began inviting me to suppers on Sunday nights at the house in Knightsbridge where she lived with her lover. She'd starred as Nancy in the hit musical "Oliver," in the West End and New York. Her friends went silent when she sat at the piano and sang "As Long As He Needs Me."

"Look for a good time!" she told me. And I thought that was what I wanted to do. It seemed impossible for me to leave the house without meeting someone who made me think—Oh God—why not? But I knew the answer. I had a house full of kids. The bountiful, verdant city of London was doing its share, sending men to me like gifts, but I couldn't open them.

"No," I said to my son, now in the full throes of a tantrum. "You can't go!" I took him by the hand and pulled him kicking and screaming out of the kitchen, leaving them all behind looking embarrassed. I was the enemy and I knew it.

"Let them go," Bob said a day later. "Tell you what. I'll send Billy the driver with them. He can pick up a car in the airport and take them there and wait. I trust Billy. They'll be fine!"

This was true Hollywood thinking, I thought. If there's a chauffeured limousine, what can go wrong?

"Wait in the car for a week?" I asked. "Where will he sleep?"

"They'll find a bed for him. These people always do. And he can call you on the phone, give you reports."

"What phone? It's a farm. They have no phone!"

"There'll be a phone in a bar. Trust me. There's always a phone in a bar."

In the end they went without the driver. He took them to the airport and they waved goodbye from the back of the car. I watched them till it turned the corner. Inside the front door the silence was white. Billy had taken a suitcase filled with matchbox cars, but the ones he had to leave behind were lined up in the hall near the door, waiting for him to come back.

They were away for eight days all together. I'd told them no more. While they were gone I broke up with Ted. He said he thought things were getting too "heavy," that we ought to see less of each other, that his psoriasis was giving him a really hard time. An English film producer whose fiancée, an actress, had eloped with Sidney Poitier asked me to dinner, but couldn't make it at the last minute because the ulcer he'd gotten when the actress left began to bleed and he had to go to bed. He asked if I'd come keep him company. His bedside table was filled with bottles of medication and I brought him some water and held the cup for him. "Was I a shmuck to offer Sidney a job?" he asked, cramming a handful of capsules.

"Who knows about these things?" I said. "Life is so unpredictable."

"You're a beautiful woman," he said to me before falling back on his pillow. "Too bad I'm impotent!"

They came back bubbling over with stories. Every time someone official looked in their direction Carmele had invoked Franco's name. There was a pinball machine in the bar and Billy had won six games. Jenifer had learned to play Cielito Lindo on the guitar. She played it over and over. A Yi Yi Yi. Julie brought back a key chain that dangled a painting laminated onto cardboard of the Virgin Mary holding the baby Jesus. She got it when Joe's mother took her to church and for reasons which she never made clear she carried it with her for months afterwards and showed it to everyone she met until it began to disintegrate. They brought me a peaked straw hat embroidered with flowers and the name "La Coruna." Billy brought back a photograph of the dog, a black and white short-haired animal that looked mangy but shrewd. He said this picture wasn't actually his dog but its mother, but they both looked the same. His dog wouldn't stand still long enough to be photographed. His dog had no name so he'd given it one. "I named him Pal," he said. He hung the picture up near his bed and kissed it every night before he went to sleep. I had to see it every time I put him to bed, its mean little eyes looking out at me from a dusty road and a deep, blue Spanish sky.

C . I . A . . . . F . B . I . . . .

"DON'T TURN AROUND," HE SAID, pulling me to him with two fingers on my sleeve. "Just keep walking. Did you see that black car? Those guys have been following me all week. I can't shake them. . . ."

"Who?" I asked.

"C.I.A. . . . F.B.I. . . ."

"Why?"

"Honey. Who knows? They don't like me."

We were around the corner from St. Leonard's Terrace, passing a row of white houses with bright enamel doors. My psychiatrist said the black iron spokes on the fences around the houses of Chelsea and Belgravia and Knightsbridge reminded him of prison bars. I didn't see it that way at all. Everything about London thrilled me. I loved walking on a London street with a New York actor, with his messy blonde hair and beaten up leather jacket.

"Yesterday I thought I'd lost them. I went in to buy a pair of pants on Carnaby Street. I figure I'm in London, buy something on Carnaby Street. I came out, the fuckers were there. Parked in front of the store. I leaned in the car window. 'Why didn't you come inside the dressing room with me?' I asked. 'Didn't you want to check the fit?' "

"What did they say?"

"They never answer. That's how they drive you over the edge."

"Oh come on," I said.

"You don't believe me?"

"Not really."

We were getting to the King's Road, the black car parked far behind. Up ahead was the Chelsea Potter. I'd suggested we go there for a beer. We ordered two pints and sat alone at a table. He folded a hand over mine and sighed.

"Do you really think you're being followed?" I asked.

"You think I'm paranoid? OK. Try this. The first day I was in L.A. I went to the police station to turn in my gun. I'd hitched from Texas. In Texas everyone has a gun. But L.A. looks like a civilized place. I thought I'd register the gun and send it back home. They charged me with eight counts of armed robbery and locked me up. I couldn't have been in all the places they said I robbed. I was behind bars for two fucking days."

"You had an unlicensed gun," I said.

"For that they charge me with robbery?"

He took a slug of beer. "It's not only cops. Did you see *Hud*?" he asked.

"Yeah."

"Like it?"

"Yeah."

"After *Hud* opens I run into Paul Newman. I hope you like Hud, he said to me. Because that's you. I was flat broke. So why didn't you lay some of that bread on me, I asked him? I should get at least 10 percent. He laughed. Big joke."

"I didn't think Hud was like you," I said.

"I didn't either," he said. "The joke's on him."

He laughed and patted my hand. "Want another beer?" he asked.

"I haven't finished this one."

"Can we go back to your place?"

"I have kids."

"When do they go to sleep?"

I shook my head. "Late. Very late."

"You going to stay in London?" he asked.

"Yeah," I said.

"Your husband is a jerk. Most producers are idiots. That's why movies are so bad. You know anywhere we can go?"

"Not your hotel. I don't want to run into your wife."

His wife was an actress, working in London.

"No," he said, laughing. "You don't want to do that. She's some proposition, that one. Guess we're out in the cold." He patted my hand again and tossed me a regretful smile.

He swallowed the last of the beer and ambled over to the pub door and peered out. I watched the way he moved, the way the leather jacket hung on his shoulders, the way his hair curled over the collar and hung shaggy on his neck.

"They're gone," he said, his eyes flashing blue.

"See!" I said.

"See what? They went for lunch. They'll be back."

We walked towards Hyde Park. I thought I'd walk with him for a while, then head back home. On Sloane Street he bolted and broke into a run after a passing black car. He chased it all the way up the block towards Knightsbridge, slivering through the chic women and tony-looking Englishmen on the street. I watched the way his body moved, so light and electric. He caught up to the car, ran shrieking into the street and banged his palm on the back fender but the light changed and the car turned and kept going. Coming back to me his face glowed with exertion. "Mother fuckers!" he said.

I felt an impulse to put my arms around him but I did nothing. He was beautiful to look at but too crazy for me. I'd had so much fun the day I met him with Allie and Mike. I had said yes right away when he called and asked to see me. But anything more than a beer and a walk would never work out. I imagined us in bed, him on top, looking down at me, his blue eyes close to mine, the F.B.I. breaking in the door of her Ladyship's bedroom, guns drawn; Joe, Carmele, and Emilia peering behind them, the kids behind them. He looked over his shoulder and collapsed on top of me. "Aaah shit!" he said.

I saw him twice after that. He told me he'd been in a play with Norman Mailer and Mailer had taken a bite out of his ear.

He said that every time he drove to Mexico, the agents at the border made him get out of the car for a search. The last time one pulled a gun on him.

"I slammed out of the car and began to scream. Go ahead. Take the fucking car apart. Hub caps. Engine. Whatever you want. I don't give a shit what you do. What the fuck do you think you're going to find? You know what the stupid bastard said? It's those parts you play. Perverts. Criminals. All those lowlifes. For Christ's sake I'm an actor, that's pretend, you moron, I said."

Bob was convinced the I.R.S. was watching our bank accounts. My psychiatrist thought he was being persecuted by hospitals, universities, governments, prisons. Ted closed the shades on his windows when he took his stash from a drawer. Even Mike peppered his speech with talk of "the fuzz." What was it that made men so paranoid? I thought of the protesters in front of the American Embassy in Grosvenor Square. I'd gone past them the day they were burning their draft cards. The world was changing fast, old rules I'd thought sacrosanct stripped away overnight. Someone had to feel guilty.

Or maybe he was just nuts.

THROUGH THE PRISM

I ASKED DAVID IF HIS marriage was unhappy, if that was why he'd left his wife and family, and he said, "On the contrary. I was very happy. Too happy. But I couldn't just be happy. Happiness wasn't enough!"

He was my analyst, the anti-psychiatry psychiatrist. We were in his office in a house in the North of London, in a working-class neighborhood so far from Harley Street and so anti-psychiatry that even the legendary knowledgeable London taxi drivers had trouble finding it.

Bob had come to him first. He'd begun seeing him to get permission to do what he wanted. When I found out that anti-psychiatry was behind what had happened in the closet ("There are all kinds of arrangements, all kinds of possibilities, monogamy isn't the only way to live," Bob had said) I'd called David up, gone to see him, and screamed, "Who are you to break up a marriage with three children? Go fuck yourself!"

He'd sat in his sloping, decrepit armchair, lighting cigarettes. He'd smoke one Gauloise down to the end, till I was sure he'd burn off the tip of his finger, and then he'd toss what was left of the butt into an overflowing ashtray and light another. "Don't blame me," he said. "Blame marriage!"

I began to see him. I wasn't alone. Half of London, especially the half in show business and publishing, traveled up to that house. Ted and Georgia and God knows who else. He lived there with his feminist girlfriend, seeing patients, writing books, smoking dope, drinking, and taking the occasional acid trip. It wasn't only marriage that bothered him. "We should get rid of all repressive institutions," he said. "Universities, schools, governments, mental hospitals—the lot!" His waiting room was scattered with copies of the *International Times*, *Gandolf's Garden*, and *Suck*. Occasionally his snake slithered across the sisal rug followed by a procession of cats. His hair was wild and red and he had a woolly red beard and moustache. He wore only black—a turtleneck shirt and corduroy pants—because black was "all colors." A sign on his wall read in French, "Those who speak of revolution without making it real in their everyday lives speak with a corpse in their mouth."

Where else could I go? He was the man of the moment. "Experience will save you," he said. "Break out. The nuclear family is over! Try something new."

At first I argued. "I don't want anything new. I want what's old. I wasn't so happy when I had it but if I could have it back I'd know how to appreciate it. " I longed so fiercely for everything that was gone that I dreamed about the past every night and even hallucinated that it was there. Sometimes I saw Bob and scenes from my past life superimposed on her Ladyship's house; he was sitting on the sofa, floating above me on the ceiling, perched on the side of the bed. I would try to speak but the words would remain stuck like gobs of glue in my throat; I'd reach out to touch and the specter would evaporate. It was then that I'd realize I had no choice but to listen to David.

The streets of London beckoned; the acid sound of Dylan, The Beatles, The Stones, and the Band throbbed from the Chelsea Drugstore where you could buy a delicate roach holder or a transparent map of the body, rainbow veins, muscles, and arteries seen through the prism of acid. There were handsome men prancing in the King's Road with hair curling down their necks, tight body shirts and bell-bottomed jeans clinging beneath their sheepskin coats from Afghanistan. There were Julie Christie look-alikes with long hair and miniskirts and angel-faced girls in boots and long skirts with dangling earrings and Indian scarves wound round their necks. The streets were a round-the-clock party of seduction and temptation, always calling out to me.

Before I took acid David advised me, "You can do it! Don't worry! You're ready. You'll be fine." I prepared as if this was college and I was taking a test. "Just be careful around the sixth hour," he said. "That's when you may start to see some things you don't like. But it doesn't last long. Just stay calm. It will pass!" He smiled like a father sending me off to a dance and lifted his arm as if in salute. The cigarette dropped a large turd on the rug. "Great!" he said. "Good luck!"

I was taking the acid with Mike. We'd become lovers. After the afternoon with the actor I'd begun to think of Mike differently and when I saw him coming towards me one afternoon in the King's Road I felt like fate was sending me a sign. He was carrying a rolled up copy of *The Village Voice* with his latest "Outside London" column. He'd just picked it up at the bookseller in Sloane Square. Writing about London for people to read in New York suddenly seemed the most glamorous life imaginable, much better than anything else I could think of—even being a movie producer. In his tinted aviator glasses with his sheepskin jacket swinging he looked sophisticated and sexy, as if he had all of London in his back pocket. "Come back to my flat. I'll make you a cup of tea," he said. "I'll show you my column," he joked. He was clumsy, half laughing, both of us knowing what might happen. I laughed too, whether out of nervousness or because I was thinking of Allie I couldn't be sure. I followed him up the steps to a one-room flat in a turreted red brick Victorian house behind Sloane Square. Inside, he bent to kiss me and I felt myself melting towards him. I thought of all the bantering we'd done on her Ladyship's sofa while he was waiting for Allie. How many boyfriends does Allie need? I thought. Why can't we share him? She'd let him go without a thought and then decided she wanted him back. Well, too bad. Bob was right. It *was* a new world. Everything's different. But new world, old world, what did it matter? Another woman had taken my husband. Why shouldn't I take what I wanted? Everyone else seemed to do it.

In bed afterwards, wound around each other, he'd said, "Let's trip together." And I'd said, "Yes."

The kids were gone for a weekend with Bob. Mike brought a small, clear bottle of liquid wrapped in brown paper to the house. "Sunshine acid," he called it. We built a fire in the fireplace and swallowed it down in distilled water. He'd done this before, but was very careful, measuring the water, pouring the liquid. We waited. Minutes passed. Ten. Fifteen. Twenty. Twenty five. Nothing. This was it? Thank God! No Experience. I'd knocked at the door but been turned away. Sitting on the toilet my eyes fastened on a drop of water. It clung to the lip of the faucet without falling, expanding like a wine skin growing tumescent. The drop got larger and larger, clear as a diamond faceted with shimmers of pale rainbow colors. I began to think it would never drop off. How long had I been sitting there? How long could this take? With a rush of comprehension I knew this was it—I was on an acid trip and there would be no turning back.

The marriage was over. The new world was here. Liquid sunshine had ushered it in. Inside the fireplace the flames were 3-D. Music, Leonard Cohen, came at me through a long tunnel. "Suzanne" was a foghorn calling to a place by the river. We made love with a red glow around us. I could see through myself; veins, arteries, muscle, texture of skin, youth, and old age seemed to join in my hands. The sounds of children running by in the street sounded like applause, the inside of my body felt like velvet. Afterwards, outside the streets were bathed in a golden glow and shimmered with lights. It was hard to know which direction to go. In a Knightsbridge mews a fourteenth-century panel of Christ in an art gallery window superimposed behind a twentieth-century parking meter was a revelation. We couldn't get past it. We marveled at the juxtaposition. Mike checked his watch. "It's six thirty . . . but not for us . . . only for the rest of the world," he said, wrapping an arm around me. This seemed profound. A pink blouse in a Beauchamp Place shop revealed iridescent blue in each fold of the fabric. We stood rooted there, amazed at the sight.

In Mike's flat there were snakes in the folds of the red velvet drapes. They came right on time at the sixth hour. The cracks in the ceiling were ominous. My shirt felt dirty, my hair oily and limp, my face cracked apart in the mirror. Mike gave me his sweater. I gave him my felt hat with the python band and my silver chain necklace of large hammered links. It had broken during the acid trip and he fixed it with a paper clip which I found very touching. I told him he could keep it. "Baby, you gave me your chains! Heavy!" he said. It was silent as we entered the restaurant. No sound but the forks and knives clinking against the plates. Nobody spoke. I thought they were staring at us but couldn't be sure.

We ordered a ton of cheap Indian food. The spices clung to my tongue and the roof of my mouth. I thought this taste will stay with me forever. I'll never forget it as long as I live.

Both of us drunk now on food, Mike took me to meet his friends Jay and Fran. He wrote about them often in his columns. Small twinkling lights flickered behind my eyes all the way up to Islington in the taxi. And they continued to come and go, sparkling like tiny diamonds as I sat in Jay and Fran's dim living room on floor cushions and a velvet-covered mattress pressed into a corner. A big mirror with an ale sign that they'd brought with them from a nightclub they'd owned in St. Louis, The Crystal Palace, took up the opposite wall. A Tiffany shade over a round oak dining table cast a burnished glow. Jay sat in a barber chair looking down from a high platform, long legs crossed, one wing-tipped Gatsby-style shoe from the Camden Passage Market swinging back and forth. "You're no good for me," he said, looking at me with lifted brows and the trace of a smile. "Get out of here before you drive me crazy."

I began to laugh and the little twinkling lights raced by as if I were hurtling past stars on my way through the universe. They continued to appear on and off over the next three or four days . . . until finally the trip was over.

"How was it?" David asked Monday morning. I'd arranged to come back right away. I had to report. His eyebrows lifted, waiting. A Gauloise burned in his fingers.

"It was a drug," I said. "It was great! I'm not sorry I tried it— but I'd still rather be married and happy!"

"I doubt it," he said. He smiled. A genial Santa. "Give yourself time."

I reached into a bag I'd bought in a rug shop in Knightsbridge. It was made of an Oriental carpet in shades of red, green, blue, and gold with a black leather shoulder strap. I'd begun carrying it all the time. I pulled out a St. Moritz and lit up. The room filled with smoke.

JAY AND FRAN

AFTER I MET JAY AND Fran my London life was never the same. I fell in love with them and took to visiting them when I was free in the evenings after the kids were asleep. They had the kind of house you could drop by any time of the day or night. Someone would always be there on the living room cushions eating the macrobiotic brown rice Jay sold and Fran cooked every night, often with broccoli, or smoking the dark hash they melted from lumps and bars and mixed with tobacco. They seemed to know every fringe character in London, the famous and far out from the worlds of music and art, politics and literature, and film. I never knew what conversation I'd stumble on when I dropped down onto the floor pillows. Jay would be in the barber chair, long legs crossed, half smiling at his own questions: "Will the counter-counter culture make the counter culture irrelevant?" "Is the common man too common?" (Way too common, Fran said.) "If you could turn back the clock where would you turn it back to?"

In Jay and Fran's living room I met Carolee Schneeman, an artist, famous in London for painting herself as Eve in the nude festooned with snakes, and filming herself in erotic love scenes. I listened to a churlish American novelist with the romantic name of Chandler Brossard and to Germaine Greer, a weedy Australian who'd written a feminist book that had become a rallying call, *The Female Eunuch*. One night a handsome screenwriter friend of Jay and Fran's from L.A. named Fred Siegel, whom they called "F. Scott Fred Siegel," took us all out for an Italian dinner in SoHo. On another evening the glamorous girlfriend of a defunct finan-cier, Bernie Cornfield, swept in from Paris. Fran had written a poem about her, "The Princess From Flatbush."

> She's got a bracelet from Cartier's and beauty and wit
> She's got a dozen new lovers but none of them fit
> She's got two eyes like black olives and very nice tits
> She's just a princess from Flatbush who stays at the Ritz
>
> She came a long way from Brooklyn without a career
> She's busy hiding and seeking and fighting her fear
> She's got a house on the lakefront, a plum tree with plums
> But all her elegant dinners still taste of the slums
>
> She settled in Geneva beside a crooked man
> Goes skiing in the winter and keeps her perfect tan

The crooked man has vanished and left her lots of bread
She's reading Krishnamurti to straighten out her head

She studies chess with a master and soon had him beat
But all her really good gambits she learned on the street
I go to faraway places and find far out chums
But I remember her kisses that taste of the slums

Fran was a lyricist. Her songs had been recorded by Sarah Vaughn and Ella Fitzgerald, Tony Bennett and Chet Baker—and jazz musicians recognized her name right away. She and Jay had written a musical, *The Nervous Set*, that had an off-Broadway run, and of their two sons, Cosmo and Miles, Miles, the younger, was named after their friend from St. Louis, Miles Davis. The night we met Fran gave me a book of her lyrics and poems. It was a little softcovered book Jay had published and by the end of a week I'd read every verse in it dozens of times. The book was tattered and frayed from my handling it. I read the poems to everyone I knew. Sometimes I cried when I read them. "All the sad young men, sitting in the bars, knowing neon lights, looking for the stars."

In the photo on her book cover Fran was drenched in sunlight; blonde, glamorous, and camp with long hair Veronica Lake style and a big straw hat with flowers and a double strand of pearls. She wore a fitted polka dot dress with a slim bodice. But on the nights I came up to Islington she was always curled up against the living room pillows like a turtle about to withdraw into its shell, her tapestry bag in her lap. Fran carried that bag everywhere, hunched over it as if for ballast as she went from room to room. Inside the bag were the bars of hash, speed—diet pills she got on the National Health, sucaryl tablets, fags, and low calorie chocolate from Boots, the chemist. She was only forty-two and still pretty, but seemed permanently stooped. In her bedroom one night, on a bed covered with even more velvet and pillows and shawls than the living room mattresses, Fran told me that she had a stash of pills too . . . in case she wanted to "off" herself. "I'm not that fond of life," she said. "I'd never hang around if things got too tough." Her contemplation of suicide was opaque to me, as dense and black as pitch. It made her mysterious and sophisticated, fascinating and baffling. I didn't understand her, but I never wanted to stop listening to her.

They had lived in this North London house around the corner from the Angel Tube station and the Camden Passage Antique Market for five years when I met them, had bought it with the proceeds of the St. Louis nightclub, The Crystal Palace, they'd sold. Jay came from a family of antique dealers and he'd furnished the nightclub with gaslight-era appointments, Tiffany shades and stained glass, some of which he'd brought to this house. Barbra Streisand and Elaine May and Mike Nichols had played that club, and Lenny Bruce and the young Woody Allen. Fran hinted that she'd had a love affair with Jack Kerouac; "He was such a beautiful boy," she said wistfully. I thought that was where her song "All the Sad Young Men" came from, from Kerouac . . . and from Jay. She said I was right; the song takes place in a bar. "I grew up on Central Park West and escaped to the village. I put in my time at the San Remo bar," she said.

Jay brought Fran tea on a tray every morning and went out to sell brown rice; he had a typewriter in a basement office and said he was writing a novel. He had a girlfriend too . . . a painter named Marcia. Fran called her "the bitch." Sometimes she called her "the witch." I asked her how she tolerated Marcia and she said, "I have to. . . . If he couldn't fool around . . . neither could I. I'd never end my marriage over her. I'll be here long after she's gone."

Their bathroom was plastered with graffiti and postcards from friends traveling in Marrakesh or Katmandu or Ibiza. Sometimes I spent a half hour in there just reading the wall. They went to parties and London happenings in their antique Bentley or Jay's big bus, Fran dressed in vintage shawls and dresses and jewelry from the Camden Passage Antique Market. For dinners out they went to The Seed, a macrobiotic restaurant frequented by George Harrison and John Lennon and Yoko. One night I joined them and Jay picked me up in his ancient yellow bus in front of the elegant Dorchester Hotel. "Madam," the doorman said, unflappable in his top hat, holding the door open as I stepped up and settled myself on a worn plush seat.

Still, they talked about the past as if their lives were behind them. "Norman Mailer said that Fran and I were the ones who started it all," Jay would say. He'd roll his eyes. I could never tell when he was joking and when he wasn't, how much he meant and how much he didn't . . . and I never asked. I understood regret— but not the kind that cancelled all possibilities. I didn't like talking about hope but I secretly nurtured kernels of belief that something good was in store for me. But loss was in all of Fran's poems . . . a past redolent with intractable mistakes and squandered opportunities. *The year's half gone and what have I done, I went to Cannes and sat in the sun, The year's half gone and what's there to show, I fell in love with a man made of snow.*

And . . .

All the good tunes have been written. All the good songs have been sung.

Somewhere we took the wrong turning. Long ago when we were young.

I took Jenifer, Julie, and Billy up to Islington to visit Fran and Jay one Sunday afternoon. They invited me to come, but didn't tell me they were going to be on an acid trip. Jay and Fran made fun of Mike for wearing a watch, for getting his columns in on time, for taking only half a tab of acid and sharing the other with me. Their attitude towards drugs was a lot more casual than mine. I was glad I'd dropped acid but I had no need to do it again. I'd never been in their living room in daylight. It looked comfortably beaten up and less mysterious than it did at night. Shafts of sunshine came through the windows lighting the rumpled pillows. Jay and Fran's faces looked smooth and unlined, even radiant.

We went for a neighborhood walk and to the park, all of us hiking in a line on the narrow paths. Jay led the way calling out sights like a tour director. The kids laughed and shouted back at him. "Buckingham Palace! Westminster Cathedral!" Jay and Fran put their arms around each other, and then around us; they never stopped smiling. "You are all so beautiful," Fran said to the kids. "Your faces are unearthly. I wish you could see yourselves. You look like angels!" "We can see each other," Billy said. "Not the way we do," Fran said. "You sound a little crazy," Billy told them. "I know," Fran said. "I am a little crazy!" "They've taken a drug," I told Billy. "It makes them very happy." "And crazy," he said.

Bob came to pick up the kids for dinner that night and in a spurt of generosity I gave him Fran's book to read. I was sorry as soon as I'd done it. Her poems were like the starbursts of light I'd seen on the acid trip, flashes of a new life I wanted to keep for myself. I walked all over London that evening thinking of Bob reading, "Would You Dance with a Man Who Used To Be Handsome?" and

"Where Are You, Darryl Zanuck? I've Been Waiting for Your Call" and "The If Game". . . . *That plane we missed . . . If you had found . . . If I had read . . . If you hadn't run, if I'd been more free, you wouldn't be you, I wouldn't be me.*

Later that week Billy the driver dropped the book off with a note. I found it on the hall table. "These are wonderful. Thanks for letting me see them." They were in a manila envelope, like 8-by-10 glossies and a resumé returned by a talent agent. I'd thought about what would happen when Bob went back to L.A. as he would when the film was finished; there would be an ocean and a continent between us, but even now, living in the same city, the distance was widening.

WOULD YOU DO IT ON SPEC?

THE WIFE OF THE DIRECTOR of Bob's film, a German woman named Carlotta, invited me to Sunday lunch with a songwriter from L.A., a former trombone player in a black leather jacket and dark blue jeans named John. He also wore a copper bracelet which he said would deflect negative ions and cure everything. He'd won an Oscar for one of his songs, "The Shadow of Your Smile," and I liked him when he said that he had a recurrent nightmare in which Richard Nixon in a TV interview names "The Shadow of Your Smile" as his favorite song and then plays it on the piano at a White House dinner.

Carlotta felt sorry for me and sat next to me at the lunch table and made a point of "drawing me out." When no one was looking she put her hand in front of her mouth and hissed "Bob is a fool! The girl is stupid. A child!" She clucked her tongue and shook her blonde head. She was a thickset woman and I could tell she'd insisted on inviting me and the director was embarrassed to have me there; Bob was his producer and setting his producer's exfacto wife up with a musician from L.A. was the last thing he wanted any part of. He had one of those ruddy English complexions and while he was tough on the set, he could barely look at me at the table. His skin just turned redder when I was in his sight line, even his thin, pinched nose reddened. Fortunately, he and Carlotta had a brood of kids that ran around a lot and distracted everyone.

It was a big, wandering house in Bloomsbury, paid for by the film company, a dark green living room of formal English furniture which the kids, English housekeeping, and the carelessness of privileged film people had left pretty much in disarray. Nothing hung together; the whole lunch didn't hang together either. Even the musician let drop over the English joint and Yorkshire pudding that he never dated Jewish women; "We're just not interested in the same things," he said. "Why is that?" Carlotta asked. "Don't know. Just never happens," he said. When I said I knew Fran . . . he sat up. "The lyricist?" he said. "You know her?" "Yeah," I said. "Very well." "I'd love to meet *her*," he said.

John gave me a ride home from Carlotta's lunch in a plush record company car that made me think of L.A. As soon as the car glided off he leaned over and kissed me. The kiss happened so fast I had no idea it was coming but it was exciting and I didn't stop him. I liked when unexpected things happened and being without Bob they seemed to happen more often. He had white skin and a sturdy muscular body which I'd seen when he took the leather jacket off at lunch. After the kiss there was another kiss and then another and then his hands began to move along my body. I began to think about marrying him. I wondered if he lived in Laurel Canyon which was the right place for a musician, but we'd need a larger house, probably in Benedict or Coldwater. I wondered if he wanted a child. I wouldn't be too happy about that but thought that the child might have musical talent. Between kisses he told me he was in Reichian therapy and had his own orgon box in L.A. He'd had it built. He sat in it every day. Since he'd been sitting inside the box he felt better about everything. In Reichian therapy he took off all his clothes. "You strip naked?" I asked, imagining him tossing off the leather jacket and flinging himself down on the couch. "Sure. After a while you don't even think about it," he said. This wasn't the first I'd heard about the Reichians. Bob had visited a Reichian analyst several times in L.A. after he'd heard about it from Sarah and Noel Harrison and Georgia told me she'd had a Reichian analyst for a while too. As I understood it, once you were naked you also got punched at various "pressure points" to release negative energy. I couldn't imagine taking my clothes off in a psychiatrist's office. Baring my body would be much worse than baring my soul. Not think about it? Naked, I'd think of nothing else. But I told John about David, and he nodded sympathetically when he heard I was in therapy.

"Hey. Any chance I could meet Fran?" he asked as we pulled up to my house and unglued ourselves from each other.

Two nights later I took John to Islington. It had become my second home. He sat down on the cushions and Fran passed him a joint and they swapped names of people they knew: Miles Davis, the Smothers Brothers, Dizzy Gillespie, Louis Armstrong, a long entourage of musicians about whom they exchanged anecdotes. "I could never make it in California," Fran said. "Promises, promises . . . none of them kept." "They're all that way out there. You get used to it." John shrugged. "They don't know any other way to be," he said earnestly. They looked at each other through the smoke. "I'm doing a recording for a TV pilot," John told Fran. "It's about a bunch of army doctors. It's called 'Mash.'" The sweet smell of hash was drifting over the room and Jay had broken out the apple juice—their macrobiotic treat. We weren't supposed to drink too much. . . . "Too Yin," Jay said. "It could throw the entire chemistry of your body out of whack." "Any chance you'd like to do a lyric for the flip side?" John asked. "You can do whatever you like. It's yours . . ." he added. "The thing is I can't get you any money up front." He looked really apologetic . . . his face folded together with the apology. . . . "You'd have to do it on spec. . . . but I have a lot of influence." "Mash? Stupid name," she said. She was leaning back against the cushions, smiling dreamily. "I don't think I'd want to do anything on spec. . . ." "Think about it," he urged. "I'll think about it," Fran promised. She didn't look too excited. "But I have to warn you . . . I'm gun-shy about Hollywood."

On the way home that night in the car John's kisses became sweeter and more insistent. He said how much he wished Fran would write the lyric for his record. He repeated how sorry he was he couldn't get her any money up front. I thought about how little it would take for Fran to write the lyric. She wrote all the time. She spent every day up in her bedroom with a pen in her hand and a pad on her knees. I didn't understand what she had to lose. She wasn't getting paid for what she wrote now. Why couldn't she just give him one of her lyrics? If it were me I would do it in an instant.

As we got close to my door John said, "Hey. I'm going to Cannes next weekend for a record convention, want to come?" "I thought you didn't date Jewish women," I teased.

"Jewish women have moustaches and thick ankles," he said. We both looked down at my feet. "But you don't. . . ." He reached over and picked up my right ankle and cradled it in his palm. "See," he said. I sat with my leg outstretched. The haunting melody of "The Shadow of Your Smile" floated across my brain. How could such a song come from someone who sat in an orgon box? There was a lesson here about art and life.

I shook my head. "I can't leave my kids."

He put the ankle gently back down on the plush floor of the car. "Can't you get a sitter?" he asked.

My lawyer, Ian, had warned me to be careful about where I went and with whom, never to risk getting caught with a man. "If things get nasty with our dear friend Bob, it will be a bloody mess," he said. Bob could call me an adulterer and try to take the kids. "No boyfriends until I say so, dear girl," Ian ordered.

I'd already stretched that rule . . . but a weekend away would be going too far. Still, who would know? I could leave the kids with Emilia and Carmele—or even send them to Bob. I'd be home Sunday night. Nobody had to know who I was with. Bob had been to the Cannes Film Festival twice and told me how beautiful the south of France was and how exciting the festival—everyone making deals, writing on matchbook covers. Envy and desire rose inside me. I wanted to go.

"OK," I said. "But Sunday night I have to be back."

We flew from London to Paris and from Paris to Nice. At the Nice airport a car was waiting to drive us to Cannes. We stayed in a room overlooking the sea that made me think of Matisse. The convention was jammed with musicians, all friends of John's. One evening they drove up into the hills for dinner at a restaurant where a basket of crudites the size of a flower bed waited on the table, every raw vegetable imaginable, the first time I'd ever seen such a display. John's friend, the musician Quincy Jones, had a room next to ours which he shared with a ravishing blonde girl as thin as a pencil. Each day she set up an easel on the promenade and painted the sea. When we were alone John said I'd changed his mind about Jewish women and asked if I'd come to L.A. to see him. I said I'd think about it. I didn't want things to get too "heavy" as they could with Jewish men.

On the way home the flight from Nice stopped in Paris. From there we'd board a connecting flight to London. In Paris the airport seemed to be whirling. A crowd surged towards the Air France counter waving tickets and passports. People were shouting, pushing their way through to the front of the line. "A strike," someone said. Planes weren't leaving the ground. The French stewards in their neat blue uniforms shrugged, offering no answers, cool and remote. "*Demain, peut-être.*" Flights might resume tomorrow. Or they might not. They couldn't say. I stood in the middle of the crowd, people swirling around me. I had taken only one little bag, just a few changes of clothes, knitted pants and a long jacket, not even a dress, which John said was a turn-on; traveling light, not something a Jewish girl would do. I'd had so many possessions while I was married, so many articles of clothing and shoes. Things had weighed me down. I wanted to own little, carry less.

The bag had hung easily on my shoulder, but now it seemed heavy, like dead weight. Sweat broke out on my forehead and under my arms. I'd told Bob he could bring the kids back that evening. I'd said I'd be back home by seven or eight. "What should we do?" I asked John. But he looked bewildered, as if I was asking him the equation for splitting the atom. I thought of the record company cars, the hotel room, the drivers to take us to airports, the reservations he hadn't made, all the things he never had to do. There was a lost quality seeping from him like water from an overflowing bathtub inching under a door. I took a closer look at his hairline. I'd thought there was something strange about it but until now I'd ignored it. Up close there appeared to be a row of little plugs along his forehead sprouting tufts like miniature whiskbrooms. I wondered if he'd had a hair transplant. I'd heard about them but never seen one up close. For this I'd risked my children?

There were ten people ahead of me at the phone booth but I waited, counting down as they finished their calls. I was sweating and my stomach had gone into a spin cycle. I clutched a handful of francs. "I'm sorry," I said to Bob, keeping my voice light. "I'm in Paris. A strike. What a pity," I said, making a joke. "*Quel dommage!*" It occurred to me that the first time I'd seen Paris Bob and I had been together. We'd stayed at a tiny hotel on the left bank with a pull curtain around the toilet and bidet and gone to the

Champs Élysées at two in the morning to look at the Arc de Triomphe. Sweat was pouring off me and the little bag on my shoulder was digging into the blades like a knife. I saw myself in a courtroom, the kids being taken away, Julie and Billy holding out their arms to me, being led by a stern-faced matron, Jenifer, her innocent face stony and unforgiving. I saw myself completely alone, a cloud of vapor wrapped around me like white steam and not a person in sight.

John and I spent that night at a grim little hotel across the street from the Gare du Nord. The room's walls were paneled with cheap wood. I lay on the bed without taking my clothes off, the bag at my side. "Don't come near me," I said to John. I had liked him in the hotel room in Cannes, but that was over. I had done everything to get us back to London. I got the boat train schedule to take us across the channel and located this hotel. I got us onto the first train out of Paris in the morning and at Southampton onto a train into Waterloo Station where I fled into a taxi. I kept my back to him during the whole trip, not speaking except to warn him never to tell anyone that he'd spent a weekend with me. "If you say a word I'll kill you," I said.

"A strike. That's typical," Bob said. He was very forgiving. If he suspected I was with someone he never let on. He said, "Europeans don't want to work. That's why the whole fucking continent is falling apart. Too much socialism. They have no ambition."

John called Fran before he left London and asked her again to write the lyric to his record for "M*A*S*H," but she said, "No. I just can't work on spec." To me she said, "He's a great musician but what's with his hair?" "I don't know," I said. "What did I tell you?" she said. "Everything there is fake." John called me too but I repeated that I just wasn't ready for anything heavy . . . or for that matter anything at all. He called me again from L.A. "It wouldn't have to be heavy," he said. "I'd just like to see you." I'd calmed down by then but I still said no. Carlotta called me too and when I told her things hadn't worked out with John she clucked and predicted Bob would be back. "But if it has to end," she advised, "make sure you get the house. Or enough money to buy one. Darlink," she said . . . I could hear the kids screaming around her . . . "remember what I am telling you. A woman alone should own real estate. Do you know an agent? I have one. I'll ring him for you."

NAMES

I ASKED THE KIDS TO call me by my name.

"Why?" Billy asked.

"Because it's my name," I said. "I have a name."

"We know that," he said. "You think we didn't know?"

"What's my name?" I asked.

"Phyllis," he said.

"Great," I said. "Call me Phyllis."

"We can't call you Mommy?" Julie asked.

We were watching TV in her Ladyship's bedroom. *Gentlemen Prefer Blondes*, Marilyn Monroe and Jane Russell flashing across the screen. Their lush bodies and legs. Julie was barely watching. She had a trail of miniature animals that she was parading across the pale blue rug. The line stretched from the bedroom door around the bed and to the windows overlooking St. Leonard's Terrace.

"I'd like to be called by my name," I said.

"Simon and Katherine call their Mom and Dad Sara and Noel," Jenifer said. "And so do all their friends."

The kids played with Simon and Katherine Harrison, Sara and Noel Harrison's kids. For a while Bob had managed Noel, a singer who accompanied himself on the guitar. He was the son of Rex Harrison. It was at Simon's birthday tea that I'd met Ted.

"I don't want to," Julie said.

"It's stupid," Billy said.

Jenifer said nothing. She'd moved to the end of the bed, close to the TV, her eyes wide, her chin tilted upward. Marilyn was singing "Diamonds Are a Girl's Best Friend," like a little girl imitating a grownup.

"You can think it's stupid, but I'd like you to do it," I said.

"Wait . . ." Billy said. He'd gotten bored with the movie and knelt down to rearrange the line of animals.

Jenifer's eyes were pinned to Marilyn.

"Don't get too close to the screen," I said.

Julie abandoned the animals to Billy and hung onto the bed looking at me, her arms on the quilt, her legs stretched out onto the floor. "I'm not doing it," she said. The heels of her cowboy boots knocked into the line of animals.

"Julieeee," a shriek from Billy.

"Fix your parade," I said.

She righted the little figures and then came back, spread herself across the quilt.

"I'll call you Phyllis if you call me Phyllis," she said.

"Phyllis isn't your name," I said.

"It's not fair," she said. "How come you get to be Phyllis and I don't?"

"That's the way it works," I said. "I can't be Julie. Everyone only gets one name."

"Square cut or pear shaped those rocks don't lose their shape . . ." Marilyn lisped.

"You like her?" I asked Jenifer.

"Yes." She threw me a complicit smile. "She's beautiful."

"She died when you were little."

"Why?"

"She was unhappy," I said.

"You can die from that?" Billy asked.

"You have to be *very, very* unhappy," I said.

"Like you?" he asked.

"I'm not that unhappy," I said.

"You were," he said.

"She's not anymore," Jenifer said.

"That's right," I said.

Jenifer moved back alongside me at the head of the bed. I put my arm over her shoulders and we watched, propped against the pillows.

When they called me Mommy, I didn't answer. Sometimes they didn't remember and they called me four or five times. When they said my name I answered right away. Billy and Julie made faces. Phyllis. Phyl. Pill. Pilly. Fill-face. It was a big joke.

Jenifer never said anything, just looked at me and corrected herself. My name from her mouth floated like breath on the air. Not responding to Mommy was hard to do even though their calls were usually for minor requests. The demand to answer them roared through me like heat.

"It won't kill them to know you have an identity other than Mommy," Georgia said. "Seeing you as a person will be good for them."

My psychiatrist said, "You're setting a good example. You're showing them how to unglue themselves. If you can do it, so can they."

He lifted his hands, a big smile on his face.

At the end of a month they were calling me by my name. "Phyllis . . . Billy hit me . . ." Phyllis. . . . Do I have to? . . . Phyllis . . . Dad wants us to go there for lunch . . ."

"What's with Phyllis?" Bob asked.

"Why not?" I said.

"I don't get it . . ." He paused.

I waited.

"Do you have any interest in having me take them?" he asked.

"Don't try it," I said.

"Very nice," he said. "A pleasure talking to you."

THE SPICE KING'S DAUGHTER

I WROTE LETTERS TO MY mother and father. "Dear Mom and Dad," I wrote, although my father never answered. My mother replied for both of them. She didn't actually sign his name. She always signed "Love, Mother," but it was understood that she was speaking for him too. That was their arrangement and until the advent of David—the anti-psychiatry psychiatrist—and his list of the many ways in which marriage was responsible for the "death of the self," I'd never questioned their melded personalities.

My parents lived in Brooklyn in the one-family house they'd bought just around the time I started high school. The house was smack in the middle of the borough, on Bedford Avenue between

Avenues M and N, a block that my friend across the street, Toby Zeller, called "The Ritz block of Brooklyn." In fact, it was a nice block but not all that ritzy. There were a lot wealthier neighborhoods than ours. Our next-door neighbors on the left, the Kaplans, had four children and Gene Kaplan owned a plumbing business about which there always seemed to be something mysterious and precarious. I'd see Mr. Kaplan with my father, their heads bent together in the driveway or walking hands behind their backs down the street while my father offered advice.

A few houses down from the Kaplans was handsome, charming Jack Lobel, an inventor and a gambler who owed everyone money including my father. My father didn't seem to care. He even joked about it, although I got the feeling he wouldn't lend Jack any more. Jack had gray hair and a beautiful smile with great teeth and always seemed happy, which wasn't the case with his wife. Bertha was a tall dramatic-looking woman with beautiful legs and she wore deep purple lipstick and cried a lot. She was always telling my mother that she couldn't hold her head up any longer and came from a family that was "fine and cultured." After Bob and I were married she divorced Jack and moved into Manhattan and got a job at Saks Fifth Avenue. I saw her there once selling jewelry on the main floor and she asked me if I thought she was right to leave Jack. "I couldn't hold my head up," she said. "He's down in Florida, still doing the same thing."

To the right of us was the large white renovated house of Mr. and Mrs. Gardner. Marvin Gardner manufactured nylon skirts and had done well enough to afford two Cadillacs, two nose jobs for his daughters, a sunken living room with a Baldwin baby grand and a busty wife who wore high heels and full makeup and "sheath" skirts every day. Rocky Graziano, the prizefighter, lived on our block for a while until he moved away, we heard to Florida, and Gil Hodges, the Dodger first baseman, bought a house there too. They were substantial houses, set wide apart with driveways and garages and generous backyards. We had a cherry blossom tree in our backyard and pink roses climbing a lattice on the side of the garage and a flagstone terrace out back where we sat on webbed aluminum chairs and chaises on summer nights, the glow of my mother's cigarette lighting the dark. Most of the houses were two-story stucco or brick with attics and basements and sunporches in the front, although some people had broken through the sunporch wall to make one big living room. We kept our wall and renamed the sun porch a "den" and watched television there, eating cherry vanilla ice cream while Sid Caesar in "The Show of Shows" and Milton Berle in "Texaco Star Theater" cavorted in black and white across the screen of our Dumont TV.

My father had worked hard to buy that house and it had taken my parents a long time to choose it. Nothing having to do with change was ever accomplished quickly in my family. Leaving a family gathering at my grandparent's house less than three miles distant, it took hours to get out the door. My sister and I would stand by, sweating in our hats and coats, squabbling with each other, waiting to go. "Please, let's go," I'd whine, and "When are we getting out of here?"

"In a minute," my mother would say and keep on talking. My parents and aunts and uncles said goodbye but never left. Moving from a rented apartment to a house that they would buy and pay for (with a very small mortage . . . "We'll pay that off fast," my father said) was preceded by years of Sundays which we spent looking at houses. We filed expressionless (instructed by my father to show neither enthusiasm or disapproval) past mantels where a wife's and sometimes children's portraits hung, and peered into built-in closets and pickled-pine finished basements. Every Sunday I fell in love with one of the houses we traipsed through. I saw myself reading in bed in a bedroom I selected for myself, my head against the headboard, looking up from my book and through the window at the eaves of a garage and the snow-laden branches of a maple tree and imagined my friends in the new living room and my dates (when I would have them) arriving at our new front door. I could even smell the fresh paint and new carpeting we'd install over the spot where the owner's dog had left a stain. Even though my parents seriously considered many of these houses and I had all of Sunday and sometimes even Monday and Tuesday to embellish my imaginings and build a web of dreams, by Wednesday the discovery of a damp basement or a leaky roof would quash the sale and dash my fantasies. The following Sunday the whole process would begin again until my parents settled with aching slowness on the house they finally bought.

We lived in Brooklyn. I longed for a Manhattan apartment which I saw as the height of sophistication—but such a dream was truly futile ("Cliff dwellers," my father called the residents of New York City buildings). A house on Long Island was another tantalizing possibility and during the search they even toured several, but in the end they rejected them as too exotic. Except for my father's two youngest brothers, my uncles Sid and Al, who had bought split-level houses on Long Island on the G.I. Bill, we all lived in Brooklyn. The family spice business was there. Crossing the Williamsburg Bridge from Manhattan you could see the sign on the left with our name painted in white on blue across the top of a large industrial building—J. Raphael & Sons—Rayson Brand Spices—Importers—Grinders. The business originated with my grandfather Jacob from a pushcart. He had come from Europe in the bottom of a ship and after he had a job and a new suit he had come to court my grandmother whom he'd met on board. She was the daughter of a religious man. Her father had led the services on the boat. Her family offered him dinner and he never left the house. They married and stayed right there.

My grandmother and grandfather had six children, five sons and one daughter (the daughter was a mistake, my grandfather joked) and four of the five sons, my father included, remained in the family business. (The one son who escaped—miraculously, first to Columbia University and then to law school, didn't fully make it, however. He stayed in Brooklyn, a lawyer with a real estate practice down by the courts.) They imported spices from foreign lands—Europe and South America, India and the Middle East (nobody ever went there—it was all purchased from suppliers). They ground and mixed pepper, paprika, garlic, cinnamon, cumin and coriander and oregano, and sold the finished product to meat packers and canners and companies in the business of preserving foods. We were rooted in Brooklyn. Nobody ever left. Even the two brothers, my uncles who bought houses on Long Island (Queens, actually), drove in every morning to work in the Brooklyn spice factory.

I was the first grandchild in my family to move away, first to Manhattan and then to Los Angeles. My revolutionary example bore fruit for my younger sister when after a considerable struggle that elicited a warning from my grandfather ("A girl is like a diamond. One scratch . . . pffftt . . . it's worth nothing!") she managed to get a job, move out, and share a Manhattan apartment with some friends after college. While I was living in California my mother visited but my father wouldn't make the trip. He was phobic about traveling and never went on a subway, a bus, or even a taxi. Airplanes and tunnels were not a consideration. His only mode of transportation was a car that he drove himself. A string of Pontiacs, a Hudson and Chevys, all smelling of spices, streamed through our lives. Once he drove all the way to Detroit, Michigan, to attend a wedding of one of his customer's daughters. An automobile was the only way he could get there.

When my mother visited me in L.A., my father had a breakdown. He called and begged her to come home. "I'm not going to make it," he said. The experience of her leaving—of separation—drove him over the edge. He had to see a psychiatrist (standard issue, no anti-psychiatry psychiatrist for him) for a while and took to guarding my mother to make certain that she didn't post any letters in a mailbox or put their clothing in the washing machine—two precautions that he was never able to explain adequately to any of us.

In the letters I sent my mother and father from London I told them about the things we were doing; I told them about taking the kids to Madame Tussaud's Wax Museum and the Tower of London and London Bridge. I sent them photographs of the kids standing at attention alongside two big beefeaters. I told them about the changing of the guards at Buckingham Palace, the cucumber sandwiches at tea at the Dorchester, about the Regent's Park Zoo, the Battersea Fun Fair, and Joe, Carmele, and Emilia, Arantja and Baby Arantja and Carmele's "husband." On the movie set one day we'd seen Marcello Mastroianni, the star of Bob's film *Leo the Last*, the story of the final scion in a long line of Italian noblemen. Marcello was outrageously handsome I told them, and had smiled at Jenifer as he passed by. I told them about buying mini dresses at Biba in Kensington High Street and antique shawls at the Portobello Road open market. But I never mentioned that Bob had gone to live with an eighteen-year-old actress on the other side of town in a flat in Russell Square.

My mother's birthday was coming—February 12th—Abraham Lincoln's birthday ("He freed the slaves but not me," she would say as she served my father dinner). She liked to read, novels mostly (anything—*Forever Amber* to *Catcher in the Rye*. Somerset Maugham's *Of Human Bondage* was a favorite. She hated Mildred), and had taken me to the library across the street when I was six and gotten me my first library card. I had the thought that perhaps I should send her a copy of *The Golden Notebook*, but doubted the notion of "Free Women" would appeal to her. "I couldn't get into it, Phyl," she'd say. I decided I'd just send her something expensive and pretty from Harrod's.

In my mind I saw her in her little golf socks with the white balls at the back at the kitchen table while the black cat clock above the sink rolled its eyes and waved its tail to mark the passing of each second. She was a pretty woman in her late fifties and she'd only just begun to "sun tip" her hair to cover the gray. She had been sixteeen and a model in the garment industry the summer she met my father at a dance at a resort on a lake where he was "the boat boy." (The story we'd grown up with was that he saw her coming down a flight of stairs and said to his friend, "That's the girl I'm going to marry.") I could see her reading my letters over coffee, the racing page of *The Daily Mirror* with the horses she'd picked alongside her, the smoke from her Pall Mall rising from an ashtray. That afternoon she'd tee off at a golf course she drove to on Long Island and tell her friends that she'd just gotten a letter from her married daughter in London. At twenty-six my sister was still single. No. I couldn't tell her. Not for her sake. Not for mine. Not yet.

GETTING A JOB

GEORGE WAS HUNGARIAN, BORN IN Budapest, a writer, an actor; a man of the theater, a man of the world. He'd lived in London, Hollywood, Egypt. He was tall and thin and graceful, his body a long elegant stalk. He had had a love affair with Greta Garbo and I could see what she saw in him. I could see what anyone saw in him. The first time I saw him it was a summer night in New York and he was wearing a white linen shirt with full sleeves like a gypsy. He was backstage at *Brecht on Brecht*, a collage of the theater pieces of Bertolt Brecht that he'd put together. Brecht's sinister characters—thieves, hookers, and beggars—swirled around him. His hair was copper, his moustache flourishing, his nose like the Matterhorn. His elongated eastern European accent was laced with culture and subtext. He said "Hello" and that was all you needed to hear.

Bob was doing some work for George's second wife, the Swedish actress Viveca Lindfors. That's why we were there. Her translucent skin looked as if it had been poured over architectural bones. They invited us back to their brownstone in the east nineties hung with theater posters and cluttered with books, photographs, and memorabilia. There were other people there, all ages, all accents, all talking. Books. Films. Theater. They all knew each other. There was food spread out on a table and two handsome children, a boy and a girl with their friends in the living room. I had never seen people like this before and I thought to come from such a family would make it possible to do anything, go anywhere, live a charmed life.

In London on his way to Berlin, George stopped by to see me. Since my separation from Bob I'd learned there were people who still spoke to me and people who no longer bothered. Of the people who still spoke to me, some of them even talked to me more than they had in the past.

We were in the house late at night. "Tell me about Garbo," I asked. He had settled into the couch and looked as if he'd been born there. No one I'd ever seen fit more perfectly into the aristocrat's house.

"I was in Los Angeles writing a script," George said. "I met her in Malibu. She was living in the beach house of Salka Viertel. They were not alike, but very good friends. Salka was earthy; always barefoot, a screenwriter—she'd be writing and at the same time cooking, stirring a pot of something on the stove, children running around, lovers in and out of the house, a different one every week. Garbo . . . was Garbo . . . off in an ivory tower. Salka, she would ask, How do you love? You just . . . love, Salka would answer.

"She wanted me there all the time. I was always leaving the typewriter, driving to see her . . . back and forth, back and forth. She was like a hothouse orchid, she needed constant care. One day I got a cable. In those days you got cables. My first wife was dying of cancer in New York. In New York Hospital. She'd asked to see me. She didn't have much time. The flight to New York was twelve hours then. I'd have to be gone three or four days. I knew when I told Garbo there would be trouble. At first she didn't say anything. But that afternoon she lost a ring on the beach. She was very upset. We searched everywhere, retracing our steps. We were sifting the sand with our fingers. She said, 'Don't go.' Only once. 'Don't go.' 'Don't be silly,' I said. 'It will only be a few days. I'll just see her, turn around, and come back. . . . She's dying,' I said.

"She drove me to the airport and waved goodbye at the gate," he said. "In those days you came out to the gate and waved as the passengers boarded. The whirring propellers stirred up the wind. Everything blew. She was wearing a white scarf and it billowed behind her. I stood at the door of the plane and waved and she waved back. But I knew it was over . . . that I'd never see her again," he said.

I waited.

"That's it?" I finally said.

I had trouble with this ending. I wasn't expecting it. I hated to see things end. I always thought there was some way to save love. If love had once been there, how could it simply one day be over? In books I closed the pages when passion died. When reading epic novels I refused to move on to the next generation. I was always loyal to the first. This was Garbo. How could he let her pass out of his life?

"What do you want?" he asked.

"Didn't you call her?"

"Of course I did."

"What happened?"

"She wouldn't speak to me."

"How could you let her go?"

"It was useless," he said. "That's how she was. She was inse-cure. It would always have been that way. If not one thing, then another."

"But she was Garbo!"

George lifted his palms and dropped them in his lap. I could tell he didn't agree with me. I thought he should go to the ends of the earth to keep her. Surely, he could make her understand!

In the hall I helped him on with his coat. I was still smarting. The chapter wasn't yet over. The ending was so unsatisfying I needed to keep him there. I didn't want to let him go so I thought of something to say. I'd been meaning to mention it anyway.

"I'm looking for a job," I said.

"For God's sake why?" he asked. His eyebrows lifted like little fur collars.

"I'm going to put the children in school and stay in London. I need something to do."

"What for? You'll have enough money. And you'll remarry," he said. He tied an elegant paisley scarf around his neck and but-toned his suede coat.

"I never want to get married again," I said.

"You'll change your mind," he said, smiling.

"No," I said. "I won't."

This was true. I'd thought about it. I wasn't interested in a revolution like David's. But to my mind marriage seemed like an unfair deal, you gave too much for what you got in return. I thought I'd have lovers, each one for as long as he lasted.

"Call my brother," he said. "He'll give you a job."

"You have a brother in London?" I said. "What's he doing here?"

"Another Hungarian Jew who ran from the Nazis. What else? He's a writer," he said. "He's always writing something . . . he can always use help."

He fumbled for a pen in his breast pocket and scribbled on the inside cover of a matchbook from a Knightsbridge restaurant everyone was going to, Mr. Chow. "Call him," he said, kissing my forehead before he pulled on his soft leather gloves and went out the door.

BOB

IN THE SPRING OF MY freshman year at Skidmore College
in Saratoga Springs, a girl named Liz Salomon who sat next to me
in an Oriental culture class and was going with a Union College
pre-med asked if I'd like a date with one of her boyfriend's fraternity brothers. Liz was a sophomore and wore her boyfriend's
fraternity pin on her left breast in the spot just where the tip of
her pinkie would fall if her thumb was pressed at the space between her clavicles. She said my date-to-be wore glasses but was
"cute," and on that basis I said yes.

He was "cute." She was right about that. He had a low-key way
of delivering funny lines and he was tall with myopic blue eyes

behind a pair of very thick, heavy glasses. His eyes were so bad that he was classified as 4F—"legally blind," he said, and didn't have to be in the army reserves. "They'll take women and children before me," he said. He had a redhead's complexion, white skin bathed in an unending spray of pale freckles and the kind of red hair that doesn't make a statement. He was awkward and there was something inaccessible about him, something that gave me to understand that I'd never know where I stood with him. But I found that appealing. I liked being kept off balance and was bored if I wasn't. We went to the movies in Saratoga and I hoped he'd call me again. By the time he did, two weeks later, I'd nearly given up on him. The phone we got our calls on was in the hall outside my room and when I picked up and he said his name I felt a burst of pleasure and then anxiety. I knew what was coming and my mind was already clicking away on the potential problem. The next week was the last one before final exams and the end of school. I knew he was going to ask me out for that Saturday night and I was busy. I had a date with a "platonic" friend who was coming down from Williams. I couldn't break it. There was nothing for it but to take a major risk. "I can't make it on Saturday," I said when he asked me out. "How about Friday?"—an unheard of piece of boldness but I was willing to chance it. I wanted to see him. "No," he said, and his voice bent the sentence in two. "I'll ask you," he said.

I was in a new dorm the next fall in an old Victorian house and up on the third floor where I lived was a pretty, arty, literary girl named Alida whose father owned a service station in Monticello, New York, in the Catskill Mountains. She was dating a boy, also from Monticello, who went to Union College. Gerry came up to see Alida the day after she and I got back to school. Alida and I were making plans to work together on the campus literary magazine when he arrived and she asked me to come downstairs to meet him. He was in a car parked just outside our dorm—a light blue Buick with a flashy silver grill and red leatherette seats and behind the wheel was Bob, the boy I'd been set up with the previous spring—the one who'd rebuffed my request for a Friday night date. He and Gerry were in the same fraternity and he'd driven Gerry up to Saratoga to see Alida. He looked even "cuter" than I remembered. There was something more self assured about him than there had been when I first met him. His face seemed somehow less rounded, as if his cheeks and jaw had lost their last baby fat.

"Nice car!" I said, deciding immediately that I was going to keep this meeting brief. I'd made myself available last time and it had gotten me nowhere. I wasn't going to make the same mistake again. After a spot of conversation ("How was your summer?" "How was yours?") I said I had to leave to go to the bookstore, pleased to see the flicker of disappointment cross his face.

I'd evened the score. When he called later that night and asked me out for the following weekend, a football game and dinner at his fraternity house, I said yes. That week Alida told me all about Bob. His Uncle Charlie, Charlie Rapp, was a show business agent, she said, a very big deal. He booked the acts into all the hotels in the Catskill Mountains. Singers and comics and dance acts and animals, harmonica players and "The Dancing Waters," people who sent fountains of colored water into the air to the sound of waltzes, the "Chevals de Chanson," twelve singing, marching men dressed like tin soldiers who traveled in their own bus—all worked for Charlie. Every Saturday night he sent them to entertain in the nightclubs of the resort hotels of Sullivan County: the Concord and Grossinger's, the Laurels, the Pines, the Nevele and Kutsher's Country Club.

Bob had worked for Charlie that summer and gotten paid a lot of money, a thousand dollars she'd heard. One part of his job was driving Charlie back and forth between the Catskills and his office on Broadway across the street from Lindy's restaurant and another part was ferrying the acts from hotel to hotel with their glittery costumes and musical arrangements, their tuxedos in suit bags and their wigs in hat boxes. Charlie had bought the snappy baby blue Buick for that purpose and let Bob have it for the winter when his business slowed down and he wouldn't need it.

Alida had a soft, low voice and big eyes that widened when she mentioned the names of the acts. She was pretty sure Bob had driven Tony Martin, she said. He might even have driven Sammy Davis Jr.

I'd spent the summer earning thirty-five dollars a week typing out bills of lading in my father's office in Brooklyn, driving back and forth with my father, stopping to pick up my Uncle Mac and my grandfather in Crown Heights, listening to conversations about the price of paprika. There was nowhere to go in Williamsburg on my lunch break so I sat around the spice factory and read. That summer I read all of Jane Austen and the Brontës and started reading Dostoyevsky. I loved *The Gambler*. My young uncles, Sid and Al, kidded me about my reading all the time, but they were also sweet and we all rooted for the Brooklyn Dodgers and called them "The Bums" and followed every game. I'd just gotten my driver's license and after we dropped off my grandfather and my uncle every night, my father let me drive the car the rest of the way home, calling me Barney Oldfield the racing car driver if I got up any speed at all. I'd wanted to go to Europe that summer but my father had refused to give me the money for the National Students' Association Tour I had in mind. I'd known it was a waste even to ask. On weekends I'd had some fun when Dick Lobel, a boy on my block, was invited to the El Patio Beach Club in Atlantic Beach and took me along. But hearing about what Bob had done, the bills I'd typed to Hygrade and 999 Provisions and Hebrew National and Katz's Delicatessen and The Pastrami King suddenly felt like a deadly noose. There was a better life elsewhere. I knew it. I'd been in the Catskill Mountains with my parents once and loved the glamour of the flirting waiters, the cha-cha bands, the dance lessons, the poker games around the pool, the manicured women in high heels and diamonds and the prosperous, joking, golf-playing men, and the feeling of sex in the air. Just being near someone who was up close to such a show business life felt exciting.

Pretty soon I began going down to Union regularly. Alida and I would take the bus every Saturday morning from Saratoga to Schenectady, she to see Gerry and I to see Bob. Bob would be working when I arrived at the Phi Sigma Delta fraternity house. He had a job at a laundry in Schenectady and when that was over he served lunch at the fraternity house. He sold jackets to the Union College bookstore and he was also the Chesterfield representative on campus and distributed free sample packs of Chesterfields and got a monthly check for that even though he didn't smoke. After lunch we would go to a football game if there was one at home and sit up in the stands with his fraternity brothers and their dates, swigging from a flask someone would pass which didn't prevent us from getting very cold in the thin, upstate late-afternoon fall sun. I looked forward to those weekends, the sun on the red and yellow leaves as Alida and I talked nonstop on the bus, the slanting light falling on the green lawns and white-trimmed buildings after the football games, and the fraternity party afterwards with the keg of beer and the same jokes all the time. The one weekend I couldn't see him because the platonic friend at Williams had asked me up for homecoming, Bob sent me a telegram that arrived the morning before I left. I hope you have a miserable time and it rains, he said. For that morning at least I was euphoric. I knew exactly where I stood.

Bob shared his room with two roommates—Gerry was one of them and there was another one, a small thin boy named Arnold. Bob had gotten the largest bed in the room, a double bed, alongside it a chair piled with all his books and clothes; the joke was that at the end of the year he wouldn't even bother to pack, he would just pick up the chair and take it home. We'd neck in that bed—often Alida and Gerry at the same time in the one across the room and sometimes the third roommate would be there as well. The sex was always incomplete but powerful and hard to stop though we'd decided we would—but it went on for hours and started up again and again. In between we'd talk. His father played the bass in the New York Philharmonic, a profession that brought with it the genteel poverty that explained all the jobs Bob did to put himself through school. His father wanted him to be a doctor—a surgeon—he had the hands for it, thin and tapering. But not the temperament. He couldn't see himself in medical school. His mother, Uncle Charlie's sister, from the side of the family with all the red hair, didn't care what he did, he said. As long as he made money. All her friends' husbands were pharmacists or furriers or jewelers and they all had more money than she had. Dmitri Mitropolous, the world-famous conductor who her husband always referred to respectfully as "Maestro," and the entire Philharmonic orchestra were nothing in her life, he told me. Her message was, just don't be poor. And no, he said late at night in the big bed. He hadn't driven Sammy Davis Jr., although he'd sat once at the same table with Eddie Fisher and Elizabeth Taylor.

We had trouble leaving each other. Late at night we four, Alida and Gerry and Bob and I, would drive back to Saratoga in the blue Buick, navigating the icy roads as it got colder, sometimes racing faster than we should to make the midnight curfew.

That Thanksgiving Bob came to Brooklyn to take me out. He had to take three trains from Kew Gardens to do it and the price of the tickets he bought to take me to see *The Lavender Hill Mob* with Alec Guinness at the Paris Theater in Manhattan cost so much more than a local movie, it shocked him. My mother was in the habit of commenting about the boys who took me out but this time I warned her; "Don't say a word," I said. "I'm going to marry him." In the bed at the fraternity house one February weekend he pinned his fraternity pin on my left breast in the correct spot. We were engaged to be engaged. I was nineteen and he was twenty one. He had applied to law school at Columbia for the coming fall and I filled out a transfer application to Barnard. I didn't want to be in Saratoga without him. I was typing bills of lading in my father's office that summer day when my mother called to say the thick envelope had come that signified I'd gotten in. I felt as if the white paper and the pink and yellow carbons of Hygrade and 999 Provisions and Hebrew National were fluttering in pieces all around me, like confetti.

TEACHER

MY MOTHER NEVER TOLD ME outright to be a teacher . . .
but she didn't say much outright. She was the high priestess of in-
nuendo, the great goddess of implication. "Teachers go home at
three o'clock every day," she said. "And they get summers off and
a week at Christmas and Easter. Where else could you find a job
like that, perfect if you want to raise a family?" She never directed,
just made remarks, like the one she made about a boy I went out
with in high school. I had fun with him. We sang show music together and danced on subway platforms. "It's very clear, Our love
is here to stay," we sang.

"Is his father a barber?" my mother asked, dragging on a Pall Mall, her legs crossed, the smoke rising around her.

"I don't know," I said, although of course I did. His father's shop was just under the subway station at Avenue M.

"I'm just asking," she said. "Don't get huffy! We don't know any barbers," she said.

To be eligible for a substitute license I had to take a physical at the Board of Education in Brooklyn. It was a rainy day and I was wearing high rubber boots. My blouse and bra were off for the heart and lung part of the exam and the nurse asked me to jump. Bare-breasted, jumping up and down in a curtained cubicle my mind shipped out to another place, a better world. This doesn't matter, I told myself as the rubber boots sprung up and down off the linoleum floor; this doesn't count.

The school on Amsterdam Avenue and 106th Street wasn't far from our first apartment on Riverside Drive, an old red building that smelled perpetually of empty milk containers. There were twenty-six seven-year-olds in my second grade classroom, among them three girls named Nydia and one autistic boy named Henry. Henry was a light-skinned Puerto Rican with a head shaped like an egg and big teeth. His large eyes were fringed with long, thick lashes and his hair was cut in a spiky crew cut. He looked like a child's drawing of a child. He was neatly dressed and well cared for and his grandmother brought him to school and picked him up every day. She didn't speak English and Henry never spoke . . . not ever. His normal expression was a half smile of such infinite vagueness that you felt as if you could travel along it for a thousand miles and never reach a destination. The most emotion he ever showed was to pull away his arm when I had to direct him somewhere. His face would darken, his brows would knit and the smile would disappear, but that expression never lasted. Five minutes later his normal vacant look would return along with his inclination to wander the classroom—a stroller on the boulevard of second grade.

Henry fascinated me but he was the least of my troubles. The out-of-controlness of the classroom was my real problem. Twenty-six children, all with different ideas of what they wanted to do and where they wanted to go. I'd learned enough pedagogy in my education classes at Barnard to be able to teach but getting them to sit still so I could give a lesson was another story. In the beginning they trampled over me. It took a year to learn the tricks of teaching second grade, a year of bringing Henry back from the classroom door or from the floor of the coat closet, a year of separating Nydia Perez and Nydia Ramirez when they tore at each other's hair, a year of asking kids why they'd missed school and having them say "No shoes," a year of learning the magic power of routine and how standing silently at the head of the class and ringing a bell might work . . . or might not.

Harriet taught across the hall. It was her first year of teaching too, but she was prepared. On the first day of class she put on a light blue smock over her clothes. She had dark hair pulled back in a barette and looked like Virginia Woolf with bad skin. Her husband was an engineer. She was planning to teach for four years and then she'd have a baby. On winter weekends she and her husband went skiing at Catamount State Park. She had things under control. Her classroom was quiet. When she turned her back or sat down at her desk the kids read or drew. They didn't fly around the room like mine did with Henry wandering off like an unraveling shoe lace. Over bag lunches in the teacher's lunchroom she explained that the reason the kids said they had "no shoes," was because they expected me to buy a pair for them. "Any white person who looks clean could be another social worker," she said. "Wait till Christmas, they'll all give you soap."

Harriet taught me the trick of the bell and of talking softly and waiting quietly and clapping my hands twice . . . just twice for attention. Harriet—like blonde, curly-haired Edna who taught first grade and was married to a customers' man on Wall Street who took her to the San Juan Hilton over Christmas, and tall, glamorous redheaded Dana who bought orthopedic shoes so she could stand all day in the classroom—were meant to teach. Dana wasn't married yet, but she would be. I could see her in a Colonial house in Connecticut in a skirt and sweater, ascending to a supervisory position, driving her car to school and leaving her orthopedic shoes in a locker in her office. In Puerto Rico Edna said they swam and played tennis all day. Every evening, like clockwork, there was a brief thundershower and then the sun returned so they could see the sunset. Dana's and Edna's classrooms were like Harriet's—organized. By the end of the year I'd learned some tricks, but nothing I did came from the inside; it was all sleight of hand, not mine; none of what I knew belonged to me.

When school ended in June I operated the switchboard in Uncle Charlie's office. Charlie paid me fifty dollars a week (fifteen more than my father had for the bills of lading, but this was show business) plus dinners and taxis home on the nights we worked late. Bob got me the job. Now we were both on Charlie's payroll. The switchboard—active though it was, humming with a zillion calls—was a relief from second grade. Until I got the hang of it I made mistakes. When three or four calls came in at once

I'd panic and freeze. Charlie was not the world's most patient employer; "If I knew I was going to have all this free time, I would have gone for a massage! Just put the plug in, honey!" he shouted from the back office. But once I learned the technique I preferred the switchboard to second grade. The switchboard was abundant with surprises. Every time it buzzed it could be anyone. "Rapp Enterprises. International Talent," I'd say (he booked the Catskills and Miami), and wait for a split second wondering whose voice would be on the other end. It could be the actor Zero Mostel. "Put Rapp on," he'd growl. "Let me speak to that cheap, miserable bastard!" (Zero had been blacklisted by The House Un-American Activities Committee. Charlie was the first to give him work but couldn't get much money for him and Zero took the jobs—the only ones he could get—but he was perpetually furious. One day Zero took me to lunch at the tiny Gaiety Delicatessen on 47th Street. "My Inamorata," he introduced me, to the dozen people he met on the three-block walk, his arm over my shoulder, a hand groping for my breast.) Or it might be one of the hotel owners conniving to get a free midnight show. If the acts would come and hang out in his nightclub when they'd finished their shows and then "just happen" to get up and perform he'd pay back with free food and booze and accommodations for the night for everyone.

Sometimes it was Charlie's girlfriend, Mignon, a French dancer with a poodle who claimed she used to dive for coins off the cliffs of Acapulco. "Let mee speeek to Charlas," she'd say. But even more than the element of surprise, what I liked about operating the switchboard was the low responsibility quotient. All I had to do was connect the caller with the callee—in this case Charlie or Al or Jimmy (the other agents) or "Chickie" (Charlie's office manager, the only person I ever saw talk back to him. She wore high-heeled mules). When the switchboard wasn't buzzing I could read *Anna Karenina* or the plays of Chekhov, praying Anna would curb her ardor for Vronsky (her foolish obsession would lead to trouble, I could tell), furious with Arkadina when the pistol shots rang out. Unlike teaching second grade where a mistake could carry heavy consequences, operating the switchboard did not impact upon the fate of the earth. In second grade a kid could hurl a block at another kid and put out his eye, the classroom could erupt in chaos, the kids could learn nothing—no math or reading all year—bad things could happen because of what I did or didn't do. But the switchboard was its own safe little kingdom; just connect people or get rid of them if Charlie didn't want to talk. That was as far as it went. Anything further had nothing to do with me. Sometimes on Thursday nights when bookings heated up for the weekend shows I had to work late. It might be nine or ten o'clock before the office staff went to Lindy's or the Spindletop Steak House for dinner. In the windowless reception area at 1650 Broadway without air-conditioning, with just the fan whirring above me and a ventriloquist with his dummy waiting for hours on the couch ("Come back in December," Charlie would say as he strolled past the poor performer on his way to dinner or a poker game at the Friars Club), I'd plug in and out, not exactly happy, but hardly discontent.

STARTING OUT

"IT'S NOT FOR ME," BOB said. He'd passed the bar exam on the first try, got a job with a Wall Street law firm, bought a pipe and knockoff Paul Stuart suits at "Merns" the discounter, played squash at the Columbia Club. He wanted to give law a try. It was a two-partner firm and they liked him—there could be a partnership down the road—but days in the law library drove him nuts. He left for work early, came home late, and said "This is a joke!" Law was slow, antithetical to his nature. It took so long to see results. He'd suspected all along he wasn't meant to be a lawyer. In law school he'd been interested but hardly diligent. He'd made it through by pulling all-nighters. He'd sweated out a few exams but always passed. Now here he was, up against the choice! Three years in law school! I mourned all that tuition, but wasn't shocked. By then we'd had numerous conversations; "It's Columbia Law school! It can't be a total waste! Better to have the degree," he said . . . "You never know!" At the end of six months on Wall Street he bailed; he had an idea; he'd manage the acts he'd met through Charlie, push them, promote them, help them write material. He'd take ten percent. Charlie said he'd filter acts in his direction. He'd use his law school expertise to negotiate their contracts. "People in show business are impressed with lawyers. They think they know something," he said, laughing.

From behind his bass in the living room of their Queens "garden" apartment (up three flights), his father smiled gamely. You could see this decision broke his heart. "Bobby can do anything," he said. (The entire family were musicians . . . his uncle Hymie had fiddled for the Czar. To have a profession, medicine or law, was close to being God.)

"Which acts?" his mother asked. She was stringing beads, squinting to put one through the needle. Her friends admired the necklaces she made. Occasionally she sold them. She looked up, her beautiful, delicate face as alert as a beagle at a hunt. As soon as she heard her older brother's name, she knew there would be money. Charlie was the family's big success, trailing clouds of gold. To travel in his wake was like owning shares of AT&T. "I've already got a comic," he said. "Personal Management," he called it.

I'd imagined myself in the role of lawyer's wife with liberal politics and a brownstone in the village, children in progressive private schools. Now I'd have to find another role. Although imagining new identities for myself came easily enough, I couldn't see much for me in Bob's new plan.

"You think this will work?" I asked. As a career, "Artist Management" felt flaky and insubstantial, like a Kleenex mopping up a flood.

"Why not?" He shrugged. I didn't argue. From the safety of teaching second grade (at least we'd be able to pay the rent), I took him at his word. His father was probably right, I thought. "Bobby can do anything!"

I'd seen him on vacation, at the blackjack tables, a glass of free casino scotch in front of him, smoke from a free casino cigarette drifting upward. By then he'd gotten contact lenses and looked sophisticated with a gambler's easy charm. He took risks far beyond what I could tolerate. Watching him my fingertips turned cold. My throat got tight. We had no money, nothing to fall back on. The pile of chips got smaller and still he'd ask the dealer to hit him one more time. When he won I was relieved. The night was over and we had more money than we'd started with. When he lost I sulked and cried and begged him to give it up. He said, "I could tell you that I will . . . but it wouldn't be the truth."

Flying back from Puerto Rico we hit an air pocket and the plane dropped. I was certain this was "it." "Aah shit!" he said. His glass had slid along his tray table, nearly dumping ice and water in his lap. He was annoyed. The turbulence had inconvenienced him. I envied him his attitudes; somewhere I knew that this was what life takes; I didn't have it, his willingness to risk, the impulse to put his comforts first.

We got married while I was in college and he was in law school and our rise, from my teaching second grade and summers driving Route 17 to the Catskills stopping at the Red Apple Rest for lunch, was meteoric. This was less due to any efforts of mine than to Bob, who was able—as a sixth grade teacher beloved and often quoted by my father said—to "keep his eye on the apple and shoot the nail through its head."

The man I'd married was his mother's son; she a Myrna Loy look-alike, of red hair and tiny, exquisite features, Charlie Rapp's baby sister, the youngest child of an enterprising candy store owner who sent his children (there were ten of them) down dark stairwells and into the streets at 5 a.m. to pick up the newspapers for the other Bronx candy store owners, saving them the trip for a dollar a week.

Our first apartment was on Riverside Drive in an old white-stone building, once a mansion, now divided up into apartments. Ours was in the back with no view, but it had a large living room, a working fireplace, and a window seat looking into a back alley with fire escapes. Brought up on movies of the forties and fifties I thought fireplaces and fire escapes were romantic and took this as a good sign. The building was sandwiched between a Buddhist Academy and another old mansion divided into apartments and owned by Duke Ellington. In the courtyard alongside us a giant stone Buddha gazed serenely out across the drive at sunsets on the Hudson; on our other side limousines pulled up from time to time discharging the Duke's elegant sister, the landlady appearing for a visit, her shapely legs in high-heeled shoes came first followed by her sleek beige sharkskin suits and hats with flirty veils.

Bob's first office was small . . . on Fifty-seventh Street opposite The Russian Tea Room. He got on the phone, spent his nights in clubs, ate lunches with agents and entertainers, watched performers in basements and on Bleecker Street, checked out acts he heard about in Las Vegas lounges and saw on *The Ed Sullivan Show*. He worked night and day and weekends; he was never home and back on the phone when he was. Acts swarmed around us with their songs and jokes, their musical arrangements and material, plastic garment bags with their costumes slung over a chair in the living room when they'd stop off to see Bob on their way to a club date in the "hills." He spent a lot of time in coffee shops; the acts drank coffee and ate danish. Prune. Apple. Custard. Cinammon with slick, buttery tops. Sometimes I came along although there wasn't much for me to do but sit and listen to "material." One of those bug-eyed comics peered over the top of his glasses as he flipped through the packets of sugar in our booth until he found the one he wanted; "Phyllis, I have your file right here," he said. "I hope you get whatever you want, and whatever you want I should also have," said another. "I can't tell you how lucky you are to have me here tonight!" They grabbed your sleeve and pressed their faces so close you could smell their breath, need and desperation flowing from every pore; "Tell me the truth! Is this funny? How about this?"

I went to City College, took enough education courses to ex-change my substitute license for a full-time one. I enrolled in a masters program and started taking psychology courses leading to a degree in "School Guidance Counseling." But the choices I'd made began to wear on me; they were automatic, the expected, sensible thing to do. I'd made my plans figuring that we'd have a normal life . . . which ours was not turning out to be. How did ambition feel? What was it like to want something as much as the acts did? And Bob? Anything I vaguely wanted seemed unattain-able, utterly beyond my reach. I couldn't even speak such ideas. I liked books and plays and paintings but had no convictions, no way to find myself inside a life that centered on those things. I wanted romance too, but Bob was on the telephone. I'd plan din-ners, get theater tickets to plays at which he'd always arrive late.

I'd sit at restaurant tables sipping water while waiters hovered and the minutes ticked by, stand in theater lobbies as the crowd filed in to see Jason Robards in *The Iceman Cometh* . . . worried that if Bob didn't get there we'd miss the whole first act. I waited, pacing in the lobby, my shoulders electric with anxiety. When he raced in he'd be apologetic; a comic . . . or an agent . . . or a phone call had kept him in the office. He couldn't get a cab. Sometimes he'd just point to his watch. "I'm not that late . . . relax . . . ten minutes . . . not even ten. (It was always more, much more.) Let's have a nice evening . . . I'm sorry. I'm sorry. . . . Come on. Give me a break!"

Loretta Lombardo and Mitch Marks were a singer and comic, married to each other. Bob handled Mitch but Loretta came with the deal. We'd rented a house on Fire Island for just a week . . . that's all we could manage in time and money. But Mitch needed to work on material. "I have to have them out," Bob said. "It's just a day." The house was on a dune, overlooking the sea, a yellow house with Mexican furniture and rugs the owner had brought back from exotic trips. Loretta wore high heels and shorts, a skin-tight tee shirt, her breasts extending like a table top, a belt cinching her waist. She was a forties pinup girl . . . in full makeup . . . her lashes glued on. Her legs were white as just picked gardenias. On the way from the ferry her heels kept getting caught in the boardwalk. Mitch caught her arm to keep her from toppling over. She was sweet though. She kept saying how nice Fire Island was, how much she liked it. I took her to the beach, covered her legs with a towel, and gave her a big hat while Bob sat on the deck with Mitch all afternoon working on material. Mitch was dressed in black, black pants, black dress shoes and socks, a gold chain around his neck. His hair was black and glossy and wavy, his forehead was like a furrowed field waiting to be planted. Mitch drank coffee and ate Entenmann's coffee cake. They wrote out lines on yellow pads. The day was glorious, the sky was blue and the beach and water perfect. But how long could I keep Loretta there? She could burn, her white skin could fry right off. I took her inside the house and we talked about her act, her gowns, her rendition of "Begin the Beguine." She sang it for me, using a Mexican maraca as a microphone, holding out her hand to me and whipping a pretend microphone cord around ("It brings back a night of tropical splendor, it brings back a memory ever green") as the afternoon, one in only six we had . . . drifted away.

"This is so nice," she said to Mitch before they left. "We have to do this, honey, don't you think?" she said. Zipping piles of yellow pages into his black briefcase, Mitch nodded yes, his forehead rippling. "Great stuff, Bobby," he said before they boarded the ferry. "I'll call you," he promised, giving Bob's arm a final pat. "Don't worry, I'm not angry," I said as the boat pulled out and we stood waving on the dock. And the fact was, I really wasn't. I'd grown accustomed to the way things were and felt that between all of us, Bob, the acts, and me, we'd work things out.

Two years out of law school Bob started making money. New acts began to come to him, not him to them. He took a larger office on 56th and 6th and hired a secretary to field the phone calls. Pregnant, for the first time in 1960, I bought a black dress. It was sleeveless and hung to my knees with a black ruffle all around the hem. I wore it every night. It was my uniform for being out in clubs, for hanging over the piano in the lounge of the Blue Angel on East 53rd Street while Bobby Short sang, "We'll turn Manhattan into an isle of joy." In the nightclub, behind the double doors where it was dark, at tiny tables where the audience drank scotch sours and rye and ginger ale, I heard Barbra Streisand, draped in an old feather boa, sing "Secondhand Rose," and Lenny Bruce talk about the biggest lies: "I'm glad I'm Jewish". . . and "Just let me put it in for a minute. I won't come. I swear I won't come." Bob was managing a "girl singer" named Felicia Sanders. I went to hear her whenever I could. She sang a song that went, "I wish you bluebirds in the Spring to give your heart a song to sing and then a kiss, but more than this, I wish you love." Whenever I heard it I cried. I taught second grade till I was in my sixth month, then gave it up. I was happy being pregnant and stopped thinking about what I wanted. Having a baby I thought would be enough for me, enough for anyone.

ACTRESS

JENIFER CAME FIRST, BILLY TWO and a half years later, Julie a year and a half after that. In between Billy's arrival and Julie's, I registered for an acting class at the HB Studio on Bank Street. I loved my kids but thought, just let me do one thing. Something. Anything.

"Technique" was the easiest class they had. Walt was the teacher. He was studious-looking and pale with clear eyeglasses and sandy hair. He wore corduroy pants. Our first exercise was to learn a cup; "everything you can find out about it," Walt said. "I want you to know that cup in your sleep."

I chose a brown earthenware mug, green on the inside, heavy and thick. I examined it while I was in the kitchen feeding the kids. After I'd put them to sleep I carried it around the house, running my fingers over its surface, memorizing its heaviness and studying the way the glaze shaded from dark to light. I held it with my left hand and my right, I rubbed it against my mouth and my cheek.

The class was held in a cavernous basement studio, brick walls, no windows, spotlights flooding down onto the stage area and a grandstand for seats, Walt off to the side at a desk. We had to "work" with the memorized cup. On stage my feet felt like lead, my head as cold as an ice cube, as if wind were blowing past my ears, a stiff blast from the north. Under the stage lights everything blurred. The audience was out in the blackness, up in the stands, watching me move. Every twist of my wrist or arch of a finger made me feel naked. Just get through this, I thought. Then you never have to come back; just pour absent milk into absent coffee and stir absent sugar into a cup that doesn't exist except inside your head. When it's over you're done!

"Good!" Walt said. "You've got it. Work a little bit more for the weight. What are you drinking?" he asked.

"Tea," I said.

"Is it hot? Let us know that," he said. He nodded, just a tilt of his head and the briefest of smiles.

We made entrances; I came on stage after being kissed by a lover, after a battle with my sister; I entered with a broken leg, a broken heart, dripping with sweat from a New York heat wave. "Turn on the air conditioner," Walt ordered. "Discover that it's broken." I entered with an armload of Christmas gifts I'd just carried up five flights of stairs, and with a pressing need to answer the phone and get to the bathroom. "More urgency!" Walt said. "As if your life depends on each step!"

We searched for lost objects; I chose keys. The exercise was made for me. I was always losing things. I searched through my handbag and pockets, drawers, surfaces, a diaper pail, a toy fire engine, a graham cracker box. My "inner objective" was to get two screaming kids to the park but I needed my keys before I could leave the apartment. The trick was not to overreact when I found them. That was the sign of a really bad actor. The keys were in the door where I'd left them. I pulled them out with the merest bat of an eyelash, the crook of a finger. I could hear the audience exhale, a flicker of laughter.

Another actress was packing a suitcase for a weekend; she held a black negligee to her body, packed garters with rosettes, preening herself, slipping one first onto a long leg. She packed sexy lingerie and a bottle of Joy perfume. She was a beautiful actress, tall and very thin with light brown hair and a mouth she could twist into all kinds of shapes. Her talent filled me with dread. How could she do this? Where did it come from? She took out her diaphragm case and opened it up. Where was it? She ran to the bathroom, came out a minute later, limping, wearing only one shoe, rummaged through her dresser drawers and bedside table; she tore back the bed covers and pulled the lost diaphragm from under a pillow; she held it up to the light and kissed it—rapturously—and snapped it into its case.

Nobody applauded. We didn't in class. But you could feel the approval, the breathing.

"How come you took off the shoe?" Walt asked.

"I had to put my foot up to look inside for the diaphragm," she said.

"Oh," he said (a laugh from the class . . . a snicker from Walt)! "That makes sense! You really endowed this exercise."

"Do anything. Just don't be an actress," Bob said.

"What's wrong with actors?"

"They're all crazy," he said. "And they drive everyone nuts!"

"I'm not an actress," I said. "I'm just taking a class. It's once a week. At night. You're not even home!"

"I deal with these people all day," he said. "That's enough! Acting is a shit life. You have to travel all over the fucking world."

"I'm going to Bank Street," I said. "Ten stops on the subway."

After "Technique" I took a scene study class with Neil. Then I took another scene study class with Bill. We rehearsed scenes with a partner and performed in class. Neil was smart. He had graduated from Columbia. In films he was the extra man, the straight man; he played the best friend or the milk toast or the wisecracking sidekick. He played in *The Misanthrope* at Circle in the Square. Bill was skinny and Irish and drank and smoked. He looked like a giraffe. He whispered in everyone's ear. "You can do this part. You know how. You have the talent." His eyes twinkled. I was never sure if I could believe him, but I always tried. He weighed a hundred ten, maybe.

In class I played Gittel. I played Annie Sullivan. I played in *No Exit*, in *Rhinoceros*. I played the Elaine May part in *Luv*. I played the ingenue in *Barefoot in the Park* and Miriamne in *Winterset*.

I auditioned for Uta Hagen's class. When she said "O.K.," her voice was like a command. Her legs were made for black tights. She had played St. Joan and looked like her with her short hair and loose shirts. She'd been married to José Ferrer and I'd heard she'd had a love affair with Paul Robeson. I thought she must live on a higher plane than the rest of us, at a level of artistry I could barely imagine. I was the only one in her class without a SAG card, without even an Equity card. I didn't rush to the newsstand for copies of *Backstage* and *Variety* the day they came out. I didn't go to casting calls. I'd never been in a showcase or tried to get an agent. I didn't have a job like the other actors as a cabdriver, a waiter, an office temp, or a paralegal. I had no 8 × 10 glossies. In the morning I took Jenifer to nursery school and pushed Billy's stroller through the supermarket. Afternoons I spent in the playground in Riverside Park. When I went out to dinner, with my husband who could afford to pay for me, a guy from my acting class, Judd Hirsch, waited on my table—twice . . . in two different restaurants. "Hi, Judd," I said. He shifted his chin in my direction and hoisted the tray onto his shoulder.

Uta assigned me a monologue, Sabina, the maid in Thornton Wilder's *The Skin of Our Teeth*. "Oh, oh, oh, six o'clock and the master not home yet. Pray God nothing has happened to him crossing the Hudson River," Sabina says, the opening lines of the play. "The whole world is at sixes and sevens," she declares. "And why the house hasn't fallen down around our ears long ago is a miracle to me." How could I speak those lines in a short black uniform and a frilly apron, flitting around the stage in high heels with a feather duster? I was too sober for the part, too serious. I did better playing more intellectual types. Thornton Wilder had written the play on the brink of the Second World War. *The Skin of Our Teeth* was about the history of the world and the possible end of it. What could an airhead like Sabina be saying about annihilation? I decided to forget about history and play Sabina as a flirt, a choice that made me sweat. In life I'd flirted a bit, but on stage I didn't know if I could.

I preferred to play more repressed, serious types. A librarian in a baggy sweater and eyeglasses was perfect for me . . . or a nun. I'd never been able to forget myself on stage. I was always self-conscious. I carried myself around like a packed suitcase. I couldn't dance or cry. Other actors wept long streams of water. I'd look at them under the lights, faces raised to glory, rivers running down their cheeks, and try to figure out where their tears came from. They said crying was easy. I was the lowest actor in the class—the least professional, the worst. To play Sabina I would have to imagine someone to flirt with. I chose a feckless singer and guitarist Bob managed, handsome and unattainable, and I stood him at the back of the theater, behind the last row of the orchestra. In real life I wasn't attracted to the singer. I'd rarely spoken to him. "In the midst of life we are in the midst of death, a truer word was never said," I crooned to him. I wanted to entice and lure him on. The cold wind I always felt on stage whistled past my head. I wished I were playing a scene with a live actor. I always let my partners steal the scene. I was so grateful when someone took the attention away from me. I bent over and whispered throatily; "We came through the depression by the skin of our teeth! One more tight squeeze like that and where will we be!" Scenery falls down during Sabina's mono-logue, walls collapse and doors fly off hinges. I'd asked another actor to drop props and slam doors. Finally Sabina flings down the feather duster and comes downstage; "I took this hateful job be-cause I had to," she says. "For two years I've sat up in my room liv-ing on a sandwich and a cup of tea a day, waiting for better times in the theater. And look at me now; I—I who've played *Rain* and *The Barretts of Wimpole Street* and *First Lady*—God in heaven!" I liked those lines. Without the feather duster my hands were free and I waved them about.

When the lights came up Uta was laughing. She wiped her eyes. She began telling a story about Thornton Wilder; a question she'd once asked him and an answer he gave. The class laughed with her but I couldn't focus. Her words floated over me. I heard them but couldn't put them together. I was happy that she laughed at the monologue but relieved that she had nothing to say to me. I wondered why I wanted to continue acting when I prayed to be ignored. My behavior made no sense. "That was wonderful," Uta said as I left the stage. "Don't make it any broader!" I nodded as if I understood. She thinks I know what I'm doing, I thought.

"Don't go, don't go," Billy wept every time I left for class. He held out his arms. I knelt down and kissed him. I told him I'd be home later. He screamed louder. His nose ran, his eyes ran; liquid poured down his sad, red face, squeezed tight with sorrow and rage. He was two. His eyes were as blue as the sea around the Greek islands and his hair was white blonde and he wore pale blue pajamas with feet. He held a plastic bottle of milk which he hurled onto the floor. He cried as if we were being separated at a foreign border and might never see each other again.

"Now Billy, now Billy," soothed our Jamaican babysitter, Veronica. "Go! Don't worry!" she directed me. "Come, Billy." He pulled away and pushed her, his hands pressed against her legs as if he could back her into another room or another world. She was a bosomy woman with a sprinkling of freckles and a low musical voice. She stood her ground calmly and bent to pick up his bottle and wipe up the drops of milk that had leaked onto the floor. Our apartment had a glass door with a curtain and he stood at it wrenching the curtain aside, his hands and nose pressed to the glass as I waited for the elevator. We lived in an old building with an old-fashioned gated elevator run by an operator named Margaret, a plump woman with mousy brown hair, a ruddy complexion, and a thin, red nose. She wore the building uniform with brass buttons and had been there forever. "Poor little boy," she said as she pulled the gate shut and sent the ancient wooden car with its worn velvet seat cushions lurching downward, Billy's screams following us all the way down the shaft.

After I'd been studying acting for three years—with time off when Julie was born—Jeremy Stevens, a name he'd changed from Steven Greenberg, an actor who drove a taxi and whom I'd met in Uta's class when we played Kate and Petruchio in *The Taming of the Shrew*, asked me to join an improvisation group that performed in a club in the Village. Hilly's, steps below ground level on West 9th Street, had a seedy bar and a small nightclub. Hilly, the owner, was an overweight, disheveled man who wore stained suits, and it was rumored that he lived in the club and slept in a bed with filthy sheets pushed into a corner of the backstage wall. In the beginning, dozens of actors flocked to Hilly's but gradually the group thinned and a handful of us remained: Jeremy, Kent, Zohra, Marcia, Jimmy, Michael, Bette, Jo, and me. The audience shouted situations: "On a desert island with Marilyn Monroe," and lines of dialogue: "You're a fool, a crazy mixed up fool," or places: "Niagara Falls in a barrel. . . . The Grand Canyon on a tightrope". . . or characters: "a plastic surgeon and a man with two noses". . . and we acted out a scene. Of course there was no pay.

Jeremy did an imitation of a Reform Rabbi . . . "As we gather together at the bima to consecrate this bar mitzvah boy . . . Herbert Bernstein. . . we think back to our own bar mitzvahs . . ." I played neurotic women, compulsively cleaning, organizing my wallet on a plane that was going down, spreading every credit card and piece of ID on my lap. Marcia was a six-foot redhead with a prominent chin and she specialized in long, jaw-dropping double takes. Zohra was a demented waif and shopping bag lady, Kent played interior decorators and hairdressers, Bette played intellectual ingenues, girls with looks and brains, Jo did old Italian women, and Jimmy did drunks. We performed operas where the entire cast lay dead on the stage and rose from their knife wounds to sing one more aria. We did actors fighting for billing, mothers laying on guilt trips, deceived husbands, corrupt lawyers, rude stewardesses and overly kind ones, dentists with sexy nurses, surgeons scrubbing up, removing the wrong organs and trying to put them back, fortune-tellers who changed the future for cash ("Don't ask, don't ask," Zohra would beg, turning away from the crystal ball), people about to hurl themselves off bridges, and drunken airline pilots who had to be carried onboard.

I'd been reluctant to perform in public but once I started, I didn't want to stop. The group worked Thursday, Friday, Saturday, and Sunday nights. The shows didn't begin till after nine o'clock so I could put the kids to bed before I left the apartment and on the weekends when Bob was in California, which he often was, I might improvise as many as three nights out of four. Between shows we hung out in the bar where Jeremy did his Brando imitation . . . "Oh, Charlie, you're my brother, I could have been a contender! The brilliance of Brando," Jeremy said, was that "he went for the sadness, the tragic betrayal by his brother. Any other actor would have played it angry. . . . It was a genius choice," he said. "The sorrow in Marlon's face . . . that was a great moment," he said. "Maybe one of the best of any actor on film." We talked about Lee Strassberg and auditioning for the Actors Studio, and about Stanislavsky's book, *An Actor Prepares*, and James Dean.

"Do you make everything up?" my mother asked when she came to Hilly's with my father. "It's wonderful that you can think so fast on your feet. Isn't it wonderful?" she asked my father.

"Yes," he said. They were seated at one of the tiny tables at the back of Hilly's. The room seemed to smell even worse when they were there, danker with a thicker smell of spilt rye. My father looked like a man about to take flight. At a certain point he cracked his knuckles.

"We can't stay too long," he said.

"Does everyone make up their lines?" my mother asked.

"Yes," I said. "That's why it's called improvisation."

"Who's the redhead?" my father asked.

"Marcia," I said. "She's from Creston, Iowa."

"She looks like a stork," he said. He looked at my mother. A mischievous smile played over his face.

"I think she's talented," my mother said. "She's the best one."

"Would you like to meet her?" I asked.

"No. No. No. We don't want to meet anyone," my father said. "I'm going to get the check, we have to go."

"She's great," my mother said. "That Marcia, she's going to make something of herself."

"Who's taking care of the kids?" my father asked.

"My babysitter, Veronica," I said.

"Go home," my father said. "Get to bed. You have to be up early."

Jeremy bent over the table with Marcia alongside him. He was a round man with very white skin. When he wasn't at Hilly's or in class, he drove the cab all night. At 27, his straight dark hair was thinning on top. His zippered leather jacket hung open as he bent over.

"How do you like your daughter?" he asked. "Isn't she terrific?"

"My daughter is good at everything," my mother said. "That's the way she is. A perfectionist. She works very hard. She's always been that way, ever since she was a little girl. You should have heard her teachers when I went to school."

"Really!" Marcia said. She did a double take with her long jaw.

"You were the best," my mother said. She patted Marcia's arm. "You have natural talent!"

"Oh. We all have our nights," Marcia said modestly.

"Nice meeting you," my father said. "Let's go," he said to my mother.

"Wait a minute," my mother said. "Don't be so impatient! I should go to the ladies' room. Is it OK?" she asked.

"It's OK," I said. "I'll go with you."

The ladies' room was in the basement. To get there you had to go behind a frayed velvet curtain and down a flight of rickety stairs.

"Maybe I'll wait till I get home," she said. She looked at Marcia.

"It's not a peak experience, but you'll get through it." Marcia said.

"Make up your mind," my father said. He looked as if an invisible wire was pulling him past the bar and towards the door.

"I'm coming. I'm coming," my mother said. She shook her head at me. "You know how he is," she said. "He just won't try anything new. So frightened!"

"I tried it! I tried it!" my father said.

I walked them to the door and watched them scurry down the street. I waited for their Buick to drive past and my mother waved. My father was behind the wheel, he gave me a quick smile and then looked straight ahead, thinking about the fastest bridge to get back to Brooklyn.

Bob came to Hilly's once. He said, "I spend my life doing this and when I'm free I don't want to watch a bunch of broken-down actors in a hellhole."

"They're not broken down. They're all young," I said. "I'm the oldest one."

"The material isn't very sharp," he said. "Not like Second City. This stuff has to be rehearsed. It's improv only up to a point. Nichols and May, Alan Arkin, they have it all down and their timing is perfect."

"We're just starting," I argued, but not very hard.

Bob was spending a lot of time in California and he'd been to London and met Julie Christie and Dirk Bogard and Joe Losey the film producer. Their names kept cropping up in our conversations. He'd done some work for them and someone owed him a favor so he'd produced an Elvis Presley movie and gotten a film credit. He was trying to produce another film starring Lee Marvin and it looked as if it would happen. He kept telling me we'd have to move out to L.A. but I had trouble believing it. I heard the words but the fact of leaving New York just didn't register. By then I'd had some professional pictures taken and I'd done some auditions and gotten some small parts off-off-Broadway in basements and churches and places even worse than Hilly's. I'd even managed to get into the unions, SAG and Actors Equity, although I'd barely earned enough to cover the dues. I didn't think of myself

PHYLLIS RAPHAEL

as an actress. I thought of acting as something separate, apart from anything real. Acting was no life. But I didn't want to stop. I liked doing it.

The summer Julie was a year and a half we spent a month in Malibu. The house was casual, all California redwood and you stepped out onto a deck and down a short flight of wooden stairs onto the beach. Julie couldn't stay away from those stairs. She was always going down them and onto the beach and wandering off. She made a lot of friends. Everyone on the beach knew her. I was always after her, scooping her up and bringing her back. She had a little blue sundress that she wore, her diaper and rubber pants sticking out from under it, and she looked back at me as she kept going, determined but guilty. At Disneyland Jenifer and I rode the Small World ride over and over. She didn't want to get off. "Just one more time," she pleaded every time it ended, holding up a finger in front of her freckled face. "It's a small world after all. It's a small, small world." The rinky-tink music played on and on. The sun shone every day and there were volleyball games on the beach and barbecues. In the evenings we watched from our deck as the sunsets streaked the sky over the Pacific and everyone we met had money and was beautiful.

MOVING

IT TOOK TEN YEARS TO get from our wedding at the Brooklyn Jewish Center on Eastern Parkway, where my grandfather
brought six rabbis to pray for my fertility, to Los Angeles and a
mansion on the Palisades overlooking the Pacific. The rabbis sat
in a little clutch at the end of the dais, dressed in black, eating and
drinking and swaying over their prayer books. Crumbs of food
lodged in their beards.

"They're disgusting! They don't bathe!" my mother whispered.
"I didn't know he was going to pull this! It's medieval!" she sniffed.

In California we had a dark blue swimming pool lined with
Spanish tiles, a fountain with peeing cherubs, a circular driveway,

a badminton court, lime and lemon trees, an outdoor kitchen, and a long stretch of back lawn crumbling down onto the Pacific Coast Highway. We lived over a fault line. One good earthquake could swallow us up. Some said a hamburger stand had been demolished only two years before we bought the house, but others swore there hadn't been a slide in twenty years.

It was a big house, built as the ballroom for an old-style industrialist who'd broken the estate up into little parcels and sold them off separately. Our next-door neighbor lived in the carriage house. He was the former emcee of a TV quiz show and had been discovered giving answers to the contestants. He had dark, slicked-down hair and was airwave-style handsome like an announcer for the Miss America pageant. His wife was from Georgia, charming and dimpled with milky skin and red hair. She'd been an associate producer on the show when he left his wife for her and she'd been in love with a woman. She wanted to marry, have children, live a conventional life. Now they had two children but he was barred from American broadcasting and could only work in Canada. As the former communists, the Hollywood Ten, Dalton Trumbo, Lionel Stander, Zero Mostel, began to get jobs, he thought he should be pardoned too. What was the difference between the ex-commies and him? Why should he have to fly to Quebec? One night we were invited for drinks on their terrace. The emcee was reading *Variety*, charting everyone else's jobs. The terrace was like a southern veranda, long and narrow with white pillars. We sat on flowered cushions on wrought iron furniture and watched as the sun sank behind the privy and into the Pacific. His wife was sweet and smiling, dressed in pale blue. She set out hors d'oeuvres. "It breaks my heart," the emcee said, putting aside his *Variety*. "How the hell can they keep doing this to me?"

We lived in the house a little more than a year and it had taken me almost as long to furnish it. I'd made friends with an antiquier named Bill with a shop on La Cienega. He found the old green and gold Venetian sleigh bed we put next to one of the glass doors in the living room looking out on the garden, and the stone sculp- ture of angels from the church in Europe that we hung in a large niche at the end of the room. It was so heavy it had to be anchored from the ceiling in the attic on chains. He also located the marble slab that we put on top of the cast iron bases of the ornate old street lamps from Santa Monica. The dull green bases were cut to size to support the marble that became our baronial dining room table. The living room was the size of a football field with a huge stone fireplace. A musician's balcony hung over one end of the room with carved Italianate balustrades. Bill came in a small truck, dressed in shorts, carrying fabric samples and paint chips. He sold things to us, but I had the feeling he wanted to be my friend. He was proud of working on the house and wanted to be able to tell people about it. He did more than he needed to do. He would call to say he'd seen a chair I'd like that was in a new shop . . . or a chest in someone's house that he thought would be "perfect." We should look for one like it. The grounds smelled sharply of a strange nut that fell from a tree on the property. Bill searched botany books to find its name. Sometimes over coffee he confided in me; he'd seen Marlene Dietrich at a theater downtown. Her legs were still "to die for." He knew the perfect white piano for her. Did I think he should call her?

We also had landscapers and pool men, gardeners, tree surgeons, and a house watcher named Burt, an old man who'd taken care of the property since the days of the industrialist's family and who acted as if he owned the place and I was working for him. It was Burt who'd hung the stone fresco of angels in the living room (an engineering feat that should have gotten him an honorary degree from M.I.T., Bob said). "What's he doing here?" Burt would say when Bill's truck pulled up. I wanted to get rid of Burt, but Bob said he was old and we couldn't let him go. Burt would announce that something had gone wrong and then wait for me to ask him what to do. Behind Burt's back, Bill would roll his eyes. It was a routine, the old man, bald, stooped, everything on his face hanging downward . . . a servant from Chekhov—delivering the bad news . . . a sick tree—a leak in the basement. He would say, "There's a bird's nest in the drainpipe," and then wait for me to fall to my knees and plead, "What should I do?" If there was any magic in that house at all for me—anything glamorous or romantic lingering from a lost Los Angeles and the rise of the movie industry, any remnant of history or imagination embedded in its stucco walls that made me want to own it in the first place, Burt was determined to put that dream to death.

Bill joked that fixing up the house was like a speeded-up movie; it should be a silent slapstick of a woman fixing, digging, buying, supervising, excavating for a pool, pouring gravel for the driveway, a woman always in motion. "Wouldn't it be funny if after it was all done a bulldozer came and razed it down? There could be a close-up of her horrified face. And then the camera could pan the ruins." He said this half a dozen times at least and let out a raucous laugh each time. I never got the joke, never understood his sense of humor. But in London, walking through cobblestone mews and green parks and narrow streets with their inviting small restaurants and shops, Los Angeles seemed like a cousin I'd struggled to get along with. I'd never had the courage to stop playing with her—until now.

When I said we were going to stay in London, no longer at her Ladyship's, but in a house of our own, Jenifer said she wanted her bed with the canopy, the one we'd bought in Bloomingdale's and brought from New York to L.A., and Billy requested his bike. But Julie said she had everything she needed; her blanket, her guns and holster, her cowboy hat and the small pocket size bible she'd begun to carry in the back pocket of her jeans. I could think of a few things I missed but not enough to go back for them. Los Angeles, the mansion on the Palisades, the life I'd left behind, it could all be run into the ground or swallowed up by the earth for all I cared. I'd still sleep through the night and wake to the clacking of heels on the pavement—a sound I hadn't heard since childhood—in the dark mornings when Londoners were on their way to work.

It took me all of one afternoon to buy the lease on a small house, one in a row of identical gleaming white houses with brightly colored doors, brass knockers, and geranium-filled window boxes in walking distance of Harrod's, the Victoria and Albert Museum, and the South Kensington tube stop. I wanted to act fast. I kept in mind the image of a comet streaking across the sky. I didn't want to notice what I was doing, remember the past or predict the future. Thinking was dangerous. If I thought about what I was doing, I might be inclined to stop. I wanted this move to happen seamlessly, a blank transition, as if buying a house in a country not my own was the most unremarkable thing in the world.

Number twelve South Terrace, SW7, came with a key to Thurloe Square, a thick green garden at the end of the street with winding paths and wooden benches. It was the second house I saw with an estate agent named Brian, an Irishman dressed in brown who seemed surprised by all the houses he showed me; "Oh, what have we here?" he'd say when he opened each door. "You could do worse," he said about this one. There was one other I liked in Pimlico, an area somewhere between Belgravia and Victoria Station, but a friend of Caroline's, a physician and man about London she called "The Dancing Doctor," advised against the neighborhood. "Dear girl . . . God no . . . not there!" he said. The lease cost 12,000 British pounds, about thirty thousand dollars, and for that money in 1969 I could live there till 1984 which, if I had any thought about that date at all, it was that it would never come.

I asked Bob for the money from what would eventually be my settlement. He said, "Your living here will make it very hard for me to see the kids. . . ." His words dangled precipitously, as if he had more to say. "I'm sorry," I said. "That's not my intention. I need to find a new life." "OK . . ." he said . . . "I guess. There are planes, phones. . . ."

"I knew you were keeping something from me," my mother said when I finally told her that Bob and I were splitting up. I wrote her a letter, then called her on the phone. "What did I do wrong?" she moaned.

"This isn't your fault, Mom," I said. "It's just something that happened and probably for the best."

"How can you say that?" she said.

My parents were finally leaving Brooklyn, moving to Long Island so they could play golf. "Who will take care of you?" my father asked. His voice was faint. "Come live here," he pleaded. "There are schools. You'll meet someone else. We'll help with the kids. We're near a synagogue."

"The rabbi already asked us for money," my mother said.

"I don't think so," I said.

"We have divorce here too," my mother said. "A woman at the golf club, her husband was having an affair, ten years with his dental technician . . ."

"New York is no longer for me!" I said, thinking of all the people I'd have to tell, all the explanations I'd have to make.

I wrote out the check, signed the papers, and as soon as the house was mine I had it painted by Carmele's boyfriend; a bottle-green living room, a garnet-colored bedroom ("the color of blood and revolution," David said), everything with sparkling white trim, the way they do it in London. I bought a brass bed on the street in front of an antique shop at the end of the King's Road in the place called World's End, (Lay lady lay, lay across my big brass bed, Bob Dylan sang) and some large floor cushions for the living room covered in Indian printed fabric in a shop nearby. I got some beds for the kids and some white china and a sofa in Habitat, a trendy furniture shop close to the house.

The day I moved in, my neighbor, an Englishwoman with a halo of white hair, popped her head around the yellow door and introduced herself as "Honor Earl." She was small boned and pretty, gossipy and cheerful. "Oh, you're American!" she said. "That's unexpected!" I told her I was separated from my husband, a film producer, and would be getting a divorce and she said there was one other American couple on the street, "not terribly like you at all! Older people, in finance." They'd lived here for years. Then too there were "the Tynans," in the big house opposite the square. "He's a writer, quite celebrated . . . somewhat outrageous. They get masses of American visitors," she said.

She announced that she was a portrait painter and hoped I'd sit for her. She'd like to sketch me, she said. In charcoal. A drawing. I was flattered. Several weeks later, dressed in a black turtleneck sweater and a necklace of hammered silver chains I'd bought in the King's Road, I went next door. Her house was just like mine . . . they were all the same in our terrace . . . and her studio was in the room where I'd put Jenifer's bedroom—on the first floor at the end of a long, narrow hallway with doors out to the garden. Paintings and drawings of dancers in the Royal Covent Garden Ballet were propped along the walls of the studio. She was their official portrait painter, she told me. Now I was even more impressed with her . . . and myself. I was keeping fine company. I sat on a high stool and she positioned my chin with her fingers.

"Tell me," she said as she sketched . . . the charcoal made a soft, slushy sound on the paper . . . she had set her electric kettle to boil water for tea and it steamed cozily. "Have you always been so rebellious?"

I didn't breathe for a minute. Nor move. The question was the last I expected. I hadn't thought at all of how I must look, a Hollywood divorcée with three children on this sedate London street. Her British veneer made her inscrutable. I'd had no idea what she was thinking. But what people thought of me, I understood in that moment, was no longer my problem. Opinions had no power to touch me . . . not here.

"Rebellious?" I said. "No! Actually not!"

But give me a chance, I thought.

BILLY

"WHY DOES EVERYONE WANT TO talk to us?" he asked.

"Because we're having a good time," I said. "They want to be part of it."

"How come kids always have a good time and grown-ups are always mad?"

"Grown-ups have a good time too," I said, without offering evidence.

I had taken him to dinner. A small, new Italian restaurant in Elizabeth Street, "Mimmo d'Ischia." Caroline introduced me to Mimmo the week the restaurant opened.

Billy and I had walked there. Just down the King's Road,

through Sloane Square, and into Belgravia, a right turn into Elizabeth Street. We'd walked past whitewashed terraces, enamel doors, window boxes, a tiny shop selling Irish woolens; calm, green, London, sanitarium city.

We got a lot of approving glances from the other tables, a little boy, out with his mother.

All the waiters had come over to talk to him. And Mimmo himself. Small, with dark, curly hair.

"I live in California," Billy told Mimmo. "But now we're going to stay in London!"

"Me too!" Mimmo said.

Billy pointed to me. "And her too!"

That day I'd taken him and Jenifer to visit a school for the fall. The Redcliffe School was in Redcliffe Gardens, a townhouse. Kids clattered up and down stairs, their English voices high and sweet. Kids' paintings hung reassuringly in the classrooms. They looked like kids' paintings usually look. Houses. Trees. Flowers. The sun. Arms and legs coming out from circular bodies. The kids all wore uniforms, maroon blazers, gray skirts and pants. In California my kids had worn jeans and gone to a progressive school in the valley. I'd carpooled them there everyday. Billy had told that to Lady Redcliffe. "Not to worry," she'd said, as the English always do. "You'll get used to us!"

He ordered spaghetti with tomato sauce.

I had grilled fish.

Mimmo lifted out the bone and flipped it aside. I ate with an English fish knife and fork, implements I'd learned to use, left hand on the fork.

Billy finished the spaghetti and came over and wound himself around me.

He whispered in my ear, "Can I have ice cream?"

"Yes," I said.

"Gelato," Mimmo said. "Chocolate or vanilla, my friend?"

"Both," he said.

I ordered an espresso. Mimmo sent over a Sambuca with little coffee beans in the bottom of the glass. "*Complimenti*," the waiter said.

"Are you going to divorce Daddy?" he asked.

I wasn't expecting the question, but I wasn't surprised.

"I don't know," I said.

"I don't want you to," he said.

"I might have to."

"Why?"

"Because he might want to marry somebody else."

"Who?" He looked genuinely surprised. As if the thought had never occurred to him. He'd been visiting Bob and his girlfriend for months.

"His girlfriend," I said.

"Vanessa?"

I nodded.

"Don't be silly. He's too old for her."

"He doesn't think so," I said.

He looked down at the tablecloth, just a flicker crossing his face. He marched his fingers across the white linen, a pianist playing a fugue.

I reached over and brushed the hair off his forehead.

I paid the bill with a British Barclaycard. I'd opened a bank account. Now I could have a credit card.

"Take care of your mama," Mimmo said as we left.

"She takes care of me," he said.

I took his hand walking home although after a while he broke away to skip ahead.

It was a spring evening, way past eight, but still light.

Julie was asleep when we got back to the house, but Jenifer was still up. She and Billy dropped right off. But I didn't sleep well. I kept waking up.

EMPLOYED

I BOUGHT A SMALL OLIVETTI portable typewriter in a thin blue and black case. The Olivetti was beautiful—sleek and light. It had Italian style, a worldliness and sophistication, an elitist air about it signaling that its owner was an insider, a discriminating person who knew important things. I loved its compactness, and the authoritative way the keys depressed and returned and the fact that I could carry it anywhere. I'd seen famous journalists swinging that same Olivetti through airports on their way to wars, assassinations, events that made history. And on the cover of one of his books Ernest Hemingway leaned over his Olivetti in shirtsleeves, his gaze direct and arrogant. I thought that typing on the Olivetti would do something for me, like driving a Porsche does for a car owner, and I always felt a buzz when I lifted it out of its case.

I smoked as I sat in front of the Olivetti; I kept a cigarette burning in the ashtray from a green and gold package of St. Moritz alongside me with matches from Mr. Chow, or the Club Arethusa in the King's Road or The White Elephant in Curzon Street. The smoke was part of the mystique but it was also satisfying to inhale, put the cigarette back in the ashtray, and return to the typewriter keys as I exhaled. It was a perfect little dance, a tango of breath, mind, and fingers.

The tape recorder, which I'd initially been enamored of, was a disappointment. I used it but didn't develop the deep love for it that I'd hoped for. It turned out to be merely an infatuation. When I went out interviewing subjects for the job I'd gotten researching and coauthoring a book with George's brother Paul, using the tape recorder was never a smooth operation. No matter how much I practiced, the recorder was not reliable. Either it didn't pick up voices, or the tape got stuck or ran out, or I spent the whole interview worrying about turning the tape over and lost concentration. Trickiest of all was that even when the recorder functioned perfectly, it was never honest. The spoken words might be there to the letter—but the truth was lost in the accuracy. In the beginning I painstakingly transcribed the tapes word for word, but as time went on that became unbearable and I gave it up. My sense of what happened was better than the recorder's which included every pause but omitted the lift of an eyebrow or the way a leg jiggled up and down on a chair. I still carried the recorder with me. The characteristics that had initially attracted me were still there, the official look of it and the way it hung sexily to my hip, but the thrill was gone. I used it to be sure my quotes were correct but the recorder itself bored me. It was like sex without passion or a beautiful room without a comfortable chair.

The book I was working on with George's brother was about the occult; psychics, mystics, healers, shamans, covens of witches. The paranormal was his specialty. He wrote about it all the time. Novels. Plays. Screenplays. Radio and TV. Newspaper and magazine stories. There wasn't anything he hadn't tried. I called him up, said I wanted a job, and he said, "Come and see me." His accent was softly middle European, reminiscent of a down pillow. "Gothic! Gothic! Gothic!" he told me. "The English love it! They can't get enough! What can we do? We give them what they want! Right?"

He lived in a large house in tree-lined Kensington just behind High Street and worked in a library lined with books floor to ceiling. His desk was a sea of magazines and newspapers; *Rolling Stone*, *Der Spiegel*, *Le Monde*, *News of the World*, *Paris Match*. His office looked out on a garden and a lovely London Street. How could he live like this from writing, I wondered. He must write day and night, a one-man factory of words. Or maybe there was something about this writing business I didn't know.

It was hard to believe they were brothers; George burned a hole in your mind, but if you met Paul at a party you'd forget him five minutes later. He was shorter and plumper than George, no affairs with Garbo that I could imagine; he had a solid Viennese wife. Kate. Kate in high heels and a tweed skirt, glasses dangling on a chain, a stack of index cards with her "work" in her hand answered the door and showed me inside.

I told him I didn't have much experience but I was an English major in college. "Don't worry!" he said. "I won't hold it against you."

"I can't pay you much, probably less than you pay your cook, but we'll coauthor the book and I'll put your name on the cover."

"That's fine," I said. "I'll take it."

He scribbled a name on a slip of paper. "Call Trevor," he said.

Trevor told me to meet him in a pub in Fleet Street. I said the words over and over. A pub in Fleet Street. The phrase made me think of Dr. Johnson and Trollope. As I was leaving to meet him Allie rang me up; "Gotta go, I have to meet someone in a pub in Fleet Street," I said. Trevor was a specialist in the paranormal and a reporter for *The News of the World*, a tabloid that featured stories about the birth of two-headed babies, secret covens of witches, the bad behavior of Whig and Tory MP's. Trevor was the Mr. Who's Who of the occult. Whatever you wanted to know Trevor could tell you, and if you needed to locate the healer who'd gotten the blind child to see, Trevor could direct you where you might find him. "Our friend Trevor," Paul called him. "Ask our friend Trevor," he'd say. The two shared information. They were the odd couple of mysticism; Trevor, tall, thin, young and blond, slim hips and flat belly in his reporter's suits and flyaway ties, his wife and kids tucked away in Harrow—and Paul of Kensington, short, smart, and Hungarian.

I took my tape recorder to the pub in Fleet Street. ("You use that thing?" Trevor asked. "Bloody nuisance!") I took a spiral notebook too and wrote down the names of the clairvoyants and healers Trevor told me to see. I felt light-headed researching a book with a reporter in a pub. I hoped I wouldn't say or do the wrong thing.

Over lunch—shepherd's pie and a pint—Trevor recited names; "Ann Dooley, Florrie Dott, Nora Blackwood. They'll give you a start," Trevor said. "Set your bells ringing."

Around me people who worked for newspapers were eating bad English lunches and drinking mugs of dark ale. The place buzzed with lunchtime conversation and smelled of damp beer and smoke.

"Harry Edwards. George Chapman . . . the medicine blokes," he said.

"Fag?" Trevor asked. He shook one out of a pack.

"I have my own," I said. I slipped a cigarette between my lips and bent my head to Trevor's cupped palm to catch the flame from his match.

It was almost too much.

"Nothing to it," Trevor said when I thanked him for the information. "No bother at all, mate."

I bought a car and drove out into the countryside. That was where the clairvoyants lived. They liked the suburbs. Aylesbury. Bedford. Colindale. Twickenham. Finchley. Wyvvelsfield Green. Biddenham Turn. They had houses with gardens and stone paths and parlors with plump sofas and doilies on the arms of their chairs and dark furniture and rugs with vines and flowers that looked like they came from the lobbies of old movie theaters. The psychics were mostly all women; middle-aged and older women in skirts that covered their knees and hair carefully dyed in the beauty parlor and set on rollers they'd slept on the night before. Mary Rogers was amply endowed and resembled Mae West. A large crucifix nestled between her breasts. "I'm just a transmitter," she said, leaning towards me. "My gift comes from God."

My car was British Racing Green, low to the ground with a leather top I could put up or down. I'd driven the same kind of car in L.A. If the weather was good I left the top down and raced along the motorway, thrilled to be able to drive on the right, my palm cradling the round knob of the stick shift, my foot poised above the clutch. It was a secondhand car of a kind made one at a time in the North of England and I'd bought it from a lanky, boyish cockney dealer in a mews near the South Kensington tube station. He'd wheeled out from under the car to sell it to me, his arms covered with grease, his hair in limp waves down his neck, and I knew the car would be trouble, but I wanted it all the same. My heart beat faster when he said, "Don't sell many of these to birds."

The tape recorder jiggled on my thigh when I went to see the psychics. I tramped through their gardens in my boots and sheep-skin coat and smiled respectfully when they came to the door. I tried to appear merely innocent and curious, asking questions at the same time as I watched to figure out what they were up to. They all brought up dead relatives of mine, grannies and aunts, gramps and cousins, all of them dropping the names of other family members, living and dead, many I'd never cared for or had much to do with. "I have a granny on the line," they'd say. Or, "I'm get-ting a granny who says she's your mother's mother. I'm getting a Sophie, a Sadie, an Evelyn, a Rose. They're telling me something about a flat tire, an accident, if you haven't had one yet, watch out, it could be next week."

"I'm hearing about someone called Vivian," Jessie Nason said. We were in Clapham on her tweed sofa. I'd been silent—she'd gotten everything wrong—but when she said the name Vivian I dropped my reporter's reticence and she pounced.

"My friend?" I asked. "Vivian? My friend?"

"Yes! That's the one! Your granny is worried. She says Vivian is confused. The two of you make a proper pair. Both of you muddling about!"

"You may think the family is dead," I told David, my shrink, at my next session, "but not at the clairvoyants."

Nora Blackwood and I had not gotten off to a good start. I was twenty minutes late for our appointment. I had been out with Mike the night before. We'd smoked some hash at Jay and Fran's and gotten into a long conversation about whether or not it was still possible to believe that happiness could arrive with the next phone call. "Does your heart still leap when the phone rings?" Jay asked.

From the cave of floor pillows, her carpetbag covering her lap, Fran said, "Not anymore!"

Jay flashed a cat smile; he inhaled through his teeth. "Tough question," he said. "Oh happiness, happiness, happiness. Very tough!" He shook his head. "I'll take the fifth!"

They waited for me. "I guess not," I said. "But I can't stop hoping!"

"I'm out," Mike said. "Keep talking!" he told us. He said he was going to be an impartial observer and write a column about our discussion for the *Village Voice*. The conversation had roamed down many avenues, into side alleys, and hit some dead ends. When the hash wore off we were all hungry. Jay and Fran's macrobiotic household had only brown rice, popcorn, and dried apples to snack on. After we'd devoured all that, Mike and I drove back to my house where we tore into my kids' stash of McVities Chocolate Digestive biscuits. I kept packages in the house especially for Billy; he was addicted to the sweet, crunchy taste.

I'd overslept that morning, taken Julie to school at the Chelsea Open Air Nursery, and lingered with her teacher. She was a comfortable woman in a smock and soft leather "earth shoes." She presided placidly over the school in a mews off the King's Road and was calm as a lake though surrounded by children. How did she do it? Julie had initiated a game of Superman with her friend Bobby Found—they pretended to swallow a seed from a laburnum tree in the garden and turned into supermen—"She has her own ideas, that one," said the teacher as the children swirled around us, pulling and hiding behind her skirt.

I'd been cavalier about time and now I was going to miss a chunk of my session with Nora Blackwood. She had a client coming after me and wouldn't extend my hour. "It's your loss," she sniffed.

"I'm so sorry," I said.

I followed behind her like a child being punished. "It's simply your loss," she tossed at me again.

She had the same coloring as my mother-in-law. Red hair and fair skin. We sat down and she asked me for something of mine to hold. I pulled from my finger three silver rings linked together as one. I'd bought them in the King's Road, the same shop where I'd gotten my necklace of hammered silver chains. She clasped the rings inside her palm and closed her eyes. Her pale face was bare of expression—smooth. A few minutes passed.

"I have someone here who says she's your granny. She's worried about you . . . I'm getting a break in your life. . . ."

Oh please, I thought.

"My granny was an immigrant," I said. "She barely spoke English. I'm touched that she's showing this enormous concern for me now that she's dead, but frankly it's a case of too little too late!"

"Keep a civil tongue on you, miss," Nora Blackwood retorted. "Your granny says you were no rose yourself! She did her best but you were not easy!"

Yes, there had been a "break," I said, and then—trying to mend things—I told her I was separated from my husband. I regretted the words as soon as I spoke them because I had given her something to go on. Now my granny had plenty to say; there would be "a deed of agreement" signed in a few months and I would have furniture shipped from California. She was right. My lawyer was drafting a "separation agreement" and we would soon sign it. These women are clever! I nodded yes.

"Speak up," Nora Blackwood commanded. "They like to hear you!"

"Yes," I shouted. "It's all true!"

"I have a man here who says he's your husband's father," she said.

My father-in-law? Here?

Bob's father had indeed "passed over" as the psychics say, of a heart attack when Jenifer was a baby, late at night after too many trips up the stairs with his bass.

"Your husband is in the entertainment business and there is a link with music," she said. "I see an orchestra. . . ." She appeared to be listening intently to what was coming from the other world.

"He says you didn't get along with his mother."

Tell him neither did he, I nearly said, but didn't.

"I'm getting the names . . ." She rolled off a list that included two of Bob's aunts, Leah and Ann, and his brother-in-law, Joe. Not bad, I thought, although all the psychics tried Joe. Who doesn't know one?

"Yes," I shouted again. For a minute she had me.

"Your father-in-law says living with his son wasn't easy for you. It was like living on top of a volcano. You never knew when it would erupt." (Softening me up after putting me down, I thought.)

"Now he's going around saying it's all your fault. It's not your fault, he says."

I looked at her closely. Her eyes were still closed. Her pale complexion was flushed.

"He's not a promiscuous man," she said. "Your father-in-law says he's just infatuated! This girl has him over the moon. He doesn't know if he's coming or going."

She laughed and hooked a thumb over her shoulder. "She's a tart," Nora Blackwood said, giggling. "That's what he called her. A cheap tart!" (In death, my father-in-law from the Bronx had picked up a British vocabulary!) "He's very upset about this," she went on. "He believes in family unity. Your husband loves the children." She paused and her face drooped. "I'm sorry to say he doesn't see a reconciliation." She shook her head. "No. You won't get back together. It's not going to go well for your husband. She cares nothing for him, she broke up your home without even a thought and when she's finished with him she'll leave him just as she found him. She's an actress, isn't she?" (A snort.) "I should have known. It will be through a job. She'll go off with another man. And she wants everything. Honestly, her name should be 'I want.'"

She paused. Little muscles in her face quivered.

"He's going to want you back," she said. "He's going to need you because you're the best friend he has." (I doubted it, but relished the thought.) "I don't see it happening. No. I'm sorry. He says he has to go . . . he's fading away . . . I'm losing him." She sat, unmoving, her white hands folded in her lap. "Let's wait. Maybe he'll come back. They sometimes do." We sat in silence till she shook her head and opened her eyes. Her face looked soft and blurry. She was prettier than I thought at first, a lot like my mother-in-law. I didn't know how she'd known all that she did. I didn't trust her but I had to respect her. It had been quite a performance! She reached for my hand. "But you're going to meet someone who will love you for yourself, for who you really are. . . ."

"I am?" I said.

"Yes," she said. "And when you do you're going to have to make a decision. When that time comes, come back and see me."

Her face was shining. She's forgiven me, I thought. She handed me back my ring and I dug into my carpet bag and gave her two guineas. Outside, a woman with long, shiny blond hair falling like sheets of rain on her suede coat waited. She was right on time and Nora Blackwood extended an arm to greet her. "How are you, luv?" she asked. The woman's car, a little black mini with tinted windows, was parked at the curb, just behind mine.

At night after the children went to sleep I tried to write about the healers and mystics and psychics. I sat in front of the Olivetti smoking and clicking the tape recorder on and off. I didn't believe any of them—some averaged out better than others, like Nora Blackwood—but as a group their performance was unimpressive. "The English love Gothic," Paul had said. "They can't get enough!" On this subject the English and I would have to part company. Gothic? I would keep the Brontë sisters, Mary Shelley and Daphne Du Maurier—but they could have Rose Harley, who put a handkerchief over her head, rocked back and forth, and told a woman in a mink coat and Gucci boots that she didn't have money problems. And Jessie Nason who as a child pressed an imaginary button in her navel and brought forth her spirit guide, a beautiful woman dressed in gossamer green. Still, I wanted to write well about them, even though I thought they were scamming.

Dr. William Lang died in 1937, but twice a week he trailed through clouds of mist from the spirit world to a consulting room at the back of a large house in Aylesbury where he prescribed cures for the sick and operated on those in need of surgery. I went to see him there. The room was lit by a single red lightbulb that cast an eerie pink glow on his face as he sat on an old-fashioned couch with photographs of his colleagues from the London Hospital in Whitechapel and the Central London Ophthalmic, framed behind him. The room was furnished with the examining table and equipment from his original office that his medium, George Chapman, an ex-prizefighter, had bought from Dr. Lang's son Basil before Basil too "passed on." Dr. Lang's face was shriveled up like a dried fig, and behind his spectacles (I wasn't sure if he brought them with him or left them behind when he returned to the land of the dead) his eyes were shut tight. "Do you understand?" he asked when he explained it all to me, the way he spent time in the spirit world with all the physicians he worked with in London. They all sat in the hereafter discussing his cases—he could call on spirit surgeons, confer with spirit specialists about the cases he was treating. And when he did surgery he conferred with them too and snapped his fingers so they passed him the necessary spirit instruments. (He didn't do fractures, he said. For that a bone specialist was preferable. Spirit healing was more effective with cancerous growths, twisted backs and spines, vision problems, and such.)

"Life in the spirit world is just as it is here—no different," he said. And since he returned twice a week to heal and much of his healing was on other doctors, he learned the latest medical techniques while he was on earth. "Fair is fair, I say to the doctors who come here," he told me. "I've helped you, now you must give back. Do you understand?" he asked me.

The way Doctor Lang returned to earth was by entering George Chapman's body. After I'd met Dr. Lang, George Chapman telephoned and asked if he could visit me in London. I wasn't thrilled with the idea. But I was surprised when I opened the door. He was a handsome man, in his late forties with a full head of gray hair and long sideburns. He was dressed in a stylish brown corduroy suit, matching overcoat, and knitted tie. Still, I could see that if he was an able actor he could turn himself into a nineteenth-century physician, long dead. There was enough physical resemblance between them so that with a practiced stoop and a scrunched-up face the transformation was possible. I'd seen Lon Chaney do it in the movies enough times. He had independent income, he told me, and ran the healing sanctuary as an act of good will. He just made expenses. Twice a week he went alone to the consulting room, lay down on the couch and let the trance come upon him; he saw Dr. Lang coming towards him through clouds of mist and their bodies met and he knew no more.

It was while he was under this spell that Dr. Lang did the healing. He never remembered it. "Going under you feel as if you're being smothered," he said. "And when you're coming out of the trance again you start seeing the smiling face of a doctor—you see the mist going away and you see yourself coming as though this body is something unimportant you carry about and two people can use it, like an overcoat." When the session was over he was drained as a limp cloth and needed to rest. His son Michael drew him a hot bath and brought him some tea and it took an hour before he could speak. The aroma of his cologne floated towards me in my London living room. He said he sprayed it lavishly on himself to refresh himself after the sessions, to wash off the illnesses the spirit healer treated. He hinted that the best healers worked in Brazilian jungles—they had a particular kind of gift—and could lift tumors from internal organs without cutting through flesh—he'd seen it himself. Perhaps we could go to the banks of the Amazon deep in the jungle to witness these miracles? He could promise I'd never forget it.

"I don't think so," I said.

"But the true beauty is that my legacy will continue. When I pass over, my son Michael will take over for me. Michael is being trained now to go into a trance and the spirit of Dr. Lang's son Basil will enter Michael's body and continue his healing. It's a bond between our two families," he said. "Do you understand?" he asked.

"Of course," I said.

After he left I opened the doors and windows to clear the air of his perfume. A breeze blew through the sitting room taking him away. I didn't know how to write about these people. Did they believe what they were doing, or was it sheer conning? I smoked packs of St. Moritz and shredded papers and carbons. I had no idea how or where to begin. I'd gotten a job, a typewriter, and a recorder. I wanted to be a professional but it felt like an impossible goal. One night I looked at the picture of Hemingway posed on the book jacket over his Olivetti and thought of him crafting lean sentences out of plain words. He'd started out as a reporter, I remembered, writing stories for the *Kansas City Star*. In college I'd read *A Farewell to Arms* and the opening lines dropped into my head. It didn't seem possible that I could remember them but I

OFF THE KING'S ROAD

knew them by heart. "In the late summer of that year we lived in a house in a village that looked across the river and the plain to the mountains. In the bed of the river there were pebbles and boulders, dry and white in the sun and the water was clear and swiftly moving and blue in the channels." Just describe them, I thought. Just say what you saw. Use as few words as you can and put your opinions to rest. Write clearly. Think of crystal.

THE MOONWALK

THE KITCHEN OF OUR HOUSE was in the basement, with a window looking up to the street. In the little alley below street level outside the kitchen door every morning the milkman left cold pint-size bottles with clotted cream floating on top. Bending to retrieve them, the street above was often white and misty, like the movies I saw in childhood of London shrouded in fog. The kitchen had wooden cabinets with round wood knobs and an old sink. You could send plates of food through an opening between the kitchen and the dining room where I'd put an old pine dining table.

At the opposite end of the room I'd put some floor pillows and butterfly chairs and a studio couch covered with a thick Spanish brown and black and gold throw that Bob had sent when he emptied our house in California. Above the couch I'd hung the ubiquitous super-size black and white photo posters found in every catchall shop in New York, L.A., and London; Marlon Brando in a leather jacket and motorcycle cap, Mick Jagger, scruffy and evil. Alongside the couch were French doors leading out back to a garden with roses that needed tending. The whole garden needed tending. But in rare sunny weather you could sit out there and read.

TVs were too expensive to buy. Everyone rented. Ours was on a big brass rolling table and on the flickering screen we watched Neil Armstrong and Buzz Aldrin walk on the moon. It felt as if the BBC would play the film forever, grainy pictures of slow-moving men in bubble suits, tanks on their backs, floating in space. You could hardly make them out, the universe behind them, the pockmarked face of the moon beneath their thick feet.

We watched the images over and over. Mesmerized like zombies. "How does the spaceship get there?" Julie asked.

"It blasts off," Billy said. "And goes a zillion miles." He made an exploding sound, the sound boys are born knowing how to make.

"Why are they walking that way?"

"There's nothing to hold them down," I said. "On Earth we have a thing called gravity. It keeps your feet in place."

"Why?"

"The Earth is different from the moon," I said. "There are different rules."

"Is London Earth?"

"Definitely," I said.

"Do they miss their children?"

"Sure. But they'll come back," Jenifer said, quick to salve the worry.

"How do you know?"

"Julie,"—exasperation from Billy—"they have a spaceship."

"They can start it?"

"Yes," Jenifer said. She put an arm around her. "Don't worry." Julie popped her thumb into her mouth and pulled her blanket under it.

We kept on staring, watching the blurred figures lumbering through space. I thought of my mother taking me to the Automat. It was a miracle when the little door opened and you took the sandwich out. Now it was the age of Aquarius; men could walk on the moon and there was the hope that if you tore the old world down the new one would be better, maybe even perfect. I drew a picture for Billy and colored it with bright chalks of Neil Armstrong floating to the lunar surface wrapped in a star-filled universe. Anything could happen. Who knew what the future might hold? "To Billy," I wrote on the picture, "who will go to the moon and bring it home with him . . . London, July 1969." He liked it and hung it beside his bed and then he drew one for me of a spaceman and his bicycle and I propped it against the old-fashioned alarm clock on the wooden steamer trunk beside my bed.

THE QUEEN'S ELM

THE QUEEN'S ELM. ELM PARK Road and Fulham. South
Kensington. I could never figure out what made it so popular.
There were prettier pubs. The Bunch of Grapes in the Brompton
Road. And The Chelsea Potter. All pubs were disappointing at
best. The food, even when it looked promising, always tasted fla-
vorless and what the pubs called salad was all mayonnaise and you
had to fight your way to the bar and then stand to drink.

But the Elm was worse than most with dun-colored walls hung
with a collection of old pipes and a big stretch of damp floor and
few places to sit. And it always smelled dank with an inch of piss-
colored ale swimming on the bar. But everyone went there. After

the Sunday morning softball game in Hyde Park the Elm was the place for the agents from the London Morris office, the visiting movie stars and screenwriters from Hollywood, for hip Americans and for Georgia and Gareth and their friends, the jazz singer Annie Ross and her boyfriend Sean, to go for a pint before a long Sunday lunch and an afternoon that stretched into forever. The Elm was a real pub. You could find Welshmen and poets and musicians and painters and sculptors and lyrical Irishmen with beards grazing their torn shetlands smoking Gauloises and passing out in the corner.

Terence was an actor. He got small parts as detectives or cops on TV. I met him at Georgia's one Sunday night when she sang. On odd nights he'd call me. "Phyllis. Great news. The Elm is open tonight!" he'd shout. After the kids were in bed I'd walk down the Fulham Road and find him at the bar reciting Dylan Thomas or Yeats, complaining about a part he didn't get. "Aahh, there she is . . . she walks in beauty," he'd say and hang an arm over my shoulder and order me a pint.

What did he want? I always wondered. We talked about books and plays and actors. He liked women—but I never saw him with one. He lived in a bare flat in a proletarian block off the Fulham Road, two rooms, a bed, a table, a tea kettle, and books. He talked sometimes about an old girlfriend, a Jewish girl named Lila who had run off with someone named Stanley. And he gave me advice he got from his mother. "Send your kids to your ex." He chortled. "Me mum says just pack them up and send them to him and his girlfriend. That'll fix him!"

He was tall and very thin with unhealthy-looking white skin that reddened easily and streaked sleek dark blond hair combed straight back. He always wore an old scarred brown leather jacket.

At a certain point in the evening he'd confide a joke we were both supposed to get: "Phyllis! Thank God I don't drink. I've seen what it does to people! Thank God. Just thank God I don't drink!" Soon it would become a bellow . . . a roar . . . "Thank God I don't drink!" His eyes would begin to look glassy, unfocused. Before that happened I'd know it was time to leave. "Don't go," he'd shout as I kissed his cheek. I'd leave behind the pint I'd been nursing and set off for home.

Good-looking people would be spilling out of the little Italian restaurants in the Fulham Road saying goodnight, and I'd stop on the way and look in the windows of the boutiques. One shop, Annacat, was just steps from my house. Soon after Bob left I'd bought a pair of skin-tight tomato-colored overalls and a creamy satin blouse there and a pair of high-waisted black plaid pants with a long matching coat. The shop carried clothing with labels that said, "Zandra Rhodes," a designer I'd read about in *British Queen* and in *Vogue*. I'd press my face against the window in the dark and peer inside.

In New York or Los Angeles I'd never spend an evening like this—taking a walk, drinking beer with an alcoholic actor in a pub—but in London it was enough to make me content. Upstairs, in bed I'd light a St. Moritz and open a book.

GIVE HER A MASK

I GOT A SECOND JOB writing letters for *Penthouse* magazine. I got it from Hal, the former producer on the same TV quiz show as my ex-neighbor in California, the emcee who gave the answers to the contestants. The emcee went to Canada, but Hal went to London, to *Penthouse*, a new British edition. Before I left California the emcee's wife gave me Hal and his wife Lucille's number. I never called them and probably never would have, but Paul was writing an interview for *Penthouse* (Pierre Cardin, Couturier) and one afternoon Hal stopped by to see him. "My coauthor," Paul said, introducing me with a wave of his hand, half Hungarian, half patriarchal.

When Paul asked if I'd work on the book he said, "I can't pay you much, probably less than you pay your cook, but I'll put your name on the cover." But when Hal offered me a job he said, "How much do you want?"

I'd gone to see him and I was sitting in his small glassed-in office; I acted casual and shrugged as if I hadn't really thought about it, but the question sent a rush of blood to my head. I'd always been told what I would be paid, but no prospective employer had ever asked me what I wanted.

To Paul, I was an abandoned housewife, one he could get on the cheap. But to Hal I was worth something.

I was a pro. I could set my price—a modest one—but my price.

The idea of getting paid did a lot for me. For the moment I had enough money but I was not looking forward to negotiating with Bob. He was a money expert; he'd been making money and thinking about money all his life; when he talked about convertible bonds or a deal or a percentage or a package or a tax deduction or a diamond mine in Africa, his face took on a smooth, soft look, a sweet melting happiness. I had been taken care of by my father and I was not the better for it. I had the fiscal aspirations of a schoolteacher or a civil service worker. I liked to spend money but I had no head for finances and little interest in how money was made. I knew I had to think about my economic future; up in working-class North London even my psychiatrist who owned one shirt kept telling me to get on my toes; "Do I have to get a divorce?" I moaned every week, tears brimming over. He had no Kleenex so I brought my own and fished them out of my carpet-bag and by the time the session was over dozens of little crumpled soggy white clumps floated like mini polar bears on ice caps over the Arctic sea of the sisal rug. "It would be best to set the wheels in motion," he'd say. His voice was deep and his diction was perfect (David was originally from South Africa but his British speech was impeccable). His King's English made his orders sound as if they were endorsed by the Crown. "Do it now. Do it quickly!" he advised.

"Why so fast? What's the rush?" I asked Caroline's friend, the dancing doctor, a short, compact Englishman with khaki hair and a Harley Street practice who wore blue blazers and drove a Ferrari. He'd put my house on the list of places to stop by late at night after he'd been to the ballet in Covent Garden or a hot party in Mayfair. This was the way of certain single men, I'd learned. Stopping here. Stopping there. Carrying gossip. "Mia's just had twins," he told me once. "I've been waiting at the hospital, with Andre." It made London feel like a small town. I'd pour him a brandy and he'd offer advice. When he'd had enough brandy I'd see him to the door and help him on with his coat. "Dear girl, You must act now while he's still feeling guilty! If you wait you'll have to battle for every shilling! Say 'Darling, it's for the children' . . . that sort of thing!"

Writing for *Penthouse* wouldn't make me rich; it would barely make me anything. Still, getting paid was a good habit to get into and I told Hal, "Yes."

"I'll bill you for my time," I said.

The *Penthouse* offices were in W14, Bramber Road, a neighborhood I could never quite place although I learned how to get there on the tube. Not far from the building were familiar haunts; Kensington, Fulham, Earl's Court, places I knew. They were just beyond reach and if I could find them I could go there for a walk or for lunch—but in which direction to go? Even the trusty "A to Zed" maps made the area seem close by but still far away. The vagueness of the neighborhood gave my three day-a-week job (I left at three to pick up the kids at school) a sense of dislocation, as if it weren't part of my real life, something removed, out of time, out of place. The office was a high, long narrow room with a lineup of desks, sometimes occupied, sometimes not. There seemed to be no logic to how people came and went. The walls were scattered with tacked up photos of "Penthouse Pets" photographed by Bob Guccione the publisher, pretty girls, some innocent looking, others wise and jaded but always with large breasts, half visible, partially covered by open shirts or deftly veiled in gauzy blouses.

Occasionally Guccione himself marched through the office in a tight white shirt open to the navel, a gold chain and medal gleaming in the V. His dark hair glistened like oil on spaghetti. He wore a leather jacket and boots that crunched rhythmically along the floor. He looked neither to the left nor the right. If on that day there were employees at the desks he never acknowledged them. A girlfriend, Kathy, was always behind him in spike-heel boots and a mini mini, hoisted as high as a skirt could possibly go and still qualify as a skirt. She had long baby-doll hair the color of tarnished brass and wore makeup that concealed every flaw. Her heels clicked in staccato, much faster than his. I could tell when they'd entered the room even with my back turned, hunched over my desk. They paraded to Hal's office, shut the door, and never stayed long. After a while the door would open and they'd come out and proceed out of the long room, crunching and clicking, him first, she deferentially behind, guarding the jewels. I always had the illusion she was carrying a whip which of course wasn't so.

Hal handed me stacks of letters from readers. Some were hand-written in cramped script on onionskin, others typed and scored with erasures and whiteout. There were letters on yellow legal pads, twelve-page epistles with dozens of misspellings, and others that were perfectly composed on expensive vellum with engraved initials. Some were fully descriptive, like novels ("That night, for the first time my stepmother opened her robe, I'd never seen a woman of her age naked before . . ."). There were straight-forward letters, written by pragmatic information-seekers ("My mates and I want to know the size of the largest willy on record? Colin, one of our mates, says he heard of one thirteen inches long when it's up? Do big ones really matter to birds?"). Still others disclosed New Age sensibilities, an affinity for the trends of the day ("At the end of the dinner, after a few dances, my friend's wife suggested with her husband's agreement that we should change partners. . . . At first my wife was horrified, but finally she agreed to try it and now we must confess that this was for us the most unforgettable experience of our life. We have never been closer"). Some writers reported on undergarments. Knickers were big ("Oh, the delights of taking them off," wrote S. W. from Glasgow. "How warmly she loves me after I expose her bare bottom over my lap and treat it to the crisp smack of a spanking"). Many of the letters were about punishment; the readers couldn't praise it enough. Canes and whips and humiliation, spanking, obedience, and bowing and scraping and crawling ("I have used a slipper, a hairbrush and oh how she squirms in anguish, but accepts her punishment; we leave the lights on because it heightens the enjoyment," sang T.R. of Tivdale, Worcestershire). Other readers found inspiration in the news of the day ("I have been masochist inclined for years but until I read reports of Dr. Ward in the Profumo case I could not find the courage to disclose it to anyone. I always believed that if I could find someone to give me a good beating it would cure me of wanting another. Eventually, I found the courage to go to a call girl and put my cards frankly before her. She shattered my hopes by telling me that however hard anyone beat me it would be no cure. She seemed to be talking from experience so I did not face the further embarrassment of having it off with her. If any reader knows the cure, I hope they will write to you").

I told Hal I didn't know much about sex. I was more than curious myself. I'd just read *Portnoy's Complaint* which Mike had brought back from a trip to New York and it came as a big revelation. I'd read it over and over. So this was my problem! I'd never understood it although Bob had hinted for years. I was too Jewish and too clean! My spelling was perfect. No man would ever masturbate dreaming of me! When he left me in the closet Bob said that with his teenage girlfriend he'd found what he needed, an elusive ecstasy that I'd never provided. "We never had it. We were too inexperienced. What we felt in the beginning we lost," he said, as I stood in unripped pantyhose and a white Maidenform bra.

"Of course you know about sex," Hal said. He looked at me with lifted eyebrows—as if I was holding back, as if I'd been not only around the block, but around the world half a dozen times, "a lady of the evening," as my father would say. "No," I told him. "I honestly don't!" Hal tried another tack. "Just be sensitive, be caring," he said. His forehead rippled. His face moved. His hair moved. All of his features seemed to cascade like the rapids in a river. He darted into his office and emerged with a stack of books that he piled one by one on my desk. *Psychopathia Sexualis*, by Kraft Ebbing. *Human Sexual Response*, by Masters and Johnson. *The Kinsey Report*. *Open Marriage*, written by a couple with their photo on the cover in peasant shirts and Mexican jewelry. "You can do it!" he said.

I began answering the letters. I took them one by one from the pile, starting with those that seemed simplest, the ones that just needed thanks and some praise. I didn't know about sex but I discovered—as I answered G.W. from Twickenham and P.F. from Lille, France, and F.S. from Blandford Street, W1, and The Enquirers of Pontypool, Monmouthshire, Wales—I didn't have to. I could look things up and quote "experts," but my words on the page were what mattered most.

"I'll make you a sex therapist," Hal said, winking. And, as I answered the letters, I began to think of myself as one.

"We have no accurate statistics for the world's largest penis. However, interviews with women have confirmed that size is never crucial," I wrote.

And . . . "Don't worry! Punishment has long been accepted as a pleasurable manner of sexual fulfillment. Many men and women take joy and reach orgasm through being spanked or beaten."

It was easy, in that room, distanced from the familiarity of even my own unfamiliar London Street in a country not my own, to sound like another person. Like improvising, I thought, as the words slipped onto the page. Once there, they assumed a kind of power, as printed words do. I knew that in a way I was lying, but in another way I wasn't. The person I became, the sex therapist/editor (sometimes I even answered as "The Editors," creating the impression that the *Penthouse* staff was sitting around deliberating over tea and scones), felt honest to me, more truthful than I could have been. "Man is least himself when he speaks in his own voice," Oscar Wilde said. "Give him a mask and he will tell you the truth." Writing, I was another person, a sex therapist/editor, someone who knew what she was talking about, a woman who'd been there.

THREE

ONE NIGHT, WHILE I WAS still living at St. Leonard's Terrace, Caroline brought Jakov home for the night. He was a big man, electric with energy, a Holocaust survivor and a writer. You couldn't ignore him. He wore corduroy pants, a crewneck sweater, and a tweed jacket and had thick red hair and a moustache like a whiskbroom. His eyes glittered in his round face like a man with a perpetual fever.

Jakov was ten when the Nazis marched into Austria and he was sent to Holland, separated forever from his home, family, and country. He survived masquerading as a "goy" on the streets of Berlin.

I was in her Ladyship's bedroom, a book propped on my knees, a St. Moritz burning in the ashtray, when I heard him clump up the stairs with Caroline behind him. I'd never met him but my bedroom door was open and in seconds he was inside examining the Lichtenstein painting ("Art!" he snorted. "Feh!") that hung alongside the bed.

He plopped himself down on the white satin comforter and took out a bar of hash. I had a newspaper on the floor and he spread it out and helped himself to one of my cigarettes.

"So, what you reading?" he asked.

I held up *The Golden Notebook*.

Jakov emitted a giant sigh, half pained, half amused. "Doris Lessing. Doris Lessing. Very serious lady," he said. "One of the literati. Lives up in Hampstead." Another sigh. "Why waste your time?"

Caroline was stretched on the chaise longue, glamorous in her velvet jeans and a silk shirt and jacket. She made a face at me. She was laughing at him, as if he was an incorrigible child.

He finished rolling, inhaled, passed the joint to me, and began stroking my bare instep.

"You like to fuck?" he asked.

"Sometimes," I said.

"You Jewish?"

"What do you think?"

"Jewish women worry too much about fucking. The Jewish mind is programmed for guilt! What's a fuck?" he crooned. "Such a small thing! What does it matter? Think of all the times you did it and you hated it. You didn't like the guy. You had a headache. You had a cold. You wanted to get rid of him. You wanted to get it over with. This time, we all do it for fun. With me."

He held an arm out to Caroline, an all-inclusive employer. When he stopped talking I could hear him breathing. His labored breath sounded like a permanent condition, a constant reminder that he was nearby. Thinking.

His hand continued stroking my foot. It wasn't unpleasant. The sweet smell of hash filled the room. Everything slowed down the way it does when you smoke. I felt as if I were floating, half dizzy and langorous. I imagined how nice it would be to be with someone I liked, even loved, someone with hair and skin I wanted to touch. I couldn't think who that person would be. Mike, more friend than lover, came closest, but he still wasn't right.

I'd been trying men out, experimenting with Ted and with Mike. Sex was everywhere and I'd wanted to take advantage. For the first time I was free to do as I pleased. Every voice in London said that I could. I liked Mike, loved his part in my new London life. He covered his awkwardness with knowing talk that seemed to me very sweet. And he'd come when I needed him; when Julie took a fall he'd left his typewriter and raced with me to the emergency room to see if she needed a stitch. I liked the feel of his body, his bigness and strength. Mike seemed happy enough with our lovemaking—he never expressed discontent. But whatever was supposed to happen in bed didn't happen for me. I was beginning to think it never would.

Jakov's hand had moved up to my ankle. Through the haze it came to me that he was serious. He was proposing a threesome. The thought brought a cold, icy chill to my head. Inside I could feel my brain turning white. I'd encouraged the *Penthouse* readers to embark on such adventures, but for myself, even the thought filled me with terror. Once, in Puerto Rico at a party a woman had kissed me, and I'd nearly flown through the sliding glass doors out onto the terrace. My wish to know about sex didn't include threesomes or women. Who did what to whom, and when? How did anyone figure this out? And why would they want to? For me, the whole point of sex was that it be with one other person, somebody male.

Jakov leaned over and offered the cigarette. I shook my head and hoisted myself up. "I'm out," I said. "I'm going to sleep."

"No. No. Don't do that," Jakov said. "What's one more time? What's the big deal?"

In the chaise longue Caroline was smiling a sweet, slow smile. I wondered what she was thinking. Was she willing? I wouldn't ask and would never find out, but my instincts told me she'd done this before. She was daring and curious, more courageous than I was. I wondered if we'd still be friends now, or if she'd just write me off.

Jakov inhaled noisily. The roach was almost gone.

"Come," Caroline said. She'd slipped off the chaise and pulled on his hand. The other one lifted mercifully off my ankle.

"It's over?" Jakov said. "That's it?" His brows lifted. "What's your hurry? Little girls! Little girls! Shame on you! You didn't even give me a chance to reject you."

I watched their backs going up the stairs, Caroline leading, Jakov hulking behind, a woman leading a bear. Relief flooded over the blur in my head. My heart was beating quickly.

Before I lived in London I'd thought the English were repressed. But the longer I stayed, the less I believed that was true. The multi-use words "fuck" and "cunt" were mainstays of London language; they appeared as nouns, adjectives, adverbs, and verbs. Everyone talked about their sex lives and the sex lives of others. At dinner my neighbor, Honor Earl, looking pleased, told me about Kenneth Tynan who lived at the end of our sedate London street. She'd heard he liked being spanked and one of our neighbors had seen his collection of whips hung just off the library overlooking the square. Jay and Fran were from St. Louis, but England suited them. They fit right in. Whenever I told them about the men I met Jay always asked, "Was there entry? Congress?" The attitude was infectious. I picked it up. And Jakov brought it with him from Vienna, Amsterdam, Berlin, and Tel Aviv. In London he was at home.

"I'm in the Fulham Road," Jakov would say. "Is that near your house?" I hesitated. "You think we're going to fuck?" he'd ask. "Forget it! No such thing! It never entered my mind!"

He had a girlfriend, a painter named Annie, but she was often away and he seemed to need things to do. "Writers are masturbators," he said. "I call them writer/masturbateurs. Writing itself is masturbation. All day they write and they masturbate." After a day of writing and masturbating he needed to get out. He knew people in London, writers and publishers and editors and agents and he dropped by to visit. He took me to Putney, to a party for the novelist Mordecai Richler and to gatherings where I saw beautiful Edna O'Brien, an aging Rebecca West, and Doris Lessing, her hair pulled severely back in a bun. When the evening ended he always asked to stay with me and I always said, "Not this time," but no matter how many times I said no, he always came back.

"I know the Jewish mind," he'd say, tapping my forehead. "You think we're going to fuck. No way! No way we'll fuck!" Sometimes he added, "I'll put my cock in your cunt, but we won't fuck."

I asked myself why I went with him. I had no answer. Sometimes, when he was at his most extravagant, I felt a faint niggling of curiosity, like the flame from a match, but not enough to make me carry through. He was too unpredictable, too erratic and overwhelming. I had the feeling that if I ever took off my clothes he'd mow me down. I'd never resurface. His desire was omniverous. All over London I could imagine him calling; "I'm in Berkeley Square . . . Eaton Terrace . . . Mansfield Gardens . . . I'm in the Camden Passage. Is that near your house?"

When I asked him to edit my writing, he did: it was amazing to see; a few strokes of a pen, words crossed out, the addition of a comma or a colloquialism and the human voice sprang from the page where once there was wood. On the subject of sex he was crude, but when it came to writing he was elegant. One Sunday afternoon he brought his kids to my house. A boy and a girl. They were English, polite, and well brought up. He'd been married to an Englishwoman and the kids lived with her. They were older than mine but I suggested we all go to see "A Night at the Opera" at the National Film Theater, and their politeness disappeared when they laughed.

Caroline had an assignment on the island of Majorca, photographing a model on the beach in a mink coat, and she asked me along. In the airport the short Spanish policemen opened her bags and wanted to seize the mink coat. They suspected something but couldn't say what. We wore jeans and safari jackets and carried the equipment. We fussed and fumed. We threatened and screamed. The blonde model smiled silently and the police melted away, gates opened, the mink coat sailed through. After the shoot we drove to the town of Deya where Jakov's girlfriend

Annie kept a painting studio. He'd built a place for himself alongside hers, a tall, round narrow building shaped like a phallus. It reached above the trees to the sky. "Jakov's Tower," Annie said. "His erection!" The sun was hot and we all stood, three women, laughing.

"I was a ghost, a shadow, a piece of printed paper with a fingerprint and a signature . . ." he wrote in *Counting My Steps*, the autobiography he gave me. "For Phyllis, for Christmas," he wrote on the cover of the story of how he got through the war, eleven years old, masquerading as a Dutch laborer, Jan Overbeek. "I was Jan Overbeek. Yes. But I didn't look like him . . . there was something wrong with my eyes. The Germans thought the Jew was attached to his nose . . . the Jew was in the eyes . . . a certain soft, reflective look. A look of shame and humiliation, a wise look, a pensive one. All this I had to lose as soon as possible."

"Meet me at Francis Huxley's," Jakov said. "Who knows with him? The English ruling classes, they're falling apart. Who knows what he likes, what he fucks? Little girls? Little boys? Maybe nothing? You'll see what you think. But he has drugs."

Francis was the nephew of Aldous, the son of Julien, the biologist and the spokesman for Darwin. In college I'd read *Brave New World* and *After Many a Summer Dies the Swan*. The name was so famous I wanted to see him. He lived up in Hampstead and I drove with the top down around Hyde Park Corner and up Park Lane to the north, the A to Zed on the seat beside me. His flat was on the very top floor of an old house, one large room lined with books, dark old furniture covered in worn velvet, a big writing desk and Oriental rugs. One small brass lamp was the only thing lit. A large white moon shone through the tall windows. We sat on furniture placed all around the room, separated from each other by large distances. Francis himself sat in a corner in shadows. The most I could see was the egg shape of his head, dark hair, and a glowing white shirt. Why were we so far apart, I wondered. What would we talk about? I asked about his travels to Brazil, to the Urubu Indians. I'd heard he'd written a book. But he didn't say much. At least not to me. An hour went by. I thought I should go.

"So, you have LSD?" Jakov asked.

Francis seemed to be waiting for this question. He didn't hold back. He stood up, a tall, wavery figure, and took out a small bottle from the drawer of the desk.

"Three ways?" Jakov asked.

"You think it's enough?"

The two men sat puzzling over the tiny bottle. There was a large round hassock in the middle of the room and they both bent over it, studying the possibilities. Two great minds I thought, puzzling over the mathematics of a tiny vial of liquid divided by three. Perhaps they wanted me to leave? I decided I wouldn't. The moonlight shone on them as if they were under a spotlight. Finally they twisted the cap off the bottle and mixed the contents with drops of tap water.

"It should be distilled water," Jakov said. "If you don't have it, you don't have it! What can we do?"

They poured the colorless liquid into a small teaspoon, one for each. There's so little there it can't affect me, I thought, but I'll have a story to tell. I will have taken acid with one of the Huxleys. We swallowed and sat waiting. Outside the window the cold, white moon shone. I was on a studio couch draped with old throws. The hum of their voices lulled me to sleep. I'm not sure how long I was out. But when I woke, everything was just as it was. Jakov sat staring in one corner, Francis in another.

"I'm going home," I said.

Jakov raised a hand in farewell. Francis just sat. I drove through a London impossibly silent. All the tubes were shut down. Not a soul in the streets. Only an occasional black London taxi with its yellow light lit. The damp air ruffled my hair and felt cool on my face. I climbed the stairs to my bedroom and had just put my head down when I heard a noise in the street, the sound of marching feet, a parade of army boots coming towards me, pounding the pavement in rhythm. A clutch of fear grabbed me and then I understood that it was the tiny bit of acid we'd taken. I was having an auditory hallucination. The boots continued to march, getting louder the closer they got, heading straight for my door. I was tempted to get up and look out but I knew that all I'd see from my window was the empty London Street. The crunch of boots was the last thing I heard as I dropped off, the sound of my loneliness.

BERLIN

THE LINE THAT WOUND UNDER the searchlights to the checkpoint on Saturday night moved faster than I thought it would. I looked into the face of the border guard expecting suspicion, but what I saw was boredom. A quick slap of the passport and we were away from the lights and hurly-burly of the West.

I followed George and his girlfriend through the dark, narrow streets of East Berlin, scurrying through alleys and beneath a dank underpass. I felt like a spy—or a character in a postwar European movie. At a certain point we passed two soldiers in the street and I felt a chill. Could I be accused, picked up, disappear? Be thrown into prison? For what?

George's girlfriend was from New Jersey with an accent to match. Her husband was back there taking care of their son. In New Jersey she must have been exotic, six foot tall, like a beanpole with white boots, a white wool mini dress, luminous skin, and glossy lips. Her straight hair was the color of light honey.

George didn't explain. He invited me to Berlin and there she was. He'd gone from Greta Garbo to Viveca Lindfors to Arlene from Short Hills. He was as aristocratic as ever; a loden coat with toggles hung loosely on his long body.

We were on our way to the Berliner Ensemble, the theater of Brecht. "Extraordinary, darling. You must go." Georgia said. "Magnificent acting, the best in the world."

Inside the theater was full . . . a starburst of people lighting the dark. Entering from the deserted streets was like going to a surprise party when the lights are turned on. The old manager kissed George's cheeks and ushered us to third-row seats.

Like a lumpen mountain of rags Mother Courage strained, dragging the cart across Europe, doing business while her children died one by one. Her head was thrown back and her nose pointed forward like a giant beak. Her shoulders rippled like waves. It felt as if she were pulling the earth. I knew no German, but watching the actors and hearing their speech I felt my heart beating faster, as if hands were reaching to wring me out.

After the show we drank with the cast at long, scarred tables in a gloomy basement beer hall.

"Marry with me," asked one of the actors. He looked at me earnestly across the scarred wooden table and rested a hand on my arm. His face was like a peach.

"He's desperate to leave," George said, "to come to America and be on soap operas."

Back in West Berlin lights blazed on the Kurfurstendam. I felt relieved being out of the East. "The rewards of freedom . . ." George drawled, dangling handcuffs in a sex shop. There were penis rings and nipple salve and rhino tusk aphrodisiac pills and whips for sale. And linzer tortes and coffee with whipped cream in the cafes, mountains of it, enough to drown in.

CHRISTMAS, 1969

REMNANTS OF CHRISTMAS WRAPPING PAPER and rib-
bon lay on the dining room table with an open paste pot and a roll
of cotton. Julie and Billy had pasted Father Christmas beards and
snow all over the packages they brought to Bob. A velvet dress
Jenifer had chosen not to wear hung by the arm on the door of her
room. I gave Emilia the day off. For a while the sound of her
radio, Spanish music, filtered from under the door of her room,
but then the front door slammed and I was alone—and out of
Tampax. I threw on a coat and drove to the King's Road, up Sloane
Street and over to Piccadilly, to the Haymarket and the Strand,
keeping my eyes peeled for an open "chemist." I'd never seen the

city so empty. Even in front of the windows at Harrod's where mannequins stood frozen in jewels and satins, the street was deserted. All the tourists were gone. The store was outlined in white lights like a big vacant castle. I imagined the food halls, usually packed but now deserted, the jars of preserves and tea cannisters and wheels of Stilton alone and abandoned. In Park Lane I gave the car keys to the doorman at the Hilton and bought a box of Tampax from room service.

In Allie's tiny flat she was roasting a turkey. She'd invited me and Mike and a collection of guests from among the loose crowd that floated through London; Terence—my buddy of the Queen's Elm—was coming and Peter, a requisite, rough-edged, bearded Australian journalist. (The English viewed the Australians with disdain. "Don't go out there," a character in a West End play warned a departing guest late at night. "The streets are filled with Australians.")

The final guest was Claire Ann—a young American Mike had met at the bar at the Club Arethusa who told him she'd slept with Bob before our marriage ended.

"A girlfriend of Bob's?" I said. "Really?"

(How many had there been?)

"She works in the Morris office. She's nice," Mike said.

"She is?" I asked.

"Yes," he said. "You'll like her."

"I will?"

"Yes," he insisted.

(Mike was always meeting people at the Arethusa. He'd met Christine Keeler there, the call girl who'd gone to jail for passing secrets she'd learned from her lover, the war minister John

Profumo. He'd said she was "nice" too—and when she wanted to sell her washing machine he'd arranged for me to buy it. It cost fifty pounds and worked very well.)

This will be cozy, I thought, as I drove through the misty white London streets searching for Tampax; Christmas with Allie and her boyfriend Mike—who was also my lover—and one of my soon to be ex-husband's ex-girlfriends. Mike's third girlfriend—the woman in the Japanese kimono that Allie had found him with the day she'd arrived in London—had broken up with him.

"Fuck you!" she said when she found out he was spending Christmas with Allie and me.

"Fuck me? Fuck her! She wouldn't even wish me Merry Christmas," Mike said. He sounded offended. "Then she said she would wish me Merry Christmas, but she wouldn't mean it!"

"That was mean," Allie said. "What would it cost her to say Merry Christmas?"

"She could say it. She just couldn't *mean* it," Mike said.

"I still think it's mean," Allie said.

"She is mean," Mike agreed. "She's got a nasty side to her!"

We were in the kitchen stuffing the turkey. Allie wasn't sure which end to stuff. I pointed to the bottom. "If this works it will be a miracle," she said.

"It's a bird! You're a bird! You can't fuck it up!" Mike said.

Allie was pink, flushed from the heat. Her long red hair spilled down her back. A new watch from Hermes on a thick silver chain, a Christmas gift from her other boyfriend Ben who was in New York with his kids, looped her thin wrist as her long white fingers poked at the stuffing. Mike and I helped her, pushing the wet bread inside. She slid the bird into the oven, slammed the door and stood up. She swatted a dishcloth at Mike. "Three women were too much for you," she gloated.

"You can never have too many women!" Mike said. He draped an arm over my shoulder but I slipped from under it. Allie swatted him again. He grabbed a towel and they raced through the tiny flat, skirting the furniture until he wrestled her into a hold and rubbed her face as she struggled. "I give up," she screamed.

I stood on the side laughing, although I didn't think it was so funny.

Allie and I never mentioned our sharing Mike and I preferred it that way. Both of us sleeping with him was one thing . . . talking about it was another.

And what would I say? I wasn't sorry I'd done it. If she could have two boyfriends, why couldn't Mike have two women? Or more? And why shouldn't one of them be me? Sometimes—like now, as he chased her around the flat—I'd feel a twinge of jealousy, but it never lasted. The fact is I was glad he had Allie. I didn't want him around all the time.

Would I have been so casual in L.A. or New York? I didn't think so. But I was in London, another country, another time.

Mike's third girlfriend, the woman in the Japanese kimono, might have the right idea but what did being right get her? She was alone on Christmas in a deserted city. Being right had never made me happy—but maybe she knew something I didn't.

"Making love is good in itself," my psychiatrist said. "The more it happens between as many people as possible the better."

"You're nuts!" I argued. "Life would be chaos!"

"Then let there be chaos!" he said. "Chaos will do us all good!"

I was right in the thick of the revolution he wanted. It was only a year since I arrived in London and Bob and I parted. But I felt as if the world had turned a million times since that night in the closet and the person I'd been had disappeared into the past, light years away.

It wasn't till after we'd eaten that Claire Ann showed up. The dinner table looked like a battleground with blotches of red wine and the turkey carcass like the shell of a bombed-out building. Someone had brought a gooey chocolate cake which we'd demolished and the dessert dishes streaked with chocolate were piled on top of plates swimming with congealing gravy and mounds of dried-out stuffing and leftover mashed potatoes. The only untouched item was a Christmas pudding, brought by the Australian. "It's not Christmas dins without a proper pud," he said.

"But no one ever eats the bloody thing till Whitsun," Terence said. His elbow was propped on the table, his chin in his palm. His eyes rolled in loopy circles.

A thick hash joint had gone around and the aroma floated over the room in a sweet enveloping cloud. Everything was happening at a very slow pace. Someone would say something and we'd wait for what seemed a full minute before someone replied. The doorbell rang and Mike moved slowly to get it. Suddenly Mike was pushing a blurry figure towards me and she held out a small white hand, the childish fingers circled with silver rings.

Blood rushed upward, shooting like a geyser through the haze in my head.

"Oh . . . it's you," I said.

This was Claire Ann?

It took some seconds to reshuffle her in the files in my head.

I'd expected someone exotic—someone I'd envy and want to be—but Claire Ann was an everyday blonde, a girl who could have been in my college dormitory, downstairs in the smoker late at night wrapped in a bathrobe, studying for a midterm, or at a weekend in a fraternity house. I'd see her coming out of a suite with a dopey-looking boy whose chin and cheeks were sandpapered pink with lipstick. She could have been on the cover of a Sears Roebuck Catalog opening a refrigerator door or pushing a lawn mower—a pretty girl with wavy shoulder-length blonde hair, brown eyes, and a sweet smile. She wore boots, a vest, a long coat that she dropped over a chair. If I saw her on the King's Road I wouldn't look twice.

Maybe she played tennis or spoke perfect French. Somewhere she must have a secret, something I couldn't see.

She pulled up a chair and put her head close to mine.

"How are the kids?" she asked.

Claire Ann was from Texas and had a sweet southern drawl and a smile I couldn't get behind, a smile that admitted no other possibilities. Behind that smile was another and then another. If there was an end to that smile with something behind it, I'd never know. She said she sang in her church choir. But she was restless in Dallas and after college she had come to New York and then to London.

I tried to see her with Bob. My head was still hazy but even inside the fog my imagination had fled. I couldn't imagine them together. What did they talk about? Maybe they never spoke, just jumped on each other and ripped off their clothes. But I couldn't imagine that either. All I could see was blank space.

"Bob had so many girlfriends," she said.

"Bob?" I blurted.

Bob? The awkward boy in the Buick peering out from behind his thick glasses. The boy whose white skin burned in the sun and who jumped rope every morning in his boxer shorts? The man who got colds four times a winter and filled the bedroom with the smell of his vaporizer. The man who ate everything my mother put in front of him, six slices of brisket? I'd been married to Bob for twelve years but the man Claire Ann was describing was someone I'd never met.

"Are you sure you have the right Bob?"

I told her his full name, height, weight, hair color.

"That's him." She smiled. "I liked him but . . ." she shrugged . . . "what could I do?"

I thought of Bob on the dance floor doing the twist. Or at the bar of the Club Arethusa chatting up women, buying them drinks. I tried to imagine him saying . . . what? What would he even think of to pick up a woman?

Jealousy, my psychiatrist said, was what made all the communes fall apart. He listed them in a deep solemn tone; Stockholm. Paris. Berlin. I saw them all crumbling, men and women running from doorways, buildings flaking to dust. "But," he added, "Jealousy isn't really the problem. After years of work you can deal with sexual sharing, but love is more difficult; to be able to love requires a revolution in our society."

Claire Ann kissed me goodbye when we parted. Her brown eyes looked into mine and her lips grazed my cheek. "I'm so happy I met you," she said. She placed her small white hand in mine and I pressed her cool palm.

"I knew you'd like her," Mike said. And I replied that I did. But inside I felt blank as a white canvas waiting for paint. I wasn't jealous . . . just mystified. I had no idea who I had married or who I'd just met.

Outside the streets were still empty as Terence and I walked home through Fulham, he singing "It's a Fine, Fine Life," from *Oliver*, slurring the words, making up those he'd forgotten. "For the likes of such as meeeee, it's a fine, fine life." He grabbed my shoulders and looked into my eyes with drunken fervor. At his corner I kissed him goodnight, pushed him towards his flat. Lights were shining in rooms, splashing the darkness with bright shots of color. Up ahead a man in a Burberry under a puddle of light from a streetlamp was walking a dog. Everything felt as if I were seeing it from a great distance; being open about sex was supposed to bring people closer . . . but I'd never felt further apart.

In England the day after Christmas is "Boxing Day." We didn't know what it meant. "Maybe it's because they put all the Christmas stuff in boxes," Allie said.

"Does it have anything to do with boxing, the sport?" she asked. Mike and I said we didn't know. I guessed that it might have something to do with the Queen.

"In England everything has something to do with the royal family," I said. We were watching *Breakfast at Tiffany's* on television.

Audrey Hepburn, in her black dress and cigarette holder singing "Moon River" on her fire escape, seemed like a lost world.

In Fran's bedroom we stretched out on her bed. "Boxing day is the day you're supposed to give boxes of food and gifts to the poor," Fran said. "It started with the Victorians."

"See! I knew it had something to do with the Queen," I said. "Some Queen! Any Queen. It doesn't matter which one!"

Fran's bedroom was a sea of clothing and jewelry, old furniture, shawls and antiques. Everywhere you looked were feather boas and scarves and shawls, strings of beads and old hats. The Camden market was around the corner and she couldn't resist a bargain. She prowled it all the time, buying things for 6p. She spent all her time in the bedroom writing poems and lyrics and reading and watching old movies whenever she could find them on TV. In the drawer next to her bed was her stash of low-calorie chocolate from Boots the chemist and her fags and bambu papers and her bar of hash. I always felt when I was there that I could nest there forever.

We played "If you were an animal, what would you be?"

"A dolphin," Mike said. "I've always liked them."

"Because you fancy yourself very smart," Fran said.

"Hey," Mike said, a little edge to his voice. Fran could set him off. "That's what I picked."

Jay chose a mountain goat. "They climb to high places. Very spiritual," he said. He sucked in his breath.

"Yeah sure. Spiritual," Fran said. "So you don't have to take out the garbage . . . or deal with any of yours."

Jay laughed, a laugh like a long cough. He patted her leg.

Allie wanted to be a bird. "I'd like to be able to fly everywhere," she said. Her voice sounded dreamy and airy.

"I wish we weren't playing this game," Fran said. "I'd rather play "Who would you like to spend eternity with?" I want to spend it with Oscar Wilde and Noel Coward. My favorite Englishmen. Although it does bother me that they're both gay. But for eternity I'd rather have someone to talk to than someone to fuck."

When it was my turn I said I wanted to be a leopard.

"A leopard!" Jay said. He made a long shshshushing sound.

"You're no leopard," Mike said.

"Why?" Fran asked.

"Because they're strong, and beautiful. They're stealthy and graceful."

"They make nice coats," Allie said. "Jackie Kennedy had one with a matching pillbox hat."

"You're not the leopard type," Mike insisted. "Maybe a leopard with a bird on its shoulder."

They all agreed.

"I can't see you as a leopard," Jay said.

I was beginning to wonder myself. I hadn't really thought about it before I'd been asked, but when it popped out of my mouth I knew it was the right choice. The more they pushed, the harder I stuck with the leopard. I thought of the leopard's strong limbs, and sinewy body, its silence and grace, climbing the mountains of Tibet and prowling the African bush, surviving the wild all alone, a killer when roused.

T W O

"A KISS CAN RUIN A human life," Oscar Wilde said. Two
nights after New Year's Jakov appeared on my doorstep with
Richard—a tall man—well over six foot, narrow as a playing card,
in a long dark blue overcoat and hair that frizzed out around his
head in dirty blond corkscrew curls like a wild poet, Shelly on a
bender. It was the look of the day but with an English twist, a care-
less, unshorn, Cambridge/Oxford look. Before the night was over
I was on the way to ruin, not permanently as Oscar would have it,
but at least for a time, just what I'd been hoping for months. I'd
been desperate for ruin, looking for it all over London, maybe

even stayed there just so I could be taken apart. My other lovers, Ted and Mike, had been experiments, but with Richard I wasn't trying anything out; I just wanted him.

"You're home?" Jakov said when I opened the door.

"You don't call?"

"We were in the King's Road. It's right near your house."

"I know where it is."

"This is Richard. He's just left his wife." Jakov snickered. "He wants to live a free life. You could instruct him how to begin. Maybe you could arrange for him an introduction to your psychiatrist?"

"Aaah Jakov. Always fast. Always smart," Richard said. He was laughing. He looked at me and I looked back.

The kids were still with Bob. They'd be there all week. We went to dinner at the Tandoori Restaurant in the old Brompton Road. A man wearing a turban and a white Indian tunic with a gold sash opened the door. We went down a long curving staircase to a room with low lights. Sitar music played in the background.

Richard was American, from Queens. He'd gone to Cambridge as a graduate student in literature just out of Amherst, married an English girl, and stayed on in London. He had two little daughters and worked as a producer for the BBC. At thirty one he was restless; last year his best friend had died of leukemia. And six months ago he'd died himself—of MSG poisoning in a Chinese restaurant. He'd been brought back to life. It made all the papers.

"How did it feel?" I wanted to know. I was eating Tandoori chicken, suddenly afraid of a bone in my throat.

"He was dead," Jakov said. "How could it feel?"

He shrugged. "There was no tunnel. No light at the end. Afterward I walked around for weeks thinking what the fuck am I doing? Is this my life? Do I want to live this way?"

"That means he wants to fuck you," Jakov said.

"Of course I want to fuck her," Richard said. "Why wouldn't I?"

Good, I thought. I'm happy to hear it.

I asked them both back for a drink. I had started keeping jugs of white wine in the house. On the way we passed my car, parked in the street near my door. Richard tapped the chassis. "I just ordered one of these," he said. "They're making it up. A month . . . maybe six weeks and I'll have it!"

"That one is mine," I said.

"You're joking!"

"No. It's true! I'll show you the papers . . ." I reached into my carpetbag.

"We drive the same car!" His voice ascended an octave. His face brightened to pink. He reached out and put a hand on my hand. It was the first time we'd touched. "Phyllis," he said, "what does this mean?"

"We're both crazy," I said. "British racing cars are nothing but trouble!"

"No. It's a message. These are handmade in the North, two hundred a year. What are the odds of this happening? Why did you want one?" he asked

"For fun. I wanted to drive it," I said.

"A couple of weeks after I died and recovered I was on my way back to the office from a lunch and I happened to walk past the showroom . . ."

He was speaking very deliberately, as if every word had weight. I would learn this about him. It was impossible to turn away or not pay attention.

"There was a red one out on the street. I walked inside and wrote out a check!"

I knew about him then. It took a certain kind of person to choose that car, someone like me, asking for more than an automobile was meant to provide, someone dissatisfied with their life and wanting another.

"My first one was red," I said. "That was in L.A."

"You've had two! That does it! We're fated!"

Jakov stood off to one side. "What is it?" he asked. "A fucking car?"

After Jakov left we put the top down and drove around London in the cold, through the streets of Knightsbridge and Belgravia. The air was damp and my face felt wet. We drove to the King's Road, quiet in the darkness, and over to Cheyne Walk, to the embankment and along it to Waterloo Bridge. On the South Bank we stood on the promenade outside the Royal Festival Hall.

"What was it like to live in Hollywood?" he asked.

"I didn't like it," I said.

"Why not?" he asked.

"It's a company town," I said. "Everything is about the movies. There's no other life. Books are called properties, even classics, *War and Peace*, *Sons and Lovers*, properties become projects, projects become packages. By ten o'clock everyone is asleep, nobody walks in the streets. You can go watch the sprinkler water the lettuce in the all-night supermarket on Santa Monica. That's about it."

"You know what John Cheever said about Hollywood?"

I shook my head.

"I'd wake up, order the most elaborate breakfast I could think of, and try to make it to the shower before I hanged myself . . ."

"That sounds right," I said.

"Wasn't it exciting?" he asked.

"Not for me."

"Don't you have any desire to go back, not even a drop?"

"No," I said. "I wasn't happy there. I want a less important life, but I want it to be mine."

"I think I'd like it," Richard said. "I'd like to be an agent . . . or a producer . . ."

"Good luck," I said.

He leaned to kiss me then. I knew it was coming. It was quiet along the embankment and I could hear the water lapping. I was wearing my sheepskin coat and I took my bare hand out of the pocket and reached up and touched his soft hair and his neck. We stood pressed against each other. He was much taller than I was and I had to tilt my head back.

"Hear the water?" I asked.

"No," he said, and kissed me again.

"You're just not listening," I said. "Try harder."

Back at my house he walked me into the darkened hallway. He ran the back of his hand along my cheek. "I think I should go home now," he said. "I'll call you."

"I'm an Oblomov. You're an Oblomov! But Richard is not an Oblomov," Jakov pronounced. He liked this description and looked gleeful, but with characteristic literary restraint didn't repeat it.

"What's an Oblomov?" I asked.

"A book. You should read it!"

The next day I picked up a second hand copy of *Oblomov* by Goncharov in Foyles in Charing Cross Road. Ilya Ilyitch Oblomov, I learned, was a man who spent his days in bed always promising to leave his bedchamber but never actually managing to get out of his dressing gown. I didn't think I was exactly an Oblomov but I got Jakov's point. There were Oblomovs—and people like Bob and Richard who never let up.

"Richard's ambitious. He has bridges to burn," Jakov said. "He's a man in a hurry. He wants to fuck you."

"So what!"

"He asks questions about Hollywood and your husband."

"Maybe he wants to fuck my husband," I said.

"He would if he could."

He liked that answer. He snorted. "All he needs is a chance."

"I want to see you," Richard said the next week. He said he'd like to come Friday. He was separated from his wife, but only mid-week. On Saturday mornings he went back to her and his kids in St. Johns' Wood. The weekend is two days, I told myself. The work week is five. "Phyllis," he said. "I like being with you. You're funny to talk to."

I didn't say anything. I just told him to come. I tried to keep my voice casual. I wanted to make it appear that I had other things on my mind. My kids were back from visiting Bob. "Come late," I said. "I'd like to take my children to dinner and put them to bed."

He brought me a book, a futurist novel by a man named Michael Frayn. *A Very Private Life* was the title and the jacket blazed with color, stripes of aqua, olive, sienna and white. On my clear lucite coffee table the book looked like a flag. If you entered that room there was no way you could miss it. Inside on the flyleaf he'd written the date—Friday the 13th and "For Phyllis. My 'property.' Richard." He explained that he'd optioned the novel for the BBC.

I put on a new LP I'd just gotten, the Band. He said he knew all about them, they were friends of Bob Dylan. "The Night They Drove Old Dixie Down." "Up on Cripple Creek." He kissed me again. "I've been thinking of this for a week," he said.

"I have too," I told him. It was true although I didn't know why. There was no explaining desire. Passion was absurd. Flights of feeling that took you places you didn't belong. There was no place an affair with Richard could possibly go. I decided I would just live for the moment. After that night I might never see him again.

He followed me upstairs to my bedroom and we lay down on my brass bed. I had put the wooden steamer trunk I'd packed when I came from L.A. alongside the bed and I lit a candle on it. It flickered against the deep red walls and sheer white curtains. The room was warm and we took off each other's clothes and dropped each piece on the carpet and I pulled him to me. I liked the length of his body, his skin and the touch of his hands. His wild hair felt soft on my face. I felt excited, high and jangled. It was like being on a high board over a perfect swimming pool, beautiful to look at but I was unwilling to fall. I wanted to say "To hell with it," but my body refused. I stood strung out, overlooking the water. Sex, even at its best, was for me always this way. The Beatles song "Come Together" could have been written for me. I never came together. I never came in the same room let alone the same bed with another person. When Bob asked me about it I always said, "I'm fine. Don't worry about me. I'm happy this way."

I'd thought about what I could do to change the way I reacted in bed, but books about sex with their clinical descriptions turned me off. So did Masters and Johnson with their new techniques. I preferred to stay as I was—flooded with desire—even if it went unsatisfied.

Afterwards I saw tears in his eyes. I was sure they were there. "This is dangerous . . ." he said.

I put my finger over his lips and put my arms around him and buried my head in his neck. I wished he would shut up. He was going to make this tough on me.

"Let's fly to New York and go to Katz's Deli," Richard said. "I want to see the sign that says 'Send a salami to your boy in the army.' We can have a corned beef sandwich and a Dr. Brown's Cel-ray."

We were lying in bed in candlelight. Outside was my prim London Street. New York came galloping back, invading my bedroom.

"My father's spice factory is just over the bridge," I said. "You can see the sign on your way to Brooklyn. J. Raphael and Sons. Rayson Brands Spices. My father sells to Katz's," I said. "But he says they don't buy the best stuff. He says they buy what he sweeps up from the floor."

"You're the movie producer's ex-wife and the spice king's daughter," he said. "What a catch!"

"Do you ever think of going back?" I asked.

"Sometimes," he said. "Do you?"

"No," I said. "I don't."

"We'll visit together," he said. "I always go in the Spring. We'll go to Katz's. Then we can go to the Village. We'll score loose joints in Washington Square Park. I'll feel you up under the arch."

"Sure," I said, believing for a minute that maybe it would happen. "That would be great!"

"He's married?" Allie said. "Are you sure you want to do that? It might not be too smart." She giggled and ran her hand through her hair.

"They're separated during the week," I said.

"Don't count on it," she said.

"I can't help it," I said.

"Then enjoy it. But don't make any big plans."

We were in her flat, the one where she'd made Christmas dinner. It was a small one bedroom off the King's Road and up towards inexpensive Fulham in a basement with windows looking up towards the street. She'd fixed it up so it was very appealing. She poured me white wine. A bunch of spring's first daffodils stood in a vase. She'd gotten a job with an advertising company. She was still dangling Ben and Mike and they all seemed content. I wished I were like her. I'd pulled away from Mike when I began seeing Richard but we were still friends.

"You have a shiksa mentality," I told Allie, like in *Portnoy's Complaint*.

She giggled again and said I was right. "See other people," she said. "Keep busy! Like the Maharishi says . . . don't think."

"Do you think I'll send you back to your wife a better man?" I asked Richard. I was joking but he got a funny look on his face. We never talked about her. Sometimes he rolled his eyes and said she was going to feminist meetings, a group she'd connected with. I imagined them as all dark and hirsute with bushes under their arms and moustaches they never removed. It was unfair. I knew it. She was probably as fed up with Richard as I was with Bob, but I couldn't help enjoying my topsy-turvy role. Now I was the other woman, the desirable, glamorous other.

"Sometimes your funny lines aren't so funny, Phyllis," he said.

"I'm sorry," I said.

"There are things I'd like to say," he said. "But at a certain point you learn not to say them."

I was smoking a St. Moritz. We were lying in bed. We lay in bed for a long time talking after we made love. Sometimes it was two or three in the morning before he went home. He always went downstairs and took a tangerine for himself and an apple for me and brought it upstairs before he left. I'd hear the door close as he stepped into the street.

I crushed out the cigarette and put my hand on his chest. We looked long at each other and I kissed him and lay back down and he folded himself over me. "I'm so fucking confused," he said.

"I know," I said.

"Tell him you can't see him anymore," Georgia said. "Just say look luv, I can't do this anymore. You have to make him see what he's doing."

"He knows what he's doing," I said. "I can't say that!"

"Then you'll eat shit!" she said. She shifted on the sofa and stuck out her legs. She was pregnant and had grown very big.

She'd told me her theory; "You can have anyone you want. It just depends on how much shit you can take." Usually I believed everything she said, but this time I didn't think she was right.

There were some people who would never give you what you wanted, shit or not.

She said that when she learned Gerry Mulligan was cheating on her she waited for him to come home and hit him over the head with a frying pan. The image stayed with me, handsome Gerry Mulligan, crumpled in a doorway, his head in his saxophone case.

She'd been with Peter O'Toole too. Lawrence of Arabia. After Georgia, was it easy putting his hand to the flame?

She shifted again on the sofa. Her ankles were swollen. "Uh oh," she said.

She grabbed my hand and fastened it onto her belly. I could feel life, kicking, thumping wildly against my palm.

"Tell him to fuck off," she said. "Don't waste your time!"

I wished I were as fierce as she was. Nothing got in her way. She seemed always to get what she wanted.

Desiring Richard raised the stakes. Life speeded up. It was like traveling on top of a fast moving, shrill-whistling train that sped through the night. I felt like I was on an amphetamine high, the eskatrol diet pills Fran got on the National Health. After work, when I'd finished writing about psychics for Paul or composing letters for Hal, I began to write for myself; I wrote letters, descriptions, anecdotes, stories, things people said, ideas and opinions I'd come to. I'd start writing one thing and discover it connected to something else and then something further than that. I'd begin at a hotel in Rome where Bob and I had a fight and end up at a shadowy place I barely remembered, a Rollerdrome in Brooklyn that I'd gone to while I was in high school. I'd start typing after the kids went to bed and when I looked up it would be one in the morning and I'd have eight pages of legal size single spaced words and an ashtray of cigarette butts on the table beside me.

When I read what I'd written I was mostly embarrassed. How could words on a page sound so bad? But I kept going; I had a sense that the trick was not to stop.

Occasionally a line or a phrase stuck out, less ragged than others, a string of sentences I actually liked. One afternoon I sent an essay to a magazine, twelve hundred twenty-nine words about being an outsider in London, the rewards to be gleaned from a life out of place. *She* was a monthly glossy for women, the same size as the old *Life* or *Look*. Inside there were recipes, fashions, advice about "slimming." A month later they sent me a letter. I picked it up from the mat beneath the mail slot at the front door. A ray of sunlight hit the envelope as I slit it open. "We admire your essay," it said. They wanted to print it. I felt a ripple of pleasure and tried to remember what I had written. By that time the month-old essay had faded. I could barely remember what I had said. My writing had changed. I was on a new tack, listening to a new voice that had begun to enter my head. She was me but a part of me I didn't know although her accent resembled one of my cousins. He was younger than I was and as a child had a nose that was perpetually running. I'd spent Sunday afternoons tormenting him on my grandmother's porch. I'd seen a lot of his back as he ran through the door screaming, "She's hitting me. She's hitting me." But now his whiny sing-songy voice had transmuted into the mouth of a storyteller. Listening I had the feeling he could go on forever; his tales came from some deep well that would never run dry. It was like going to Delphi to meet the oracle and finding out he was manic—or lying under the stars in the Egyptian desert on the night the sphinx decided to give up her secrets.

When he was around, my runny-nosed cousin, life was clearer than I'd ever seen it. I felt as if boxes and cartons of junk had been swept out of my head and all that was left was raw lumber. Stripped of veils of excess the world was awful—but funny. Alone at the typewriter late at night I'd giggle out loud. In his stories people were larger than life ever was. They resembled people I knew but they came with new names or sometimes no names at all. More charming and selfish, stupid and brutal, smarter and sweeter than life ever permitted, they distilled normal, blurry existence to an elegant scaffold. When they'd completed their escapades final words would drop onto the page and lights would flash on and off like a pinball machine at which I'd just won; they'd click into place and I'd read what I'd written. It was always just as he told it to me— something I never knew I knew—but which I recognized as the truth.

RICHARD

HE BROUGHT ME BOOKS. THEY came across his desk at the BBC and he passed them on to me, always with inscriptions in blue ink and the date, number first, then month, then the year. *For P—who listens to rivers. With love, R. For P. With love and attrition, R.* (I'd asked him the meaning of the word attrition.) *For P—The spice king's daughter. With love, R.* His handwriting slanted upward. Optimistic, I thought. Although I wished it was less narrow, more generous. Some of the books were pop psychology. Max Luscher, a Swiss scientist; The Luscher Color Test, a book about the way colors can predict personality traits. I took the test over and over, wondering what I would find out about myself and about him. His car was bright red, the color of activists, masculine, aggressive and striving. And mine was British racing green; green was the sign of spring, youth, idealism, revolt, someone who would never grow up. Blue was for the earth, eternal, nurturing, sad. Blue was really my favorite color but I wanted no part of nurture or sadness. He brought me Pablo Neruda, *Twenty Love Poems and a Song of Despair*, and Desmond Morris, *The Human Zoo*; "In our cities we don't live in concrete jungles," Morris, a zoologist, proclaimed, "but human zoos"—and *Musrum*, by Anthony Earnshaw and Eric Thacker, authors with names so British they could have stepped right from Dickens. The book was a piece of British science fiction, an alternate universe with a mouse hero, gnomic and weird. The edition was expensive and had dozens of intricate line drawings and was printed on thick parchment like paper with a clear plastic cover to save it from harm. Richard pored over it, chuckling and pointing out humorous pages—but like much of English humor I never really got the joke. That night he sat down at my Olivetti and typed "an apple . . . for an apple . . . from a tangerine" on a strip of paper and taped it to the apple he brought me before he left. I took it off and tucked it inside the book and put it on top of the pile that was growing on the wooden trunk beside my bed.

"See other men," Caroline said. "As many as you can." We were on the telephone, static crinkling across the Atlantic. "And don't be at home when he calls! Tell the slave (Emilia) to say you're out, she doesn't know where. Be busy at least fifty percent of the time!"

"I can't do that," I said.

"Sure you can." She sounded encouraging. "Torture him. Men are happier when they suffer. Masochists way outnumber sadists. A cruel woman is hard to find!"

Then she told me about all her boyfriends. The ones she liked best were Irish. One owned a bar, Bradley's, on University Place. She called him "Craggy Tower," because he looked like one. Another was an "Irish Mafioso" in the concrete business. He took her to Twenty One and Toots Shors and called her "Gypsy" because of her wandering ways. "If you want to turn an Irishman on, make him wear a condom," she advised. "It reminds them of their Catholic girlfriends in high school. They think they're sixteen again."

"Thanks for the tip," I said. "I'll keep it in mind."

Sometimes on weekends Richard invited me to bring my kids along with a loosely knit crowd that went on excursions. He brought his daughters. His wife never came. One afternoon the group took a boat up the Thames to Kew Gardens. On another Sunday we all drove out of London and into the country. I melted in with these people, identifying myself vaguely as "a friend." I didn't like pretending we were friends. Being in a large group with him made me uneasy. I wasn't sure how to behave.

I had a camera and on the afternoon of the boat ride someone snapped Richard and me together on the embankment alongside the Thames. He was looking down at me, his arm around me, our eyes riveted on each other. It was an unseasonably warm spring day and the buttons on his tan safari shirt were open and my head was in the crook of his arm at the level of his bare chest. The space between our faces was narrower than good sense should allow. Could anyone not tell that we were lovers?

On another afternoon Richard took a picture of me with Julie and one of his daughters lined up in front of me on the terrace of a country house, my hands on their shoulders, his little girl rubbing her eye with her fist. Afterwards I cleaned a speck out of her eye with a Kleenex, my fingers grazing her cheek. A feeling of tenderness welled inside me touching his child.

The house we were visiting had a pasture and a small, closed corral with a horse. I turned my back for a minute and when I looked back Julie had climbed up on the horse, she was astride, bareback, her hands clutching the withers. She looked happy, bent over the horse's neck as he sauntered around the corral. She was wearing a suede cowboy jacket Bob had bought her with fringes and her hair had grown long and streamed over her shoulders. No one was near by. Everyone had gone inside the house through a pair of French doors.

The horse was a tired-looking brown animal with a look of sad resignation in his eyes. But a river of fear streamed from my chest down to my legs. My throat tightened up. Julie had been eyeing that horse all afternoon. I should have known this would happen. I wondered if I should scream, but for whom? From time to time I went riding with her in Hyde Park, the two of us with a sturdy, horsy blonde woman, one of the instructors with chunky legs and a thick blonde braid down her back. But I was no good in the saddle. I liked striding through Knightsbridge in the helmet and black velvet jeans, but the horse itself intimidated me. Why did the instructors at the stable always put me on a large horse with a frisky personality, an animal that didn't respond when I tightened the reins? I always felt out of control. Like now, I thought.

At the fence I climbed up on the rail and held out my arms. "Come on," I pleaded. "Come back!" What would I do if it didn't? Julie edged the horse up against me so its flanks rubbed my knees. It smelled like an old rubber tire and looked weary. She slid down into my arms and I pressed her against me.

"Don't do that again," I breathed. "Never do that again!"

"It's OK," she said. "Don't be scared!" She patted the horse. He stood docilely alongside the fence.

"Don't do that again," I repeated. Her face had that opaque look kids get when their thoughts are secret. She looked innocent, rebuked, with just a tinge of shame, her big eyes staring back at me. She was five years old and competent, unafraid of horses. What was I doing? What do all human beings want, my psychiatrist asked. "Autonomy" was the answer. That was the word of the year, perhaps of the decade. I thought of Richard—with me but not—beyond my control. I talked as if I was running the show. But I wasn't.

ONLY WHEN YOU BREATHE

"FOR A MINUTE I THOUGHT we were in trouble," Sundance
says just before he and Butch run out into the rain of bullets that
end their lives. I saw the movie three times; once at a screening,
again when it opened in Leicester Square, again when I took the
kids. That's what I wanted! A relationship like the one Butch had
with Sundance. No whining or pleading, love that lived an outlaw
life. Passion unremarked upon and unspoken, scored with under-
statement. "Australia," Butch says, bleeding, half dead. "Easy,
ripe, and luscious." "The women or the banks?" Sundance asks.
"Both," Butch says. A hail of gunfire. Freeze frame.

"A true relationship is centered on itself," my psychiatrist said. I agreed with him. Love either was—or it wasn't. No bonds or ties could dictate that emotion. "I have a fantasy of driving with you on an open road," Richard said. "When I get my car that's the first thing we'll do. " I liked being the woman for open roads and excitement. I wanted to be the outsider, the adventurer, the thrilling affair that morphs into love, not the woman of habit.

It was a Saturday night. His wife was in Wales at a feminist conference. He hired a babysitter and came and picked me up and we drove to Brighton. February. The road was cold and dark and empty. We were the only ones on it. Inside, the shiny, new red car smelled of fresh leather and the wood on the dashboard was gleaming and silky. Behind the wheel, the collar turned up on his dark coat, his curly hair floating, Richard looked romantic and happy. We were together, all alone, on a road that stretched like a long ribbon into the darkness, the car bouncing over each bump the way low, springless cars do. I felt as if we could go on this way forever. Richard's hand nursed the stick shift. For long stretches when the car was in fourth his palm cupped my knee.

At Brighton we passed the illuminated wedding cake pavillion that Victoria, an adoring Queen, had built for Prince Albert. Who needed such gestures? Why should love be embalmed in cement?

The boardwalk was deserted and stark, everything shuttered. A cold moon shone above. Richard pulled me to him. His hands found their way under my coat, tracing my body. Ripples of excitement traveled from my waist down through my knees. The wind whipped my face. "I think about you all the time," Richard said. "I'm completely fucked up." I leaned toward him and kissed him but didn't answer. Why should I? What more could I ask for?

That week Richard told me that our midweek nights were over. Saturday he was going back to his wife. "I have to do it," he said. "I have to give it a try."

On Friday night he brought paté and wine and cheese. We smoked a joint and went to bed.

"I packed my things and then I unpacked them," he said. "I'm so fucked up."

I acted casual. I didn't want to behave like a wife. "I hope you'll be OK," I said. "I hope it works out."

"Am I going back to my wife a better man?" he asked.

"I'm a better woman," I said.

On the night he went back to his wife he called me from St. Johns Wood. "I miss you already," he said. "She said I'm an oppressor. Do you think I'm an oppressor?" he asked.

I imagined his wife in the kitchen, feeding the kids, long dark hair hanging down her back.

"Only when you breathe," I said.

"Will you see me sometime?" he asked. "I promise not to die at your place."

(We had a joke. "Don't die at my place." Like John Garfield in bed with a showgirl. "I don't want to have to make that call to your wife.")

Butch and Sundance, I thought. The Sheriff with the posse was right behind them. But they jumped off a cliff and into a river in one more daring escape. "I'll be in New York the same time you are," I said. "I have to see my lawyer." I gave him my phone number. "Call me," I said.

AGENT

IN NEW YORK I WAITED for Richard to call. I walked all over town, up and down, east and west, Katz's Deli and Washington Square Park. I'd followed him there—not literally—I'd said I had to see my lawyer. And that was true. But I might have delayed if Richard wasn't going to be there.

Towards the end of my stay I went to a party for a feminist writer. Caroline was invited and took me along. I was staying in her loft down in the Village on Washington Street, around the corner from the HB Studio on Bank Street where I'd taken classes with Uta and Walt and Neil and Bill and a few blocks away from Gansevoort Street in the meatpacking district where I'd sent bills

239

of lading when I typed for my father. This was an uptown party, a duplex on Park Avenue with a staircase like the one that Cary Grant carried Ingrid Bergman down in *Notorious*. Its silken walls were hung with Picassos and Cezannes, a Van Gogh and a Braque—a display that made Lady Goldsmid's St. Leonard's Terrace collection—and all of England—look like the third world.

There were writers everywhere; I spotted Jimmy Breslin and Tom Wolfe whom I'd met when I was married to Bob and there were smart-looking people talking and drinking and laughing in impenetrable clusters that sailed through long endless rooms. Richard would have loved this party, I thought; would have wanted to be here, gently cracking those little eggshells of insiders with a peck of his beak. If we were together I would have taken him. But alone—I wished I were back in London on my own quiet street or up in Islington at Jay and Fran's playing "Who would you like to meet in heaven and what would be your opening line when you did?"

The man opposite me at the end of the long velvet sofa wore shoes made in Great Britain. He bought them at Church's, in Regent Street. Whenever he got to London he picked up two or three pairs. They were expensive, but cost much less in England. He had trouble with his feet and these were the most comfortable shoes he'd ever worn. We'd begun to talk because we were the only two people on the sofa, both of us alone. I assumed he must have come with someone with a reason to be there and he was, like me, waiting it out till he could go home.

I said I understood about his feet. I'd damaged my feet wearing high heels and pointed toes while I was in high school. I knew just how he felt. "There's nothing worse than bad feet," he said.

He lifted a foot and I admired the shoe. It was beautiful, a classic; graceful but reliable, gleaming leather the color of chestnuts and thin, elegant ties. He extended the shoe from the leg of an immaculately creased gray flannel trouser above which was a blue blazer and the perfect red tie. He wore heavy black-framed glasses and had the kind of well groomed look that announced success.

I'd told him I lived in London and was getting a divorce and that's when he told me about the Church shoes. "Who is your poor soon-to-be ex-husband?" he finally asked when we'd said all we could about the shoes. When I said Bob's name he began to laugh. "I've done business with Bob. I'm a book agent," he said. Just then Caroline came by and put a hand on my shoulder . . . she was ready to leave. I asked the book agent to tell me his name. He'd told me once but I'd forgotten. "Sterling Lord," he said.

I clasped his hand, walked off, and came back. I didn't know whether to call him by his first name or his last. Both were intimidating.

"I've written some stories, Sterling," I said. I felt as if I were diving into cold water. "Would you take a look?"

His office was uptown on Madison Avenue and the next day I took an envelope up there and left it with a receptionist. I had brought stories with me from London along with my Olivetti which I typed on every morning on a wooden table at the back of Caroline's loft where she piled film and lenses and contact sheets. I didn't expect to hear from him. I thought eventually he'd just send the stories back. Or forget about them. But the next day he telephoned.

"Phyllis," he said. "I like these, but I can't sell short stories. Can you write a novel?" Something felt strange in my throat. A lump. I might be going to die, I thought. I hoped it wouldn't be soon.

"A novel?" I said.

"Yeah," he said. "A novel. A story. But make it longer than these."

"Oh. A novel!" I said. "Sure. I can do that."

AIRPLANE

RICHARD AND I WERE ON the same flight back to London. I caught sight of his wild curly head bobbing out of the crowd ahead of me just as I was about to board, a canvas backpack squared over the shoulders of his dark blue coat. I was carrying my Olivetti, pages I'd begun to write already tucked inside the case. A dry feeling took over my mouth and my head felt fluffy and light. My nose stuffed up. He turned around, spotted me and waved, and I waved back. When the plane was in the air we met in the aisle. "How are you?" he asked. And I asked the same thing, trying to make sure that the conversation remained as impersonal as I could keep it. I wanted it to seem that we'd never known each other, never made love, never held each other or touched. I wanted the fact of our driving to Brighton, owning the same cars, kissing alongside the embankment, laughing and joking had never existed, and that there had been no apples or tangerines, no books piled at my bed. Above all I didn't want to know what he'd done in New York, whether he'd been to Katz's Delicatessen or Washington Square Park or up at the Morris office turning himself into a Hollywood agent.

After a while I said I was going back to my seat. "I miss you. Can I see you sometime?" he asked. His voice seemed to come from nowhere, as if it had materialized out of vapor. A longing came over me to touch him, a longing so fierce that I could almost feel myself moving towards him, pressing my face against his chest. But just then the plane hit an air pocket and I felt as if we were dropping down into a deep, empty space, plastic glasses sliding on tray tables and tinkling bottles on the stewardesses carts jingling like bells in the aisles. It felt as if we were in free fall, the plane just kept going as if we might never stop. My stomach exploded up into my mouth and both of us swayed towards each other clutching the seats to keep ourselves steady.

"No," I said. "You can't see me. You can't see me ever again. It's over."

He looked at me almost as if he might laugh, which is what I began to do. The lights in the cabin were flickering, the seat belt signs flashing on and off.

But as soon as I'd spoken the plane righted itself, as if I'd sent it a signal. I smiled and kept moving back to my seat. Back in London he sent me a letter about what a wonderful person I was. I've never known anyone like you, he said. I tore it up and threw it away but I regretted it afterwards and wished I had saved it. It would be nice to say that material like that didn't come along every day but I was certain that just the opposite was true. There could be many letters like that, a long career of them if I wasn't careful. I should have kept it as evidence.

OLYMPIA

IF THE OLIVETTI WAS SLEEK and sexy, the choice of a journalist traveling light, the Olympia was a placid matron, the Mrs. Miniver of typewriters. Bob had a couple of them in the film office and gave one to me when he closed the office down. The Olympia was more stable, larger than the Olivetti, and the sound of the keys was throatier than the Olivetti's clinkety clank. The Olympia was made in England and had a pound key rather than a dollar sign which made me feel worldly and connected to English literature.

When the carriage stopped moving one morning—mid-sentence—the handle just would not go—I packed the Olympia up in its case and carried it to the typewriter repair shop just outside the South Kensington tube stop. I'd been there before to buy ribbons and take the Olivetti for a cleaning. It was a small shop, always busy, and there were people ahead of me. I had to wait my turn. It was a warm day and I began to sweat. I'd been annoyed when the typewriter broke down but now I was jittery.

The clerk was tall and thin with white skin that looked acne prone—it could erupt at any minute—and streaked blonde hair which he wore plastered back. He unloosened the platen knob and took out the platen and a handful of small screws. "Have a good bit of fluff in here, don't you?" he said, showing me little bits of pink eraser that floated inside. The handful of screws blurred on a little rubber pad on the counter and he wanted to tell me about something that was bent. I didn't want to hear but knew I had to listen . . . or pretend to. He said it might take a few days to repair, depending on whether he had to "ring Bristol." "How long?" I breathed. "I have a deadline," I said. He shrugged. "I have a deadline," I pleaded.

I'd told Sterling Lord I could write a novel, but in fact I had no idea how such a thing was done. The main difference between a novel and a short story as far as I could see was that a novel was longer. I'd have to keep going until I got enough pages. I checked contemporary novels in bookstores for length, wondering how writers found so much to say. Pages and pages of words, sometimes without even paragraph breaks. Where did it all come from? I'd been lucky so far—words kept pouring out. After the kids left for school I'd sit down. You can't say that. That's ridiculous, I'd think. Then . . . oh, what the hell. Go ahead. Every day was like throwing myself off a cliff.

It took two days before I got the typewriter back. While I waited for the Olympia I tried writing on the Olivetti and with a pen on legal pads, but the voice in my head went on strike. It had grown accustomed to the buxom, decorous Olympia and wasn't interested in alternatives.

On the night I got the Olympia back Jay and Fran invited me to dinner with a writer. Seymour Krim was living in London, in Kennington ("Poverty City" he called it, but said George Orwell had lived there—"When they give the world an enema that's where they'll put in the plug," Jay said). Seymour was a barrel-chested man who wore a Greek fisherman's cap and a vest and suspenders and steel-rimmed glasses. He'd written for *The Village Voice* and a collection of his essays, *Views of Nearsighted Canoneeer*, had been published in London. One of the essays, "The Insanity Bit," was about how he'd been hauled into Bellevue and given shock treatments for running around New York wearing only a towel. "Seymour is a friend to young writers," Fran said, over macrobiotic broccoli and brown rice to which she had added some codfish ("The purist days, just rice and vegetables, are over," Jay lamented. "Adding fish is 'yin'." "Like everything else," Fran said, "the *I Ching* is slanted towards men. How come everything good is 'yang' and masculine and everything evil and dark is 'yin' and feminine?" "Because women are inferior," Jay cackled).

"Writing is a struggle," Seymour said.

He said that when the poet Theodore Roethke taught at Princeton he'd periodically go crazy and rip off all his clothes and run naked and screaming across the campus in the snow. Students, faculty, locals, were accustomed to his breaks. "There goes Ted again," they'd say. The police would come and collect him as he streaked, wrap him in blankets, and cart him off to the mental ward till he calmed down.

Seymour had a gravelly voice, like a driveway under truck tires; "Writing is bloodstained," he warned. "Keep in mind," he said, "people have died for words."

I listened and nodded, feeling a wash of emotion. This had happened to others. I wasn't the only one.

It took two days until the whiny voice inside my head began to speak again. I knew it was a warning that I'd better cater to it, not anger it or get in its way. In spite of all my hours discussing "autonomy" up in North London with my psychiatrist, for now at least, I didn't own the voice—it owned me.

I went to Foyles in Charing Cross Road and picked up some of Theodore Roethke's poetry but it didn't impress me; I liked the beat poets better. Alan Ginsberg and Gregory Corso. Seymour Krim had edited a book called *The Beats* and said he preferred them too.

> *Should I get married?,* [Corso asked.] *Should I be good?*
> *Astound the girl next door with my velvet suit and faustus*
> *hood. . . .*
> *Because what if I'm 60 years old and not married, all alone in*
> *a furnished room with pee stains on my underwear and*
> *everybody else is married, all married but me?*

It was a good thing that Sterling Lord hadn't asked me to write poems, I thought. I would have said yes, but I really didn't "get" poetry and I would have been in worse trouble than I was now when all I had to do was write something long.

ENDING

I'D BEEN TOLD THAT DIVORCE is final, like the first shovel of dirt as it falls on the coffin. But I felt nothing conclusive the weekend that Bob flew to Mexico to formally end our marriage. It was June. Pale roses were blooming in the garden out back, sheer white curtains blowing at the French doors. The kids were out with Emilia in Thurloe Square. If I walked down the street I'd hear their shouts from behind the iron fence and the curtain of green. Mexico, streets blistering with heat, a dusty courtroom and a judge who barely understood English with a bottle of tequila under his desk and a big rubber stamp seemed far away and unreal. I knew that before the day ended the phone would ring and Bob would say our marriage was over—but I didn't believe it. I'd known Bob almost half of my life. What would divorce change that hadn't changed already? "The only sin worse than divorce is the prior sin of marriage," my psychiatrist said. I believed him. A piece of paper in Spanish? What could it mean?

A comedy writer from New York, a friend of Caroline's recently arrived in London to work on a film, sat on the sofa delivering one-liners while I waited for the call from Juarez. He'd gotten two Mexican divorces. "I keep a locker down there," he said.

He'd brought a bag of pistachio nuts and a bottle of bourbon in duty free and I was eating the nuts and he was drinking the bourbon. One-line jokes escaped from his mouth like prisoners from cells.

When the phone finally rang I picked it up but no one was there. I stood holding the receiver like a diploma on which nothing is written. It happened three times.

"Maybe they said no," said the comedy writer.

"Fucking phones," Bob said on the fourth call. "It's over. It's a big nothing. A lot of paper."

I waited. "Well, congratulations," I said. It didn't sound right but I had no idea what would.

"It's depressing," he said.

I put down the receiver and tried to decide what to do next. I wasn't sure if I should sit or remain standing.

"Never let the magic go out of your divorce," said the comedy writer. "Want to go out? Paint the town black?"

That night I took the kids and the comedy writer to Mr. Chow in Knightsbridge. I loved the restaurant, the glitzy entrance with its black marble and gleaming brass and curved windows jutting out onto the street. They had a dish called "seaweed," strips of something that looked like grass, fried so it was hot and crispy with just a whisper of sweetness. We ate the seaweed with dumplings and then I somehow managed to pile everyone into the car and we drove along the embankment with the top down to Big Ben and the houses of Parliament glowing pink in the dark. The kids were crammed and laughing in the back, the comedy writer hunched alongside me in the front looking anxious, his wide blue eyes open like stop signs.

At one in the morning the phone rang, splitting into my sleep. It was the comedy writer.

"What are you doing?" he asked.

"Sleeping," I said.

"I couldn't sleep."

"So you woke me up?"

"Are you alone?"

"Am I alone?"

"I don't know. I don't know what you do," he mumbled.

"I'm alone," I said.

"Want company?"

I waited.

"It's late." I said. "Some other time."

It was the longest conversation we'd had all day.

I couldn't sleep after I got off the phone so I went down to the living room and cleaned up the nut shells. He'd left me the bag but taken the bourbon with him. I thought about that; a tall silvery-haired man in a blue blazer crossing Hyde Park swinging a bottle of bourbon. He'd had two wives and lived with a third woman. Last week he'd gone to Paris with a girl named Sue who worked in publicity. And those were just the ones I knew about. I got back into bed, lit a cigarette, and leaned back on the pillows. When I was married if the phone rang late in the middle of the night it was because someone had died.

I looked at the clock. I'd been divorced for twelve hours. So far I couldn't say much for it.

HOLIDAY

AFTER THE DIVORCE I TOOK the kids to Majorca. There were cheap deals in Spain. The dollar against the pound made London life sweet—against the peseta it was luxurious. I'd never taken them on a vacation alone and it was something I wanted to do. I didn't want them to think that all holidays and treats came from Bob and everyday life was all I could offer. In London I did things separately with each of them: a bike ride with Billy in Hyde Park; tea with Julie; shopping with Jenifer at the "Way In" shop at Harrod's.

In the airport in Palma I rented a car and drove to a high-rise hotel scalloped with balconies like cake frosting and a lake-sized swimming pool with a long slide. All the guests were Australians. Billy loved it. He never left that pool. He played all day with a gang of kids and at the end of the day he had two invitations to visit Sidney. While I was spreading Noxema on his sunburned shoulders that night I told him that the next day we were leaving to drive into the country and his eyes filled up; "I've dreamed of a place like this my whole life," he said. "You always ruin things," he said.

The car was a white convertible and Julie and Billy sat in the back and Jenifer alongside me as we drove into the mountains and to the little village of Deya, a dropout paradise; it was filled with ex-New Yorkers, Madison Avenue account executives on the lam from their accounts and people who one day had just walked away from their desks at *Time Magazine*. There was a secluded cove of a beach cut into cliffs. You could reach it by climbing down a long flight of curving steps from the mountains. The water was green and clear and the kids snorkeled for hours. We all put on masks. "Come see this," the kids shouted, pulling me or each other to their spot in the sea. Even Jenifer, who normally held back, floated face down, her hair spread out in the water around the snorkeling tube. Looking up at the end of the day I saw the poet Robert Graves climbing the rocky cliff above the beach, a tall, thin, ancient, lone figure in a loose shirt and big hat.

The hotel in Deya was white stucco punctuated with arches and hung with colorful Spanish blankets and pottery. It was set in hills of olive trees and there were pots bursting with pink and fuschia blooms and cool tiled floors. The guests were all European couples in middle age, many of them German. At lunch in the dining room the kids, neatly dressed, hair still wet from the pool, filed carefully in front of me to our table. Julie and Jenifer were barefoot in identical white Mexican dresses embroidered with flowers I'd brought from L.A. In this place they were like birds of Paradise, exquisite oddities. Their legs were tan and their toes like flower petals.

Among the couples at the table closest to us was a man with a steely crew cut and an array of gold teeth. A German submarine captain I thought. The gutteral sounds of their language slid into our hot lunchtime tomatoes and noodles. He was always looking at me. When I stared back he'd avert his gaze. I'd feel his stare from behind a newspaper at the pool on a chaise alongside his neat-looking wife and from behind the blue shuttered window as we climbed in the hills around the hotel. One evening I saw his back disappearing around a corner as the kids sang their way down the corridor to our room after dinner.

They came back to Heathrow tanned and wearing straw hats. We'd shared a room in Majorca and that first night back in London they didn't want to part; they all got into my bed. Emilia came too. They told her everything. She clucked her tongue and said "Ts Ts Ts Ts Ts " as she combed Jenifer's hair. An accountant from *Time Magazine* with a boy and girl their age that we'd met on the beach at Deya was coming through London the following week and the kids were invited to tea. They discussed gifts to bring for the other kids and decided on tee shirts with Queen Elizabeth's portrait. I hoped their new friends were hip enough to get the campy joke. Falling asleep I had a nightmare about the German with gold teeth. I hit him over the head with a shovel in an olive grove and again on a New York street that resembled a nighttime painting by Hopper, but he kept coming back to life. Finally I pressed a lever and sent his submarine down to the bottom of the sea.

It was past midnight when I took them all back to their beds. Julie needed to be carried. Her arms around my neck were tight as a vise and when I put her down she clung to me, her mouth moving close to my ear. I couldn't figure out what she was saying but felt the whisper of her breath against my neck and lay down next to her till she let me go. Across the street our neighbors were saying goodbye to guests. I could hear their voices. A car door slammed and the motor started up. I live here, I thought. I have a life.

THE GREAT AMERICAN DISASTER

I STILL WANTED TO BE ruined by love, but Jay said red meat would do the job faster. When The Great American Disaster opened on a corner of the Fulham Road queues stretched half-way around the block. Hamburgers. Cheeseburgers. Ketchup. Malts and fries. Jay sucked in his breath; "It's the gateway to hell," he said.

Fran insisted on going. She wanted us to go together, she with her sons Miles and Cosmo, me with the kids. I'd never seen her want anything so much. A revival of *Lawrence of Arabia* was play-ing in the King's Road and the plan was we'd eat the burgers and go to the film. I'd already seen *Lawrence* in L.A. and eaten my share of American burgers, but if this was what was happening in London I wanted to be part of it.

Out of the house, without Jay, Fran was wary, stooped over, clutching her handbag and holding onto her kids. She spent all her time up in her bedroom writing poems. Traveling to Chelsea was a major event. She planned the trip as if she was going to another continent and told me her route on the underground at least twelve times. She hadn't eaten meat since the macrobiotic diet entered her life. She lifted the bun off the hamburger and looked at it as if it were the face of God.

After the meal the kids skipped in front of us, but I held onto Fran's arm as we walked to the King's Road Cinema, guiding her as we crossed each street. Every step seemed fraught with danger. Her eyes shifted from the traffic to the street to the passersby. I didn't want to ask her if she was OK, but finally, the words just slipped out. "For that hamburger and Peter O'Toole, there isn't much I wouldn't do," she said.

We got into the movie theater, the kids lined up in the row in front of us, Jenifer between Cosmo and Miles. They were good-looking boys. Miles, the younger one, already had a cockney accent. Cosmo was poetic, more like Fran. There was about him a sense of the aesthete. Jenifer turned to look at me, grinning.

We bought Licorice Allsorts and buried ourselves in the seats. I could hear Fran breathing softly as the film began. Her anxiety had vanished and she looked like a flower settling into the perfect vase. The horseman, at first a tiny speck in the distance, galloped across the sands, slowly growing larger inside a shimmering cyclone of sand and heat until Omar Sharif, the desert prince, finally emerged into sight. "The greatest entrance in show business," Fran murmured.

THAT SUMMER THE KIDS WENT to visit Bob. He'd bought a house on the beach in Malibu. He said it was a nothing house, a shack. He said he had no money. He had given it all to me to pay for our divorce.

"A shack in Malibu?" I said. "It's a crummy house," he said. "It's not in the colony."

"There are no shacks on the beach in Malibu," I said. "That's what you think," he said. The kids went off in a limousine to the airport. I went with them. The TWA stewardess who escorted them to the first class cabin was as blonde as the sun with a smile to match. Everything about her glowed. When she bent to greet them her skirt rippling across her thighs was so beautiful it nearly made me weep. Her legs were perfect too, the blue leather pumps fit so smoothly on her feet it wasn't clear that she had toes. Alexander Portnoy would worship her, I thought. She wasn't Jewish. She had sex all the time, none of it complicated. She didn't waste her time reading or thinking and she never cleaned. She didn't have to. Everything she owned or touched fell into place.

"I'm a big sister," she told them. "I have two younger brothers." She held out coloring books and crayons. Jenifer said, "No, thank you." Her English accent resonated with British reserve. The tones were high and sweet. She would be ten in September and carried her guitar. She had always been tall and was entering that age when girls are awkward, but she was beautiful. She knew more than she should, but looked innocent. When she wasn't wearing her maroon Redcliffe School blazer and gray pleated skirt she wore bell-bottom trousers and Indian tops but today she was wearing a sleeveless white and blue sundress. Her reddish hair hung below her shoulders and she had inherited all of Bob's freckles.

Billy said he wanted to meet the Captain.

"I might be able to arrange that," the stewardess said. She smiled brightly. All the kids sounded British. Like chameleons, they'd become Londoners. Expatriate American accents were called "Trans Atlantic," but the kids sounded British to me. I still sounded the same although English words and phrases leaked out of me; I'd know beforehand when the choice was coming; Should I say "elevator" or "lift"? "Thanks" or "Ta"? I'd have to decide quickly. I wondered if the day would ever come when I'd say "Lay the table" without thinking twice, or feel comfortable describing someone as "smashing."

PHYLLIS RAPHAEL

Jenifer said she didn't want to leave me and looked mournful.
But I knew that when she got to California she'd have a good time.
Bob would take her everywhere with him. She'd compete with his
girlfriend and win. Julie and Billy carried teddy bears with legs
that were falling off at the thighs. "What do you need those teddy
bears for?" I asked. "We just do," Billy said. "You don't even sleep
with them anymore," I said. I jabbed at the stuffing, trying to push
it back in. Emilia had washed Julie's blanket and packed it for her
but it was in shreds. I thought it was getting time for her to give it
up but she shook her head every time I brought up the subject.
When we lived in New York my mother bought her a new one
every time one wore out. She liked a particular kind of nylon ruffle
around the edge. My mother took her shopping and let her rub
the ruffles against her face until she found the right one. The
stewardess waited. The bears and children looked back at me
mutely. Julie and Billy had chosen their oldest clothing for the
trip. Bob would seize upon the wounded bears and the worn
clothes and ask me why I'd sent them off in such shabby condition. He'd hold me responsible, not them. I thought there was a
conspiracy on all their parts to make me look bad. And it didn't
take much to accomplish that goal. Guilt was endemic to parent-
hood . . . that I already knew. But divorce brought guilt to an en-
tirely new level, like a migraine that infiltrated the bones. My
psychiatrist told me I hadn't ruined their lives, that growing up
with my old discontented self would have been worse for them
than their parents living apart. I nodded in agreement just to keep
him happy, but in fact there was no way to get me to believe what
he said. I was not only divorcing their dad, but severing them from
their home, friends, and kin. I had done the worst thing a parent
could do. I had dropped us all into a country where we lived

262

without an anchor, all of us bobbing around like corks. I knew Bob felt guilty too although he claimed otherwise. "Who, me? Guilty?" he'd said to me once. "I don't feel guilty. Should I feel guilty?"

Why then did he call them every night from whatever spot on the globe he happened to be? They'd come back from these visits with extra suitcases filled with the latest toys, gadgets, movie posters, clothing, records, and souvenir menus of meals in posh restaurants. Whatever they asked him for they usually got. Until I put my foot down he'd even told Julie he would buy her a horse.

Watching them trail onto the plane, Julie's thumb wandering into her mouth, I felt like my heart was being ripped from my chest.

And they knew it. They played us both like violins. Today was my turn. I felt like shouting as I watched them being led away, "Hey! I didn't leave your dad. Let's get this straight. I may have wanted a life, work, love, all those things! But I am not the one who left. Don't try to pin this on me."

TURKEY

ON THE SUBJECT OF FEMALE orgasm Sigmund Freud and I were of the same mind; "Frankly," Freud is reputed to have said about women (late in life after he caused all the trouble), "I give up!" Simone de Beauvoir disagreed with Freud but I couldn't figure out how. I read *The Second Sex* a dozen times and still didn't understand what she was saying. The researchers Masters and Johnson claimed they could help—but you had to fly to St. Louis and check into a motel. Doris Lessing, in whom I put my ultimate faith, said an orgasm was only possible with a man you loved. This was the worst information of all.

August came; the kids were away. And Hal had a perk; free tick-ets on TWA. He gave them to his wife Lucille and she invited me along with her and her teenage daughter. She could go anywhere in Europe TWA flew . . . and she chose Turkey. "All my life," she said, "I've wanted to see Istanbul."

The city was hot. We stayed at the Hilton in a room with two double beds and an extra bed added. In the streets small Turkish men watched us from doorways. They tried to brush against our bare arms and whispered, "I love you." We went to the Santa Sophia, the Blue Mosque, and the Topkapi Palace. The sun shot down like a flame from above. Lucille lectured about the foun-tains and pools, the tiles and the domes, Constantinople and the Ottoman Empire, the harems of Suleiman the Great. Her daugh-ter said, "OK Mom, enough!"

On the third afternoon I lost them in the crowded street mar-ket among the rugs, brass trays, and vases, the shawls, scarves, and coats. At the rug stalls the merchants offered sweet, thick black coffee in small cups. They unfurled the rugs so the sheen rippled like flying carpets of the Arabian nights. On impulse I bought a black leather coat, its neck rimmed with a round, shiny black fox collar and cuffs, a coat for a woman dressed by Fellini. The leather skimmed my body and the fur felt soft on my neck. The salesman promised I'd never regret it. He said, "This is a magnificent bargain! I give very cheap price. You will wear it till you die, even in heaven . . ." but I doubted I'd wear it at all.

In the hotel elevator—with the coat in a shopping bag—my eyes locked with those of a man in an oxford blue shirt; he had curly brown hair and a sunburn. His nose was peeling and shiny. There was something familiar about him; I could have known him somewhere, in some other time, or some other place. The door slid open and I got out. I'd enjoyed the look . . . but the look was enough.

A day later we went to Tarabaya, a little port on the Bosporous. From there we would set out in a bus to explore Turkish antiquity, the crumbling remains of the past. But we could only travel one coast—the Mediterranean or the Aegean. Which one?, Lucille debated. The question was endless. "Mom," said her daughter, "A ruin is a ruin!"

The hotel had a smooth wooden deck from which you could swim out to a raft. The Bosporous was cold, dark, and mysterious. If I kept going I'd come to the Black Sea and the Soviet Union, to beaches where fleshy white-skinned Russian leaders had dachas. At a café in the port I ordered a wine and opened my copy of *The Godfather* with its flashy black and white jacket. It was too heavy a book to take on a trip, but I'd started reading it in London and couldn't leave it behind. When I looked up, the sunburned man from the elevator was opposite me, at a table with another man. There was a blur of a blue shirt and khaki pants as he came towards me; the Fire Island ferry, I thought . . . the first hot weekend in June. I lay the book over my bare knees. "You like that?" he asked.

His name was Arthur, Artie, for short. In college I'd known four, in high school at least six. He was an M.D., a researcher attending a medical convention. He'd gotten the sunburn not on Fire Island but when he'd stopped off in Athens to see the Parthenon. In New York we'd lived less than five miles apart. I might have brushed shoulders with him in a crowded theater lobby or stood beside him at a counter in Saks while he bought a Christmas gift for his wife.

At some point in the late afternoon I showed him my new coat, slipping it on over my bare skin. By then I'd peeled the flaking white skin off his nose; like parchment, it came off in one strip. He'd drawn the curtains of the hotel room and behind them the setting Turkish sun glowed like a round hot ball, sending zigzags of color under my eyelids. Everything was happening very slowly but after a while, I understood that my sex life was about to change; the information came at me from a distance, like a lazy messenger ambling along without undue haste, an employee who deserved to be fired.

This is easy, I thought, as our bodies lay pressed together on the crisp white sheets of the hotel bed. What took me so long? I'd done nothing special to bring this transformation about and the fact that it would almost certainly occur surprised me. Like everything that you discover you already know, how simple it is is the most astonishing part. I had to get used to the idea, to wrap my head around what my body was telling me. I was underneath him . . . although I'd been on top . . . and I shifted just slightly to improve my position. I remembered I'd once asked Bob to describe an orgasm and he'd said it was "like each individual brain cell was being washed in running water," but what was happening to me involved more than my brain; all of my body—even my fingernails—was flying rhythmically down a long road, riding electrical waves that began in my groin but were getting progressively higher and were speeding me towards the edge of a cliff. Nothing to do. Just hang on. Let go. And fall.

When I told Artie that this was a first for me ("In case you were wondering, I didn't fake that." "It never occurred to me that you did. Do women really?"), he believed me; his eyes widened and then misted over. I'd just lit a cigarette and he took it from my hand, killed it in the ashtray, and kissed me. It occurred to me that he held himself personally responsible for my triumph and I didn't correct him; he was an excellent lover, passionate but controlled, langorous and slow moving. I liked his body and his smile and his sunburn; the color slashing his cheekbones and the streak on the back of his neck brought back Fire Island and the sexy promise of sun and sand and coppery skin on the top deck of the ferry.

But I didn't think he was the reason for my transformation. What had happened to me was inevitable; if not him, it would have been someone else; like apes at a typewriter, given enough time I'd heard eventually one of them would write *Hamlet*. We were in a room he was sharing with a colleague, the one he'd been drinking with at the café, and he said he wanted to take another room for the night, so we could spend it together. He was eager to get downstairs to the front desk and make certain he could find us a room. He traced my body with his fingers and kissed my hair and my neck before we showered and dressed.

On the way to the lobby he put his arm around me and pulled me close to him. He returned from the desk clerk grinning and waving a key. He whirled me around in the lobby. He took me to a cocktail party and hovered over me. The wives of the other doctors were elaborately dressed and older than I. I wore a skirt and a tee shirt, bare legs and sandals, nothing but lip gloss.

I was surprised that he believed me even though what I'd told him was true. I never would have trusted such an absurd story. I was a divorcée he'd picked up in an elevator in Istanbul. I was living in Europe and claimed to be writing a novel. I was insubstantial as gauze or mosquito netting. Men were more romantic, more gullible than women, I thought, or more susceptible to flattery—or maybe just dumber.

Lucille decided we would take the bus that drove the Mediterranean side of Turkey. She wasn't sure why. The Aegean coast was equally tempting. In the end, she had to make a choice. "That's life," she said. "You can't have everything!" "Right, Mom!" said her daughter. She rolled her eyes.

The bus rattled through small towns and along a glittering coast. The sun on the sand radiated white light. The sky was blue, the water a sublime aquamarine, like a jewel. My body glowed with the pleasure of what I'd just done. We stayed at motels, some built by American oil companies. They had once been beautiful but were shabby and semi-neglected, as if run by people who had been given a gift they didn't know what to do with. I finished *The Godfather* and left it in one of the rooms. I liked the idea that a stranger might read it and be surprised by something he'd never expected to find on a trip.

At all the ruins vendors sold Coca-Cola in green bottles. The bigger the ruin, the more empty bottles. At the best sites the crates were piled ten feet high. In the small towns we passed through, young Turkish boys dressed in white tunics rode horses covered with colorful, embroidered, jeweled blankets hung with tassels. They were at the head of processions on their way to their circumcisions, flanked by beaming parents, like brides being led to the altar. Their families and friends rode behind. The processions clip-clopped through the streets. The richer and more prestigious the family, the longer and more elaborate the procession. The young boys sat unmoving, stiff as rods, their eyes dark with terror as they stared straight ahead. I'd been twenty-one when I got married and they reminded me of me, captives of a culture. "Flee!" I wanted to shout. "Leave home! It's the only way! Run! Run for your life!"

I saw Artie again a month later. He came to London in September for a medical convention and we drove to Stratford for a weekend.

We stayed at an inn with Elizabethan beams, slept in a four-poster, sat on the grass by the Avon watching the swans. We made love in every position, sometimes with eyes wide open watching each other's faces. I had gotten good at this kind of sex and made it a part of me. I didn't think I'd ever turn back.

The thirty-six hours felt like time plucked from real life, an interval between acts. I wanted to keep it that way. I thought of what happened between us as something that would end.

We saw *A Midsummer Night's Dream* which struck me as the perfect play. A hot night. The right place. A little fairy dust and magic happens with the first person you clap your eyes on . . . possibly an ass.

On Sunday night I dropped him at Heathrow. He asked me not to come inside the airport. I didn't ask why. He had told me he was separated from his wife, but had a girlfriend. Now I knew he was lying.

I'd put the top up on the car driving back from Stratford and the mood inside was leaden. I pulled up to the curb at the terminal and said "Goodbye." His smile had disappeared and his sunburn had faded.

I leaned over and opened the door and waited for him to get his bag out. Outside he bent towards the window and said "Goodbye . . ." but didn't move, just looked at me.

I put my foot on the gas and zoomed off without looking back. I wished the car would emit a puff of cartoon smoke in his face.

Two weeks later I got a letter from him asking if I'd read *The Music School*, a story collection by John Updike. He'd just finished it. What did I think? I didn't answer. A second letter arrived asking if I'd gotten the first one. I didn't answer that either. I was pleased with myself for not answering and hoped that I'd hurt him.

"Orgasm is the transcendence of the non-fucking of one's parents and the non-love of families," my psychiatrist said.

"Sex is much easier in casual relationships," he added. "Especially orgasm and co-orgasm. Intuitively you did the right thing!" He looked very happy. His red face glowed.

"Oh please," I said. "I picked up a guy in an elevator and got lucky. Nothing more."

"No," he insisted. "It's larger than that. Fucking is our revolutionary duty and we must do it with joy."

An ash from his Gauloise dropped on his corduroy pants and I leaned over and flicked it off. "I worry about you," I said. "I really do!"

TIME

I WORE THE BLACK LEATHER coat several times that fall. It was sexy, but not all that warm. Wearing it made me feel like an actress in a decadent Italian movie, Monica Viti or Anita Ekberg. The coat wasn't my style but I'd found my "true self" when I bought it and was reminded of that every time I slipped it on. Sometimes I wore the coat with blue jeans to tone down its Fellini quality—although it looked good with mini-skirts too. Mini-skirts were going out of style, however, so I wasn't sure how long the life of the black leather coat would be. Time was passing. I'd been in London just three months short of two years. Maxi-skirts were coming into fashion. I'd already bought two at Biba in Kensington High Street.

HELEN

STERLING LORD TURNED ME OVER to an agent in his office named Helen. "Helen handles our fiction," he said. Helen was blond with a nasal voice that made her sound as if her bloodline went back to the Mayflower. She told me she had a dog and I could imagine her in tweeds tramping across a field with the dog at her side.

Back in London, whenever I got thirty pages I sent them to Helen. "I love it. Keep sending," Helen wrote back. Sometimes she said she knew of a particular editor who would like what I'd sent. I paid attention to everything Helen told me. I believed in her one hundred and fifty percent. A paragraph from Helen on

Sterling Lord's stationery was enough to put me on clouds for a week. When I'd seen Richard on the flight back to London I'd told him about Helen and his eyebrows had lifted. "Helen is from Philadelphia! She's main line," he said. "She's Richard Brautigan's agent. Have you read *Trout Fishing in America*?" I shook my head. "You should!" he said.

In Foyles I looked at Richard Brautigan's photograph on his book jacket; a homespun man with long hair, a handlebar moustache, granny glasses, and a tall black hat. He looked like Mark Twain on pot. I didn't read *Trout Fishing in America*. Richard had said, "It's not really about trout fishing," but even a book about trout fishing that was about something else was more trout fishing than I wanted to read about. Still, I felt a kinship with Brautigan, as if he and I were in the same family, brother and sister, united by Helen.

One morning, two months after I got back from Turkey, the words ran out. They simply stopped. Fragments appeared like the ghosts of a dream. Phrases. Descriptions. Lines of dialogue. But nothing hung together. There was no story. The whiny voice—like an ambivalent lover—had evaporated . . . gone off to date other women, or back to his wife.

But not being able to continue writing was worse than losing a lover. A lover is alive and well, just gone someplace else. Not writing was mysterious, as if a part of me had deserted myself. I had no idea where to look for it, or if it would ever come back. And the harder I tried, the more elusive the missing part was. I'd assumed that I'd finish what I had started, but I began to understand that short of a miracle, that might not happen. Sitting at the typewriter, I felt as if I had egg on my face.

That Christmas Neil, my acting teacher from the HB Studio in New York, came to London. We'd seen a lot of each other in L.A.

The kids were in Malibu spending Christmas with Bob and I invited Neil to stay at the house. He said he wasn't sure what he wanted to do next, and he'd spent all fall traveling through Europe; he'd been to Amsterdam, to Florence and Venice and Rome, to Paris and to Athens.

During the holiday week two friends of Neil's, small, manic comedy writers from L.A., were in London and stopped by to visit. While they were there a high pitch of hysteria whistled through the house. "This place is fabulous," they screamed when they came in the door. "Where's the pool?" The writers hung a blowup of Nancy Sinatra on the front door of my house on my prim little street lined with Christmas wreaths. "These boots are made for walking," they sang. "They're crazy," Neil grumbled, but he laughed. On Christmas day, watching the Queen pacing backstage before delivering her annual speech, the writers wrote her a monologue; she had just discovered she was following a music hall act; "Philip," she shouted at the Duke of Edinburgh. "Call my agent! Get me the Morris office!"

At the end of the week my eyelids felt stiff, as if toothpicks were holding them open. My neck was a thin piece of wire. I missed the kids. I wanted them back. On the telephone they told me they were going to Disneyland and riding horses in Topanga and I felt a deep, searing jealousy. The phone calls were worse than not talking at all.

I gave Neil my pages to read. When he was finished he put them back on my desk; "Make something up!" he said.

"Like what?" I asked.

"It doesn't matter," he said. "Anything!" Out and out lies hadn't occurred to me. The couple I was writing about was me and Bob, but not exactly. I'd taken liberties, lots of them. I'd exaggerated and invented to make the story better, but I hadn't ventured beyond certain boundaries of truth. "I don't know what that means," I said. My mouth was open. I was sure I looked perplexed, probably stupid. "Just do it!" he said.

When he was directing the play I'd been in he'd once demonstrated to me how to stalk off, leaving another character in your wake, and I imagined him turning his back and abandoning me. He was smart—he'd played the classics, Shakespeare and Shaw and Moliere. He knew history and philosophy and literature. He'd dropped out of Columbia Law School to become an actor. He was depressed too . . . a romantic figure, he'd traveled the continent, his unhappiness swirling around him like a cloak. I knew he knew what he was talking about. For Christmas he'd given me the complete works of Shakespeare and an oversized *Webster's Dictionary*. "It doesn't matter what shit you write," he said, his voice dark with finality, "if you want to write a novel you have to make something up!"

I sat at the Olympia for a week trying to invent. All my fabrications sounded pathetic. I made lists of lies, none of them even vaguely worth telling. Finally, I picked the one that seemed least dangerous, a low risk, cowardly little lie but the best I could do, I made my character a screenwriter. The sad little masquerade was depressing, but what choice did I have? Slowly however, being a screenwriter began to seem comical. I could shoot down all those Hollywood types. Being outlandish made the character braver . . . the heiress to a string of "what the fuck" moments. Things began to happen. The story—based on a lie—began to feel truthful. The whiny voice came sniveling back. But this time I wasn't sitting around waiting for the creep to call me. I was making the calls.

A month later I sent Helen more pages. "I love it. Keep sending," she wrote back. I used Helen's Madison Avenue address, but
when I imagined her opening my envelope she was always standing in front of a kennel of dogs, all of them yapping. Richard
Brautigan floated downstream with the trout, smiling and waving, beckoning me into the water, his hair floating around him.

PORTRAIT OF THE SMARTEST

DEREK WAS ENGLISH. DIVORCED. AVAILABLE. He was even Jewish.

"Not unhappily married?" Allie asked. "What more do you want?"

"I don't know," I said.

And I didn't.

I'd seen his photograph in *Harper's Bazaar*; "Celebrities Talk About Decadence." We were at an opening, in a crush of people at the Institute of Contemporary Arts on the mall (The English say mal).

"Images of Women's Liberation" had as part of the exhibit a light show flashing against one of the white walls, old black and white film of stiffly parading suffragettes in long skirts, strippers and housewives, women marching with signs in front of the White House.

There was a long table with red and white wine, plastic glasses, pretzels and chips.

Derek was the director. He'd planned and executed the show.

I'd worked my way across the room, shifting from group to group till our shoulders brushed. "What *about* decadence?" I'd asked.

"D-D-D-ecadence?" He laughed right away. (Later he told me he had that stutter under control. But sometimes it cropped up.) "I've been quoting Byron; 'Nothing I say will keep down a single petticoat. '"

"No petticoats here," I said, looking around.

"That magazine story is absurd." He laughed again.

I thought he was pleased with being in *Harper's Bazaar* but didn't want to admit it.

"You're American?"

"Guilty!"

"You're funny," he said. I wasn't sure what I had said that was so humorous, but just then I spotted Richard's curly head bobbing along in the crowd behind Derek like a bouncing ball. My fingers grew suddenly cold around my warm plastic glass. I hadn't seen or heard from him since that day on the airplane coming back from New York and the thought of coming face to face with him made me anxious. Just then the slide projector behind us which had been flipping images onto a white space on the wall sputtered and fizzled. There was a tiny explosion in the room, like a dying firecracker, and the pictures careened onto the ceiling and floor and all the wrong places; Betty Friedan and Germaine Greer flickered across Derek's chest; a peace sign slid over his balding crown and down his wide, white forehead. "Dear me! I must see to that," he said. "Will you stay for the Cabaret? We've invited a stripper." I shook my head, reached into my carpetbag, and scribbled my address and number on the back of a matchbook.

"Is that South Terrace . . . off Alex*aaa*nder Square?" Derek asked without a hint of a stutter.

Nothing like the English language properly spoken, I thought as I fled. I could listen to that my whole life.

I'd come with Allie and I went to find her. "Let's leave," I said.

Richard caught up with me just as I was nearing the exit.

"I'm pissed. I'm stoned. I'm depressed and I'm mixed up as hell," he said.

"Fuck off!" I said, and kept going.

"Lovely as ever, Phyllis," he shouted after me, which for some reason made me laugh. When wasn't I lovely? I wondered. I thought I'd been nothing but. Allie laughed too. We headed out onto the mall, lit up, London's most impressive Avenue, Buckingham Palace at one end, Trafalgar Fountain at the other.

"I still miss him," I said. It had been six months but the pile of books he gave me was still next to my bed. "That shook me up," I said.

"He's not worth it," Allie said.

"I know. But knowing doesn't help."

Allie's other boyfriend, Ben, had quit his job and come to London. They were living together, crowding out Mike who had been spending a lot of time in Paris. I thought he might have a new girl-friend. Allie didn't seem unhappy about it.

"Two men. It had to end sometime," she said.

Derek lived up in Hampstead, a small basement flat lined with books and crammed with posters and prints that no one had yet thought to collect; Hiroshigi and reproductions of Klimt. Maps of the London Underground. Poems by poet friends, illustrated and written in calligraphy and propped against the wall. A pen-and-ink line drawing of a reclining female nude by an artist Derek knew. He took me to Keats' house and to walk on the Heath. "Pinter lives not far off. And Doris Lessing. And Maggie Drabble. You'd do well here among the literati," he joked.

He was a sad-looking man with large gloomy bags under his eyes. They made him look older than he actually was. Thirty-one. But when he was mischievous the bags smoothed out and his full cheeks moved upward and he looked his true age. His skin was unlined, his lips full and pink.

In my bedroom we made love by a thick candle that threw flickering shadows on the deep red walls. Afterwards we talked; Derek was always reading. Rilke and Proust, Kafka, Beckett and Brecht; ideas flew from his head like confetti. Why settle for one if you could have hundreds? No—thousands . . . whistling and fraying and sliding all over the place. I called him "portrait of the smartest," and he couldn't stop laughing. He had a smooth brown belly and I put my head on his chest and watched it move as we laughed. "You're a female Lenny Bruce," he said . . .

We played word games:

He called it a dust bin.

"Garbage pail," I said.

"Biscuit."

"Cookie."

"Flannel."

"Washcloth."

"Fringe."

"Bangs."

"Horlicks."

"Malted."

"Lift."

"Elevator."

"Boot."

"Trunk."

"Bonnet."

"Hood."

"Outside there's no time . . . nothing . . . no weather . . . when I'm with you there's only this room," he said.

He'd been married to the fragile girl he'd met at Cambridge. They'd tried but found themselves "muddled," he said. A few years on they were forced to give up. He sighed.

"I've been asked to resign from my job," he said one night. His face drooped down to his chest.

"Why?" I was astonished. His shows succeeded. Everyone went.

"*Over—reaching* they said . . . but in fact there's a new chairman and he wants to assert his authority. It's a bloody struggle."

I kept quiet. Secretly, I suspected that the new chairman might have a point. But what did I know? My husband Bob could have been called "overreaching" and who would have said that description was wrong? He generally got what he overreached for. I was a person of small ambitions in no position to criticize Derek's grand schemes. "I'm sorry," I said. I took his hand and looked into his dark, sad eyes. He was a Jew in England, not an easy place, the land of Shylock. He pressed my hand in return and looked mildly happier . . . but not for long. Soon he was out of bed in his underwear and down at my Olympia writing a letter stating all the facts in his case to the *London Times*.

I lay frozen. The kids might wake up. The idea of them seeing Derek in his underwear at my desk terrified me. Till now I'd managed to keep my boyfriends' bedroom activities out of their sight. I always made Derek leave before morning. I was sure they knew everything . . . but not because they'd seen it. And I was writing my novel on that typewriter and couldn't bear for anyone to touch it. Derek did have his ways of moving in and taking over. "Does he want his space?" Allie asked when Derek and I first started seeing each other. "No. He wants mine," I'd said. He'd once told me he thought of himself as a bulldozer, that he just kept pushing on no matter what happened. I listened to the keys clacking and tried to be understanding. It was a typewriter. That's all. And the kids never woke in the night.

From Dublin Derek brought me a suede hat and from the pornographic fair in Amsterdam an erotic Egon Schiele print, a woman with red hair in black tights. He took me to concerts and happenings, to plays and readings by poets, exhibits by painters. Anything underground . . . and avant garde Derek knew about. He took me to Chalk Farm and The Roundhouse. When he came to the house he brought food, a jar of Stilton or the season's best pears. On Sundays Derek put on a turtleneck sweater and a jaunty hat and sunglasses and went biking in Hyde Park with me and the kids and afterwards to Soho for a Chinese dinner at the Dumpling Inn. The kids were suspicious, but civil. They answered his questions and acted polite. It was, I thought, a beginning . . . maybe a life.

One night, early on in our dating, Derek and I couldn't sleep. Sleep seemed impossible so we got up and went out into the city. We drove to Sloane Square and stopped at the Royal Court Theater where the stage crew was doing an all-nighter, setting up the next play, and to Piccadilly, like an artist's print, empty and blurry in the mist, and then to Covent Garden, damp and alive in the middle of the city with bustling stalls where Derek bought me a box of yellow chrysanthemums. We drove along the silent embankment, the river lapping at our side. I felt as if I could keep driving forever, and never see all of London. I was behind the wheel of the car, the wipers clacking back and forth, and it felt warm and tender inside. As our sojourn continued I lost track of where we were and just followed Derek's instructions, turning through the damp, unfamiliar, narrow streets down to Whitechapel and back past St. Paul's. There was a closed-down cinema, The Trocadero, boarded up and lonely in the darkness and across from it the shop where Derek's father grew up, the letters of his grandfather's name fading on the front. Derek had been raised in Golder's Green but he'd told me of how his father had carried bales of cloth over Tower Bridge for his tough Russian immigrant mother. ("The shmatte business," he said . . . "What else?") I told him about my family, my "tough Roumanian" immigrant grandfather, our name and our spice business visible from the

Williamsburg Bridge. We drove over Tower Bridge, past the tower and the mint and to St. Katherine's dock. The dock was being torn apart and was a mass of rubble which we climbed over just as the sky was beginning to lighten. The last time I'd been out at this hour I'd run down King's Road from her Ladyship's house. Somehow, we ended up at Hyde Park Corner. Speeding around the turn, normally thick with cars juggling for position but now empty, I could feel my heart beating wildly. I loved owning London this way. Once, when I'd been away and returned, Paul, the romantic Hungarian, had said, "You're back in your beloved London!" The city was my beloved, I thought.

Inside the car Derek's hand was on my leg. We'd kissed several times. "I know this is a sore subject, my darling," he said, "but how would it be if I left a few things at your house? A razor? Clean underwear?" He'd been dressing at work. He waited. The car was silent. We speeded around the curve and headed towards Knightsbridge. Driving was so easy with no one around. I thought of Bob. But what did he matter? We were divorced. I was free to find a new life. "Hello?" Derek said. I kept my eyes on the road but took my hand off the wheel and patted his hand. "Let me think about it," I said.

For his final show at the ICA Derek planned an exhibit devoted to comics. This was to be his grand send-off! His statement! He called it "Aaargh!" The poster for the show, plastered all over London, was of a large, generic, superhero, masked, his head sheathed. He wore a flowing cape and boots and tights and seemed to be flying off the page, fist extended. He was surrounded with smaller comic characters of all nations—Australia and Italy, France, America, Germany, and Holland. There would be comic strips in the gallery and a cabaret show with comic-strip characters and rock musicians and dancers, poets and actors. Derek immersed himself in comic book research. His office at the ICA was piled high with comic books and posters and strips from Sunday supplements. He seemed to be swimming, even drowning, in comics. On nights when I came to meet him he'd look up from the mess as if he were coming to the surface for air. Sometimes I had the feeling that until he got hold of himself he didn't remember who I was. He discovered Mao comics from China and comic posters from the '68 revolution in Paris. "It's low culture," he rhapsodized to me. "And that's the whole point! Junk is so freeing!"

The show was scheduled to open in the week between Christmas and New Year's, the time when Neil was staying at my house. Derek asked if we'd be in the Cabaret and do a scene or a skit to represent American comics. "You can be Batman and Wonder Woman! The true American icons!" He looked expectant . . . even joyous. His eyes lit up and he waved a hand, impressario-like. Derek was full faced and full-bodied. When he was happy there seemed to be more of him, as if he'd taken on an extra persona. "Jolly good! I can see it!" he said, with a full laugh.

"Let's do it!" Neil said.

"I don't know!" I said. I felt I'd left acting behind. I'd become a writer and was relieved not to have to get on a stage and perform. And I didn't completely trust that all would go well. There was a high-flying vagueness to Derek's plans that made them difficult to understand. I thought of the night we'd met, the projector exploding to a fizzling halt, the images cascading over his head and chest.

"Oh come on," Neil said.

"Don't blame me if something goes wrong," I warned Neil.

"Like what?" he asked.

The night of the opening the ICA was packed. Everyone in London turned out. Derek had been right. He'd predicted that during the week between Christmas and New Year's people would be hungry for excitement, escape from the enforced quiet of the holidays. I thought of Christmas a year earlier, the silent morning I'd driven through London alone searching for Tampax. Now I didn't have to be alone any longer. I could, if I wished, be with Derek. The gallery was jammed with people in beads and shawls and outrageous comic book outfits. They glittered with lurex and spangles. Many were smoking, drinking, and already high when they arrived. The small cabaret couldn't hold the entire audience. Many were watching on a video hookup in a room off the gallery. Neil and I were backstage.

The audience had been promised a beauty pageant, but the "Colossal Comic-Strip Cabaret" started off with a ragtag lineup of poets, friends of Derek's with peace messages. It didn't take long before the audience became unruly. Anti-war poetry—even if it did rhyme Batman and Napalm—was not what they wanted in a cabaret. At the end of three minutes they began booing and shouting for the girls in the contest to come on stage. A minute later they were throwing the lemon slices from their drinks . . . and then the drinks. They were momentarily mollified by a cross-dresser, a beauty contestant in a school uniform with balloons for breasts, but the respite didn't last long. "Take it off," screamed a voice and the audience took up the chant. At the hisses and shouts from the audience the bags under Derek's eyes crinkled upward, as if he might fly. It seemed to me that he liked the disorder, the excitement. "It's so Elizabethan!" he enthused. Neil and I were scheduled to go on after several more acts. By the time it was our turn the stage would be bedlam. I looked at Neil and saw his eyes darting from the stage and back in comprehension and then horror. I thought of saying I told you so . . . but kept quiet. We had worked hard and done our research to put together a mélange of lines from American comics. We'd included all the classic bits of dialogue we'd grown up with, even copy from comic book ads for zit medication. Our high school days of Clark Kent and phone booth jokes, Captain Marvel, Ma and Pa Yokum, and the little comic strips inside Double Bubble gum wrappers were in the repartée we'd written. We were Batman and Wonder Woman, but our childhood autobiographies were in that script along with Boo Hoo!!, Sigh, Boing, Thwack!!!, Zoom, Kerplop, and Krunnnch!!!!

"Elizabethan?" Neil said, gazing out towards the stage. His voice was low . . . every syllable a dagger. "Elizabethan!" He dragged out the word as if it were ten miles long. "You better do something!" He warned Derek. "Somebody could get hurt! Get out there!" he ordered. "This place is coming apart!" Derek threw him a reassuring look—as if the restive audience could easily be taken care of—and stepped out onto the stage. He had a jaunty little walk and was smiling. He held up his hands as if he could arrest the uproar. But whatever the crowd wanted, they could see that Derek wasn't going to give it to them. The boos and hisses got louder, bloodier.

"We're not going on!" Neil said. "Let's get out of here!" He folded up our script, tucked it in his pocket, and did a swift little turn and flounce.

I took a last look through the curtain. "Come! Come! A little courtesy for the Artistes," Derek pleaded.

He clutched the microphone as if it were a lifeline and held up his hand, but a tall, skinny girl had just stripped down to her bra and panties and was gyrating around him like a puppet on a string. She bumped and ground in front of him and he tried to handle it, smiling, as if he were still in control, a part of the joke. The audience was shouting and screaming, egging her on. She was part of a drunken entourage, two painters that Derek knew who were engaged in a shouting match across him:

"You Fuck!"

"You Cunt!"

"You Shit!"

"You pussy!"

Now a chunky girl in fishnet tights and black leather boots was heading straight for Derek, marching through the audience swinging a whip. She was followed by a line of British actors in torn shirts—more friends of Derek's—dancing and whirling behind her. Derek clung to the microphone. The painters tried to grab it away from him but he held on, smiling frantically. He was trying to treat the bedlam as just an outbreak of spontaneity, but it was a lost cause. The comic show was in chaos. Derek looked toward the wings and caught sight of me and Neil and beckoned us on, presuming, in spite of all the evidence, that we would come to the rescue, but I shook my head. I felt a surge of anger. The audience was coming forward like a giant wave, taking over the stage. People were taking off their clothes and beneath the lights there seemed to be a sea of moving, naked flesh. Did he really think I'd go out there? Well, I'd never promised him anything. The whole time we'd been dating, nearly four months, I'd never let him leave a pair of socks at the house.

I didn't think I wanted to see what would happen next. Somehow Derek would handle this. This was his job—at least for the moment—and London was his city.

I'd worn a low-necked top and tied a band of stars around my forehead suggestive of Wonder Woman, and I felt suddenly cold, reminded of the damp chill of the London winter. In an unexpected flashback I saw Lady Goldsmid's overflowing trunk in the closet on the day we met, her elegant cashmere sleeve draped over the side. "How will you manage?" she'd asked. Well, I had managed, I thought, on my own, pretty well.

Neil and I walked all the way back to South Terrace, replaying the evening.

Everything about the comic show set us off into hysterical bouts of laughter. Tears streamed down my cheeks.

"I thought he knew what he was doing," Neil said. "His picture was in *Harper's Bazaar*."

"He means well," I said, still laughing and weeping. "He's just . . . disorganized."

Derek never held it against me that I'd walked out on him in his moment of need. He was so lost in his comic book concept he'd hardly even noticed that I was gone. I could have a life with Derek, but not one I wanted. I didn't stop seeing him although I told him not to expect much from me. Dating Derek was like being in a holding pattern, aboard a plane that would eventually land somewhere, but for the moment just kept on circling.

SPRING, 1971

AT KENNEDY AIRPORT MY PARENTS swooped down like birds with sheltering wings. The kids ran to them, with paintings from school, a wooden boat Billy had made, a macaroni necklace Julie had strung. I felt like an outsider, a black hawk, the predator who'd snatched them away. My father, in his "car coat" with the fur collar, piled our luggage into the trunk of his car on top of bags of golf clubs and whisked us to their new "ranch" house on Long Island. The sound of their happiness twittered at a high pitch, like music from string instruments. My mother was sixty and had just dyed her hair blonde. That week she gave Jenifer dozens of her gold bracelets and bangles. They whispered together like girlfriends. My mother played "tennis" with Billy in the backyard and chased after all the balls. She bought Julie the corduroy pants that she'd begged for . . . identical to Billy's. The kids loved staying with my parents, eating Kellogg's Special K and bananas for breakfast and going to their golf club. "Why can't we live here?" Billy asked. All my parent's friends cooed over their English accents and paid them endless attention. They milked it for all it was worth. My parents took them shopping for toys and to visit aunts and uncles they barely remembered. They came back glowing with family stories . . . and tales of my young cousins who played with them. Everything I'd run from . . . life in one place . . . big cars . . . split level houses on Long Island . . . a family that interfered with even pulse and respiration . . . the kids loved.

When my father pointed out houses for sale in his new neighborhood ("a backyard, near the school, a dry basement"), my mother said to him, "Stop it! She doesn't want to live here! Enough!"

At the end of the week we took the kids back to Kennedy . . . which I still thought of as Idlewild . . . to fly out to L.A. to see Bob. My father still refused to fly but he always wanted to take others to airports. "I'll run you out there," he'd say. If you refused, he insisted. "Come on! Get in the car." For a man who wouldn't fly he knew everything about terminals: where to park, who to tip to watch your car if you didn't want to go into the lot, how to talk to skycaps ("Hey pal, over here"). I watched him get the kids to the gate, my mother fussing, all of them hugging and kissing. I felt as if I was watching the scene from a distance and was startled by how old the kids had become; they were now ten and a half, eight, and six. Jenifer was tall and willowy; she still took the guitar everywhere but her tastes were widening. In London her music teacher had taken her class to Covent Garden to see *The Magic Flute* and she played the record over and over. *Hair* had come to London and she'd already seen it twice. "Aquarius. Aquarius" rang out from her room. Billy was tall and shockingly neat, with a fresh haircut he'd gotten at my father's barber. He took Julie's arm and pulled her along. Julie kept both hands in the pocket of her corduroy pants like a boy on a corner jingling change. I'd never flown anywhere till after I was married but they boarded a plane as casually as if they were going for a stroll around the block. "Don't worry, Grandma, we'll come back," Jenifer soothed my mother who stood fastened to the waiting area, waving, her eyes filling up as they passed through the gate.

Would they ever be English, no matter how well they spoke the language? Watching them, so at home with my parents, I didn't think so. They'd bubble over with enthusiasm when they brought classmates home from school for "tea" (milk and chocolate digestive biscuits). "Do you want to ride bikes? Go to the square? Play ball in Hyde Park?" They'd offer a stream of thrilling choices. "I don't mind," the well-bred English child would reply. At the Redcliffe school, clattering up and down the stairs, bare knees peeking from beneath their school uniforms, they looked like any other English child. But British reserve was not a characteristic they'd ever possess. Did I want them to? Was it better for them to tamp down their high spirits? And if they didn't, would they ever fit in?

I'd asked my parents to drop me at the train after the kids left so I could go into the city, to Caroline's, and I braced myself for their urging me not to leave. But they were still talking about the kids as I kissed them goodbye at the station, slammed the car door, and waved.

The first editor to turn down my book said it was "the voice of New York, the voice of today."

"Which one didn't he like?" I asked Helen. "New York or today?"

"Both," she said. "Don't worry. I love it. I'll sell it . . . even if it takes forty tries." She waved a hand and looked confident. She was a large woman, maybe five years older than I, with streaked blond hair that turned up just around her ears and an unmade up, round face. She reminded me of girls I'd known in college who carried hockey sticks to class and always got what they wanted.

"Who are these people?" Helen grumbled. "Are they publishing books or writing reviews?"

"I don't care what they say," I said (only half true). It was miracle enough that I'd gotten this far, that I was sitting in Helen's office, that pages I'd written were being delivered by a messenger (*a messenger*) to publishers whose names I'd seen on the spines of great books. I didn't think anyone would publish my book. I'd been lucky. But how far could luck take me? Publishers would keep turning me down and calling me names until Helen gave up. When it was over I'd put the manuscript away in a drawer and write something else. Failure didn't matter. Being rejected wasn't the point.

Helen had the manuscript retyped on letter-size paper instead of the legal size I'd used in London and she gave me back the pages I'd sent. She sent the manuscript out in a box to one publisher at a time. This could take years, I thought. Still, I felt light when I left her, buoyant, a writer leaving her agent's office; the mystique of it thrilled me and I walked out onto Madison Avenue holding the envelope with Helen's name and the Sterling Lord Agency sticker tucked against my chest.

It was a clear day in March, blinding, the kind of day when New York looks as if you are seeing it through a newly washed window.

I walked over to Third Avenue and 6oth Street where the improvisation group I'd been in at Hilly's was appearing in a theater.
They'd graduated to an off-Broadway show and called themselves
"The Fourth Wall." The poster for the show had been adapted
from a photograph that had been taken while the group was at
Hilly's and my body was still in it, my face blotted out and Jeremy's
head superimposed over where mine had been. He had two heads.
I had none. We were posed on some low steps outside a warehouse
and I was seated in the front row, my legs crossed, Jeremy alongside me in a leather jacket and newsboy's cap. I stood in front of
the poster for a long time looking at my body without my head. It
was a peculiar feeling to see myself erased from a place that I'd
been, as if I had been robbed of my past and was now the sole
owner of a memory that no one else would confirm. I felt angry
but I wasn't sure at who. I couldn't realistically blame the other
actors since I was the one who'd left.

But New York was a minefield. It was impossible to set foot on
a New York street without the past jumping up at me. "Remember everything," Georgia advised after Bob left and I was spending my days weeping. "Leave nothing out. And you'll see, being
married to him wasn't that great," she chortled. Standing in front
of the poster where I'd been decapitated, I felt like calling to tell
her she was wrong. Good, bad, it didn't matter. All memory was
an assault.

I crossed the street and went to Bloomingdale's. When I lived in
New York I'd loved Bloomingdale's and wanted to buy everything I
saw there. The money I'd spent in Bloomingdale's irritated Bob
although he never actually forbade me to shop. "Do you know what
our bill was?" he'd ask every month. On the main floor a pretty girl

stood behind a long counter of glass jars blooming with colored soaps; rose, lilac, lemon, citron, pine, peony, aquamarine. They came into view like a shimmering mirage into focus. My tears were completely unexpected; they shocked me, like an insult I wasn't expecting from a friend I was happy to see. Through the blur the toiletries and cosmetics department of Bloomingdale's looked like a wavery rainbow of desire. I wanted to grab it all and hug it to me. When I was married I'd bought these very same oval soaps, a dozen to the box, in bath size. Bob liked the pine. I could smell the scent on his cheek as he left for work while Billy was in his high chair with cereal splattered over his face and the tray. I reached into my bag for a pair of dark glasses and fled, sailing up on the escalator, above the soap into clouds of lingerie, bathrobes, up past mannequins sheathed in clinging jersey, past piles of Oriental rugs, displays of wooden ice buckets and red, blue, and yellow enamel pots, basketry and a vast garden of artificial flowers arranged to resemble the ones Monet painted at Giverny. No sooner did one display pass then you were on your way to another. Such profusion. So many things to want. On the fifth floor I walked through the model rooms. Bloomingdale's had gone Indian; behind the ropes Indian rooms glowed with pink and orange and gold shawls, brass lamps and boxes and throws and filigreed screens and tables and sofas piled high with silken pillows. Spilling from a carved trunk were lengths of shimmering fabrics laced with silver and gold. Once I had lusted after those designer rooms—penthouses overlooking Manhattan by night with martini glasses set out on a silver tray, spare modern furniture in living rooms where the stereo piped in Sibelius, French Country dining rooms with "distressed" walnut tables and chairs covered in Provençal prints. A model life. You could buy it at Bloomingdale's.

I still had a Bloomingdale's charge card in my wallet and back on the main floor I pulled it from a hidden crevice and handed it to the salesgirl. I couldn't decide which color soap to buy. I frittered away time, trying to choose. "Lovely, aren't they?" she asked. "Take them all," she suggested, brightly. "I can mix them." She opened an empty box. "One of each." Her skin was as clear as daylight, her lips shone with gloss. Where did such translucent skin come from? How did Bloomingdale's find someone so unmarked? She was in her early twenties, just a notch older than Bob's girlfriend, a model or actress; some rich man would want her. I hadn't used the charge card in nearly four years, not since I'd lived in New York. The bill would go to our old address, the apartment we'd sublet to someone else when we moved to L.A. Would it eventually land on Bob's desk?

"Your card has expired," she said. She put the telephone receiver down and made a sad face. "You can open a new account," she offered. "We can ship it to you."

I shook my head.

The box of mixed soaps was still open on the counter and she put a soft white hand on them.

"Are you sure? It won't take long," she promised.

"I'm leaving town," I said.

"We ship everywhere . . ."

Her voice drifted after me as I headed through the bottles and jars to the Lexington Avenue exit. "You could have them next week. . . ."

On the Fifty-Seventh Street crosstown bus I looked up from *New York* magazine. Bob's law school roommate, Dave Solomon, was sitting across from me. Attached to his arm was an Asian woman, tall and narrow as a pipe cleaner, her long neck rising above his tweed hat. Dave was quirky, a rich boy from a Westchester suburb with a Chaplin-like walk and a sharp nose. He wore tortoise shell glasses and was finicky, a picky eater. When we went to dinner with him he asked about every dish on the menu and took half an hour to choose. When the food arrived he moved things aside on his plate . . . bits of mushroom out of the rice . . . mashed potatoes that were too thick or too thin.

Dave had been an usher at our wedding and spent a lot of time at our Riverside Drive apartment.

I leaned over and waved a hand in front of his face and after a minute of blankness it popped open with recognition.

"Phyllis! Is it really you? I can't believe it. This is Ho Shi, my wife (she smiled and dipped her head on her long stalk of a neck. I dipped too).

"We saw Bob last month. He was in New York. We went to dinner at The Four Seasons . . ."

He was off. A long discourse followed, about Bob and his girlfriend and Bob's next movie which would star Jane Fonda and was about a dance marathon. Ho Shi sat, posture perfect, her body unmoving. Dave kept going, a monologue about Bob; his voice was like an automobile that stops and starts, making a joke or focusing on a small detail and then revving up again. When the bus got to 7th Avenue I stood up; Dave unlatched himself from Ho Shi and jumped across the aisle.

"I need to talk to you."

"Oh Dave. I'm swamped. How about my next trip?"

I said I had "business appointments," people to see. I murmured about my agent and an editor at the *Village Voice* Mike had told me to call. I flapped the envelope with my manuscript and Sterling Lord's sticker in front of his face.

"But it has to be now," Dave whined. "I have to apologize."

"For what?" I asked.

"It was my fault," he said. "Your divorce was my fault. I want to make it up to you. I want to take you to dinner. . . ."

Ho Shi put a hand on his arm. "Dave . . ." she said softly.

"Bob told me he didn't love you. It was the year we graduated from law school. He wanted to leave you but I convinced him to stay. If he had left you then you wouldn't have children. You wouldn't be in this mess. Do you realize how responsible I feel?"

"Dave . . ." Ho Shi said again. She tugged on his sleeve.

But Dave was going full tilt, no more jerkiness, he was the Twentieth Century steaming across America. "It was my fault," he moaned. His voice was tinny and the lines had deepened in his forehead and appeared to be opening like craters. "I should have told him to leave you long ago when you first had trouble. . . ."

In the seats around us an elderly woman with thyroid-popping eyes listened intently and a guy in a pea jacket with a head of curly blond ringlets was watching us, his eyes darting back and forth between us, riveted.

"That's why I have to see you. You have to tell me how to make it up to you. . . ."

"I have to go now, Dave," I said.

I hopped off the bus, Dave behind me, Ho Shi after him.

"Please," he wailed.

"It's OK, Dave," I said, sprinting towards the next bus which was lumbering not quickly enough to the downtown stop. "Don't give it a thought."

If he followed me on board I would duck under a seat. I wondered if he'd crawl under with me. My heart was beating quickly. I could hear it thunder in my chest. But Dave and Ho Shi were still trailing me. I had visions of them pursuing me downtown to Caroline's loft, Dave, waddling Chaplin-like behind me and Ho Shi alongside him, a beautiful race horse whinnying reproving sounds. "No, Dave. Stop. Stop."

The bus door opened and I climbed up on the step and turned and held up my hand. There were people waiting and I'd edged them out. "Don't follow me, Dave," I shouted. "Just don't." He froze. Ho Shi gripped the arm of his jacket, yanking him back. Irritated riders pushed in front of him and piled onto the bus, their bodies huddled together like closing gates. I scurried to the back and sank down. When I looked out the window he was still there, Ho Shi clutching his sleeve, talking softly, her lips next to his cheek. In defeat Dave's tweed hat had slipped to the back of his head and beneath it his face crumpled, like wet laundry.

Caroline's loft was empty when I got downtown. She'd left me a note that she wouldn't be home that night. The late afternoon sun was filtering through the grime on the windows and I fell asleep on the sofa under a square of sunlight. It was one of those heavy sleeps from which you try to pull yourself up, but then drop right back down. At two in the morning I was finally awake. The bar and grill downstairs had closed and the streets outside, normally clogged with trucks from the meatpacking district, were silent and empty. The room was dark except for the light from a street lamp. I switched on the TV just as the credits for the Late Late Show—*On the Waterfront*—rolled onto the screen. The sound of a bassoon—Leonard Bernstein's gloomy score—tunneled its way into the room and then came Brando's chiseled face, emotion pouring over it like falling water. Tears welled in my eyes and I wiped them away with my shirt. I watched the movie all the way through without stirring, from Brando's first guileless shout to Eddie Doyle from the sidewalk till he dragged his mangled body up the gangplank in the final scene. After the foreman shouted, "Let's go to work" and the gates slid shut, I watched the station signoff and then I watched the test pattern. I couldn't fall asleep when it was over so I lay there until it began to get light. In the instant before I dropped into sleep I had the sensation that I was driving around Hyde Park Corner before daybreak. I veered to the left and felt the car vibrate beneath me as I tapped the gas pedal with my right foot and held my left one poised above the clutch. The damp air rushed past my cheeks and the white townhouses of Belgravia seemed to be moving past me, shimmering in the mist.

Dave called me twice the next day. He got Caroline's phone number from my mother. I told Caroline to say that she didn't know where I was. The next afternoon I picked up the phone and it was Ho Shi. "I am so sorry," she said. "I say to Dave leave the woman alone."

"You know the worst people," Neil said. "It's mystifying how you manage to find people that awful. Where did he want to buy you dinner? Côte Basque? Could you take friends?"

We were in his apartment in the West sixties, laughing. We laughed about Derek and the comic book show and about the two comedy writers who'd come for Christmas and hung the picture of Nancy Sinatra on the front door. It was harder in London to find people who laughed at the same things I did; there was Jay and

301

Fran and there had been Richard. In New York humor came fast, like shorthand. Everybody got the joke.

"If that happened to me two years ago I might have jumped off the top of a building," I said. "I still might, but now I would at least think about it first!"

Just before I went back to London I saw Artie. To come upon him when I wasn't expecting it felt like having a pail of cold water dumped on my head. I was having lunch with Caroline in a crowded restaurant on First Avenue and Thirty-Second Street across from NYU Hospital and near *New York* magazine where Caroline was bringing some contact sheets. I looked up and saw him across three layers of tables.

He came over to the table and I got up and led him outside onto First Avenue and we stood in the wind, which was considerable. I could tell he was angry. He was wearing a shirt and jacket and tie and his face looked stern. His cheekbones were higher than I remembered and without a suntan his face looked urban and lean. We were no longer on the grass at Stratford-on-Avon or in the sunshine in a Turkish café. The room where we'd first made love came filtering back, even the sun beating through the drapes and zigzagging under my closed eyelids. I could feel desire lurking, ready to spring. Why was longing so indiscriminate, or did it always choose the wrong person?

"Why didn't you answer my letter?" he asked.

"The one about Updike?"

He made a face, as if I was the impossible one, as if I'd treated him badly. Just then there was a gust of wind and his jacket and tie flapped around him. He had to hold the tie down. He was wearing a wedding band.

I reached over and tapped his finger.

"Is this going to fry me?" he asked. "I don't even get a chance to explain?"

I didn't answer. We stood in the wind until I shook my head and went back inside and finished my hamburger.

I was alone in Caroline's loft the afternoon Helen called to say that a publisher, W. W. Norton, wanted to buy my novel. "I can't wait to tell everyone who your publisher is," she said. She was giggling and sounded high and girlish. It's a game, I thought, thinking of Bob closing a deal. You play it to win. After I got off the phone the loft seemed too small, as if the walls were closing in on me, so I went downstairs and walked up Bethune Street. I was feeling euphoric, as if my body had become very light and was floating above me and there were tears in my eyes and a jangling sound like bells in my head. I stopped in front of a tree that someone optimistic had planted. It was a fledgling tree attached by rubber thongs and wire to splints set in a patch of earth demarcated by a low scalloped iron fence. The cement around the fence was decorated with dog shit, cigarette butts, and a crumpled Rheingold can. I was looking at that tree when I knew I would move back to New York. The information came like a news bulletin I didn't know I was expecting until it arrived. When I tallied everything up I didn't want to live so far from my past, even if it wasn't the one I would have chosen.

DAVID

MADNESS. DAVID RECOMMENDED IT. YOU can't be sane until you've been insane.

He had opened doors for me and given me permission to do what I never would have done on my own. He'd shown me the streets of London glittering on acid and the veins and arteries beneath my own flesh. He'd helped me to claim my body—and probably my mind. I knew he was crazy, but the craziness suited me. It came at a time when I needed it. Insanity had seen me through.

Now he lay four flights up in an empty room on a bare mattress in a working class neighborhood even more remote than the one where I'd found him. He was being tended by a spiky-haired boy named Roy, all white skin and bones. A stripe of flesh gleamed like neon between the bottom of Roy's tee shirt and the waist of his pants. Roy had hammered red burlap over the windows, darkening the room with a coral glow.

He'd disappeared and I hadn't seen him in months. Finally Georgia had smoked him out. He'd moved away from his feminist girlfriend and come to live here with nothing but his mattress, some books, and his sloping armchair. A half empty bottle of amber-colored liquor stood on the floor.

He hailed me as I came in the door and Roy hoisted him from the mattress to the armchair. His pants were now red instead of black and they slipped down his bare hips. A blue/violet bruise flared from under the skin around his left eye spreading fingers onto his cheek. A railroad of spidery little red capillaries traveled from their red centers across the whites of his eyes.

I pulled up a folding chair. My heart was racing from climbing the stairs, but even after I sat down it wouldn't stop pounding.

"What happened?" I asked.

"Last night I had a near death experience and reached the cosmic endpoint. I felt love for all the world . . . but coming out I hit my eye on a doorknob," he said.

"I see," I said.

I concentrated on his voice and his diction. If I closed my eyes he could have been Winston Churchill. "We will fight them on the land. We will fight them on the seas . . ."

Alcohol, I thought. Old fashioned booze. I'd imagined a mind-expanding drug if anything, something that spoke for a larger consciousness, grander horizons. I'd thought there was complex thinking at work, not merely whiskey.

PHYLLIS RAPHAEL

I stayed for a long time as the orange afternoon light coming through the burlap ebbed. Sometime during the afternoon he had a coughing fit. He'd been swigging from the bottle and his shoulders and back heaved like a whale. The spasm seemed endless. Each time I thought it was over it started up again. He spat mucous and blood into a dirty handkerchief. Roy helped him back down onto the mattress, his arm hanging over Roy's skinny shoulder.

"Don't give me a check," he said when I tried. "Every time I go into a bank I feel like blowing it up. Give me cash."

"I'll have to come back," I said.

I came back again and then again. I wanted to say goodbye but couldn't find the words. Georgia told me that in Stockholm an audience had booed him. He'd gone out on a stage and talked about apes. He said they fucked for hours and were peaceful. One afternoon he said he wanted to bring the ape from the London zoo to live with him.

"Are you sure about that?" I asked.

"Yes," he said. He looked mischievous and we started to laugh but it ended in another spasm, more coughing, more blood.

The last time I saw him I brought Brian, my estate agent, a straight, sober alcoholic, in A. A. He was a dry man, from his brown tweed jacket and knitted tie, to his humor. His voice remained in the same register even when he smiled or laughed. He knelt alongside David. "How are you? Have you eaten?" he asked.

No expression, not even the flicker of an eyelash. Finally he gazed over in my direction and shook his head. I had betrayed him.

306

"I don't need A. A.," he said, the voice still majestic.

"What *do* you need?"

"A woman. I'm lonely."

"How about an ape?"

"One or the other."

"Not much you can do," Brian said. "You'll have to wait till he hits bottom."

"What's this?" I asked.

"He decides where bottom is," he said.

"David is switching this week," Roy said tenderly. "From a quart a day to a pint."

The room was near dark when I said goodbye. I was sitting alongside him down on the mattress, my arms around my knees. From time to time during the afternoon he shook like a seal. Now he lay with his head in Roy's lap. "I'm going home to New York and my family," I said. "Oh no. Don't do that," he moaned.

I leaned over and put my arms around him for an instant. I knew he'd try to pull me down alongside him unless I made it short. The smell of liquor mixed with stale sweat and Gauloises covered me over, like a giant cloak, and I stopped breathing until I got out the door.

NEW YORK

July 1971

LEAVING

ON THE DAY I LEFT London I knew I'd made a mistake. The house looked bereft—like a host saying goodbye at the end of a long party. There were marks on the carpet where the furniture had been and I longed to put everything back. Brian, the estate agent, had already brought buyers to look at the house. As he opened the door of the balcony off Jenifer's bedroom to the tangle of pale roses in the garden out back I overheard him say, "You could do worse . . ." the same words he'd spoken to me. ("Don't say that!" I wanted to shout. "Don't say that to anyone else!") I'd lived in number 12 South Terrace for two years and the asking price for my lease (still to run till 1984) was nearly twice what I'd paid. "You'll get every shilling too!" Brian said. I'd lived in London on American dollars as carelessly as a pasha, spending whatever I pleased, and I'd done it at a profit. Somehow it didn't seem right. Why was I leaving this idyllic life?

I stood in the bedroom inside the space where my brass bed had been. I'd discovered a few crumbs of marijuana in the corner of the built-in white drawers where I'd kept my underwear (knickers) and I pressed the grains onto my tongue and felt the sting rise in my nose. I wished the bed were still there. I wanted to do everything over—ring up one of my lovers—Mike or Richard or Derek and lie down, light a fat candle, and shut out the light.

Emilia stood weeping at the yellow front door. She would begin a new job, that afternoon up in Hampstead, but cried, "I won't love them, Madammy. I only love you." Joe had drifted away months earlier—Emilia said he had taken a job in Kent—but Carmele had said goodbye only last week, just before she went back to Spain to visit baby Arantja who she'd sent to live with her mother. "I'll never forget you, Madam," she said. She tapped her chest with two fingertips. "You will live with me always in my heart."

Jenifer clung to Emilia; "We'll come back to visit," she swore. "Promise you'll write." Emilia bobbed her head—she kissed a pinkie in faith as Jenifer had taught her to do (a letter from Emilia was sheer fiction—she couldn't write English—even her phone messages were indecipherable). Julie climbed up Emilia as if she were a ladder, her legs wound around Emilia's thick waist. As always, Emilia had washed Julie's blanket and packed it in a little bag for the trip. In fact, Julie had weaned herself of the blanket but said she might need it "to take." "Don't cry," she said, wagging a finger at Emilia. "It will be OK. Alright? Alright?" she cajoled. "Say it's alright!" "It's alright," Emilia repeated with a fresh outburst of tears.

"Madammy. Madammy," she wept, her arms around me, her rough olive skin and black hair against my face. "You cried when I came and you're crying when I leave," I joked. Emilia's body odor floated up to meet me, as thick and pungent as the smell from the inside of an old sneaker. I felt as if I could cave in against her soft breasts.

A dark blue Bentley waited at the curb with the door open. Bob had offered Billy the driver to take us to Southampton. I could see my son Billy's knees jiggling in the back seat. He had no patience for all this emotion. "Why are we always moving?" he moaned, when I brought up the idea of going back to New York. "What's wrong with us? Why can't we stay in one place?" But then I told him we could go by boat—the QE 2 would take all of our luggage, his bike, and his toys—and thoughts of the ocean liner had lured him. He'd brought brochures to show his class and promised them that he'd write. He'd begun playing soccer that year and become good at reading. I had been anxious about his reading because he inverted letters, made backward S's and E's, but the previous year he'd seemed to learn overnight. "How did you do it?" I asked. "I made up my mind," he said. Emilia ran down off the steps and offered one last hug which he suffered before stroking her cheek. "Don't cry, Emilia," he said.

I looked out on the sparkling white terrace. Honor Earl stuck her white head out the door, strode to the car and clasped my hand. "Good luck, Miss Rebel," she said. I kissed her dry cheek. "My portrait will hang in New York," I told her. "And wherever I go!" "Ready, Madam?" Billy asked. (Who would call me that ever again?) Inside the car was cool gray and plush. The motor throbbed softly like a dangerous caress. Julie leaned up against me, her head on my arm, her thumb in her mouth. The blanket sat in a paper sack on her lap. At the opposite window Jenifer looked out, her long hair glowing on her shoulders, her freckled white face looking like it belonged to a girl in a church. South Terrace glided by in a blur, like fast-moving film; enamel doors, brass knockers, black iron fences, Thurloe Square the color of emeralds, as lush and thick as a jungle. "You can always come back," I said to myself. "Nothing is forever. If you've made a mistake you can always come back."

Fran had begun doing her "act" in clubs and at "happenings" around London, wherever she could get a "gig." She said she was tired of just writing poems, she wanted to be a star. She'd discovered an arranger/accompanist, a very young man named Jason (who she also seemed to have a crush on although I thought he preferred boys) and they'd put some of her poems to music and written a line of patter. She sang her standards . . . "All the Sad Young Men" and "Spring Can Really Hang You Up the Most" and added others. She sat on a stool under a spotlight with a feather boa around her neck dressed in her 50P dresses and jewelry from the Camden Passage. She had a wispy little voice with a quaver and under the lights she looked pretty and vulnerable. I couldn't imagine why she would want to appear in public when she could write the way she could. Why would she even dream of leaving her bedroom? The places she performed were crowded and smoky and the audiences could be drunk or high. But I went to all her performances. One of her poems was about Manhattan.

My lost city
Smiling in the setting sun
Looking for a moment
As it did when I was young

My Manhattan
Hasn't got a chance they say
Still the streets enchant me
On this golden Autumn day

Like an old and jaded lady
Paying for her wicked ways
Dreams betrayed and cracks uncovered
How I miss those bad old days

Dirty sidewalks
Poison fills the air they say
Still I love this city
Just can't seem to stay away

Friends and lovers
Fleeing from their favorite town
But I will keep returning
Till all the walls fall down

Fran was right, I thought. She'd grown up on Central Park West but she'd left New York and moved to St. Louis and then to London. Except in her poems, she'd never looked back. I'd heard it said for years that New York was a jungle, but now it was true. In the West seventies Neil put six locks on his apartment door and bought a dog. In London the kids could walk in the streets . . . even at night . . . to Thurloe Square, to Hyde Park with Emilia. London was ridiculously safe. Londoners never even raised their voices. When two cars brushed fenders in the King's Road the drivers got out and apologized to each other and the police. Ask for directions and passersby stopped and walked you to your destination. "That's why they're a second class power," Mike said. The first month I was in London I'd watched the draft card burners in Grosvenor Square pelt the unarmed police with eggs. Eggs! But in Manhattan I couldn't let the kids out of the apartment alone. And after dark I wouldn't be able to walk the streets or ride the subways or be in the park. "People say London is twenty-five years behind New York, it's the way New York was in the forties and fifties," I'd heard people say. But that world was gone.

"Why am I leaving London?" I asked. We were at a table in the darkened club where Fran had done her act. "You'll be fine," she shot back. "You're going to see the city from up top. When your novel is published you'll be lionized. You'll spend every night at Elaine's, exchanging clever repartée with the greatest minds of your generation."

"Aren't they all dead?"

"There are always more great minds in New York," Fran said.

"There's a twinkling light for every mind on the Great White Way," Jay said.

"I've heard Elaine doesn't like women," I said.

"It won't matter. You're going to be a successful novelist. Men will fall in love with you. . . . You'll have whoever you want!"

"I'll be back in London in six months. New York is just a trial. . . ."

"People say that but they never come back," Fran said. "You'll have too much fun."

"You're wrong," I said. "If I'm not happy I'll leave."

I was certain this was true. If there was one thing I'd learned in my two-plus years in London it was not to stay in a place I was miserable. I never again wanted to live half a life.

There were only three places to live: London, Paris, or New York. Fran and I agreed to that when we played the "Where would you live" game. And Paris we'd said was "iffy" because we didn't speak the language and didn't like the French. "Paris . . . beautiful city," Oscar Wilde said. "A pity it's in France." That left London or New York. Now I'd made the wrong choice—and Fran had made the right one.

"Will success make you a bitch?" Jay asked. "When I come to you for a loan—just a few pitiful quid to feed my children—will you remember all the brown rice you ate under my roof?"

"Not a threepence," I said.

"Since when have you ever worried about feeding your children?" Fran asked him. "I don't recall nurture being high on your list?" Jay sucked in his breath. He rolled his eyes. We were back in their Duncan terrace house. He'd driven Fran home in their old Bentley and I'd followed in my little green car. He'd worn a tux to Fran's performance but now he'd changed into a red velvet smoking jacket with satin lapels and a sash and big dark glasses. He was in the kitchen making Mu tea, a brew that smelled like dirt and which I drank every time I went there. He brought it to us with a plate of dried apples and popcorn which he put down on the cushions.

Jay's brown rice supplier was there too, the man from whom he bought the rice he sold. "My associate," he said. Tall, bearded,

Norman Pilkington came from blue blood, a titled family. He always wore the same bedraggled jeans, dark sweater and sheepskin vest. He was only twenty-nine years old but yellow from all the rice he ate and he never bathed. He smelled like iodine or scorched ironing, I could never decide which. Jay and Fran's house had the same smell; it hit you as soon as you came in the door. "If you go macro in New York," Norman said, "It will moderate the ying in you. . . . make re-locating mellow. Place is an illusion," he said.

"Norman's right," Jay snickered.

"Oh please," Fran said. "Don't go back to New York and give up sugar at the same time. It's too much of a shock to the system! Oh . . . none of this matters," she said. "You're going to be famous. . . ."

I sat on the cushions, the cup of Mu warm in my hands. Where would I meet people like this? In New York they simply didn't exist.

I couldn't say goodbye to them so I said I'd be back over Christmas when the kids went to L.A. They offered me an extra room they had upstairs which sometimes they let to a lodger. I'd spent so much time in their house on the cushions that I thought my car must know the way by heart. The dealer who sold me the car said he'd buy it back and resell it although he complained about the condition and offered me only a little more than half what I'd paid ("Why do birds always ride the clutch? You've about burned the bloody lining to cinders"). Driving home that night I imagined the new owner when the car insisted on its own route from Islington; Euston Road to Marylebone Road, into the Edgeware Road or through the elegant streets of Mayfair to Knightsbridge and back to my house. Sometimes, still high on grass, I took a roundabout route, Fran's songs in my head; now all of that over.

"I'm moving back to New York," I told Hal. We were sitting in his Bramber Road office surrounded by magazines and sex manuals.

"Great," he said. "Would you like a job?"

No, I thought, I would not.

"Like what?" I asked.

Hal wasn't moving back to America, but he would be in New York setting up the offices of a new sex magazine. Bob Guccione was bringing the American edition of the British magazine *Forum, The International Journal of Human Relations* to New York. The magazine would feature articles and essays and answer letters from readers.

"Adultery Is Good for You," written by a clergyman.

"A Helping Hand," an article about masturbation written by a psychoanalyst.

"We want three women—British sex therapists—to go to New York for the launch," Hal said. "They have to be good-looking. We'll fly them over, put them up at the Hilton. We'll call a press conference and get them on *Today* and *A.M. New York*. Three gorgeous British sex therapists! You can be their duenna!" (Here Hal clicked imaginary castanets.) "You can coach them . . . make sure they say the right things."

"They're experts! Why do they need me?" I asked . . . (although the light was beginning to dawn. Were these "experts" as expert as I had been when I began answering letters?).

"Do you know three sexologists in all of England?" I asked. (The English tend to go their own way. I wasn't sure there were three practicing sex therapists in the country—even counting Scotland and Wales.)

"We'll advertise," Hal said. He jotted down some lines on a pad. "University women! Exciting Opportunity! Editorial and International Travel. Must have background in psychology and enjoy meeting and greeting the public!" Hal selected a redhead, a brunette, and a blonde. They were smart girls and beautiful and they looked classy. The redhead had gone to Oxford and the brunette to the London School of Economics. The blonde could have been Miss Scandinavia. If they had any thoughts about what they were doing, they didn't let on.

"They don't look like sex therapists," I said. "Sex therapists wear native American jewelry and no makeup."

"They're English. Englishwomen are more secure than Americans. They're not afraid to dress sexy *and* have careers."

He offered me a three-day-a-week job and said he'd give me a title, Associate Editor, my name on the masthead. After the sex therapists left I'd be part of the *Penthouse* staff.

New York is expensive, I thought. In London I'd taken any opportunity that came my way until something better turned up. I'd better do the same in New York.

"How about it?" Hal asked.

Don't do it, I thought.

"I'll take it," I said.

Allie and I had dinner together and walked through the mews behind Sloane Street.

"After Bob left when I began walking through London each little house I passed I wished I could go inside and try on the life," I said.

"I'll probably be back in New York soon too," she said. Her boyfriend Ben had two daughters in Connecticut.

"Look," she said, gesturing to the street of low carriage houses with brightly painted doors. "Will you ever forget it? It's Toytown. None of it real."

"Don't make me cry," I said. She put a thin arm over my shoulder and her silver bracelets jingled. Mike called her Mary Poppins. I could understand why.

"I'll miss you," I said.

"Oh . . . come on," she said. She giggled and gripped my shoulder, her white cheeks blazing red.

The QE2 steamed north from Southampton. It made one stop before setting out onto the open ocean. There was a chill wind at the pool on the upper deck where I tried stretching out on a deck chair. Someone said it would get warmer as we went further south. Someone else said "The White Cliffs of Dover," and I looked but saw nothing white.

Our second-class stateroom was the size of a closet with two double-decker beds and a tiny bathroom. Out of the portholes I could see only blank water. The kids ran all over the boat. They wanted to eat in all of the restaurants. We tried every one. But I couldn't taste food. My taste buds had died. I imagined them buried under neat little gravestones along with the rest of my emotional and sensory life.

One night in London Mike had taken me to dinner with James Baldwin whom he'd met in Paris. Baldwin had the saddest face I'd ever seen with eyes that popped out like two headlights on an approaching car in the dark. I imagined myself under their glare and thought he saw right through me. I felt silly next to him, an important writer with real things to say. Mike asked him about

American writers and if he'd read *Portnoy's Complaint* and he said that Sophie Portnoy's cleaning woman and all black cleaning women "were singing the blues."

I'd grown up with a black cleaning woman named Sarah who had worked one day a week for my mother and I was sure Baldwin's eyes saw right through me to her, ironing in our kitchen with the radio playing. (She didn't actually sing the blues. She listened to a program called "Mary Noble, Backstage Wife"). Baldwin said he was going to spend his life in Europe. No place for him in America. I knew I was nowhere near as serious as James Baldwin. I was frivolous with nothing of real importance to say, but I couldn't even say that in New York. On the ship, playing endless games of Ping-Pong with the kids, the little ball clicking back and forth over the table while outside the salon window the dark ocean rose and fell, I recited the names of all the writers who'd left the United States to live in Europe: Ernest Hemingway and Edith Wharton and Henry James, Scott Fitzgerald and Gertrude Stein and John Dos Passos. They'd all needed to see their lives at a distance. Up close I'd be blind. Once I set foot on the dock I'd never write another word.

The kids swam, went to movies, dropped oranges down a high stairwell that circled to the bottom of the boat, snuck into the first class casino. They came back to report on the glories of the roulette wheels and blackjack tables, the handsome passengers in evening clothes betting large piles of chips. One night they said they had met someone who knew their dad and had seen all of his movies. "The real world," I thought, feeling cut. Bob's fame would now follow me. In London, in the island of friends I'd created, I was exotic, desirable, a rarity, an adventuress writing a novel, the ex-wife of a famous American movie producer too—but nobody cared who the famous man was. He was an accessory—like a charm on my bracelet. In New York, all that would change; I'd still be the ex-wife of a movie producer . . . but everyone would care—down to his last credit—exactly who he was . . . and who I was not.

Derek looked pathetic when I said I was going back to New York; the bags under his eyes drooped like two sacks of wet flour. He'd walked through London looking sad and said he was seeing the streets anew wondering if he could leave them and follow me to the United States. "That's not a good idea," I said gently, and he dropped the subject immediately. Should I have stayed with him, I wondered, seeing an English life, tea and scones in a messy house with bad plumbing, no central heating, and "rising damp" climbing the walls? Unwashed artists and painters and poets in torn shetlands with beards, friends of Derek's, would come to dinner, shepherds pie on unmatched china. We'd have no dishwasher. I'd do the "washing up." Derek, out of work, his books and papers scattered all over the place. "I do love you, my darling," he said. "Perhaps you'll let me stay in your house till the new owners take title?"

"That's the Statue of Liberty," I said, pointing it out in the distance. We were all on the deck, six in the morning. I'd thought dozens of passengers would get up to see the boat steam into the harbor—but in fact the deck was all ours. I put my arm around Julie. She had a crust of sleep in the corner of one eye and I wiped it out with my fingertip. She leaned her head against my thigh. Billy and Jenifer ran up to the side of the boat and peered ahead.

Small boats scattered to each side of us as the ship swept them out of their path. I'd never seen New York harbor from this vantage point, and as it spread out in front of me I felt a sudden sharp pang of amazement and awe. To the right I could see Manhattan, clouds like little pillows clustered at the base of the island and the silvery buildings rising out of the mist. The green statue, torch raised aloft, appeared to be coming towards us as the boat moved into the harbor, the clouds parting like curtains to show her off. "Why is it there?" Julie asked. Billy and Jenifer had come back from the ship's rail to stand alongside us. "Because this is a free country," Billy said. "Wasn't London a free country?" she asked. "Yes," I said. "It was." "So why is this different?"

"Julie," Billy said, "it just is!" "There's more opportunity here," I said. "For more people to do whatever they want." But they were no longer listening.

I could feel perspiration under my armpits and where the hair grew at the nape of my neck. New York in summer came rolling back; the way the city swelters, heat rising from the pavements and the sounds of a baseball game on the radio. I was wearing a white skirt and I could feel sweat running down the backs of my legs. The ship kept moving forward, Manhattan continuing to get larger, the clouds floating away until the city was unveiled, opened up like a gift. I looked down at Julie. Her eyes were dark pools. She stood at my side, her arms around me. "Grandma and Grandpa are over there," Jenifer said, kneeling beside her and pointing ahead to a speck on the now naked shore.

Sometime after we'd gathered on the dock, my mother, my father, my sister, the kids and me, after everyone had kissed and my father had said, "Let's get out of here," and my mother had lit her first cigarette, before my father drove us to the sublet on Central Park West where we would live that year ("cliff dwellers"), there arose out of the clamor on the dock a conflagration over my containers of luggage and furniture; something to do with the union that would require money before our things could leave the boat; a twenty dollar bill pressed into a palm. Sweating, my heart pounding, I ran to the side of the boat to locate a dock worker with a clipboard and papers to sign. I recognized his look immediately. In gentle London I'd seen the same glint in the eyes of plumbers come to fix the ever corroding pipes in the bathroom or offer a solution and a price for a new outbreak of "rising damp."

Swinging over the vast hull in a net cage, dangling precipitously over a dirty swath of the Hudson was my brass bed, its head and foot and springs clasped together in a passionate embrace. A shaft of sunlight danced blindingly off the brass. The cage swung dangerously over the water, circling and spinning in an elaborate dance. For a long moment it whirled above me like a twirling, graceful acrobat, bursting with promise and wonder. Men, I thought. New York was full of them; jogging in Central Park in damp tee shirts, men in black jeans and dark glasses sipping coffee in the garden of the Museum of Modern Art, intense men typing at desks in the offices of the *Village Voice* where Mike had given me the name of an editor to call. There was even Jakov. He was about to leave for Majorca when I rang him to say goodbye but said, "I'll be in New York in September at the Chelsea Hotel. You know where that is? Is it near your house?"

I reached into my carpetbag for a St. Moritz. I'd bought a dozen cartons in the duty free shop on the boat . . . but I knew I could get more at the smoke shop in the Plaza Hotel. The bed slid gracefully down the rope and landed with a soft thud on the dock.

ACKNOWLEDGMENTS

I'd like to thank my literary agent Christopher Schelling for his unwavering support and uncommon smarts and Rosemary Ahern for her sympathetic, elegant editing. Thanks to Bob Langs and Louise Rose for patiently reading and rereading my drafts, Steve Schrader and Roger Wall for listening to them, Sandra Langs for legal advice, Susan Lehman for enthusiasm, and Laura Ross for just about everything else. I'm also grateful to Lewis Lapham and Ellen Rosenbush at *Harper's Magazine* for accepting and editing "Last Tango," Fran Landesman for permission to reprint "The Princess From Flatbush" and "My Lost City," and Hervay Petion for excavating the archives of the *Village Voice* for Michael Zwerin's "Outside London" columns. Thank you all so much. I wish words said it better.